An Education Handbook for Parents of Handicapped Children

An Education Handbook for Parents of Handicapped Children

Edited by

Stanley I. Mopsik
Judith Andrews Agard

Abt Books
Cambridge, Massachusetts

Library of Congress Cataloging in Publication Data
Main entry under title:

An Education handbook for parents of handicapped children.

Includes bibliographical references and index.
1. Parent-teacher relationships—Addresses, essays,
lectures. 2. Handicapped children—Education—United
States—Addresses, essays, lectures. 3. Handicapped
children—Services for—United States—Addresses,
essays, lectures. I. Mopsik, Stanley I., 1939–
II. Agard, Judith Andrews, 1938–
LC4019.E33   371.9   78-67848
ISBN 0-89011-511-7

© Abt Associates Inc., 1980

Printed in the United States of America.

Contents

v

Tables and Figures

Acknowledgments

This book is based upon the personal experiences and research of its authors. However, there are also many other people who have made this book possible.

Clark Abt provided continuing interest in and support of the production of this publication. Special thanks go to a number of people who provided critical review of chapter manuscripts. They are: Clark Abt, Marcia Burgdorf, Roland Yoshida, Maryann Hoff, Wendy Mopsik, Kathleen Fenton, Nancy Goodrich, Richard Anderson, and Matthew Bogin.

In addition, our warm appreciation goes to the Abt Associates Washington, D.C., office staff who helped type various drafts of the manuscript, especially Pamela E. Richards, Carole Paine, Helen Chase, and Ruth Lamothe.

Finally, we dedicate this book to the millions of professionals and parents who have devoted their energies over the decades to improving the quality of life for children with special needs. Most of all, however, we dedicate this book to those exceptional children who are coming out of the heart of darkness into a brighter and more satisfying tomorrow.

Introduction

STANLEY I. MOPSIK

During the past several years American education has been in the midst of the "Quiet Revolution."[1] The goal of this revolution is to gain the right to education for all of this country's children, especially its handicapped children. These children, also called children with special needs, include those who, because of mental, physical, emotional, or learning problems, require special education services. Their number is estimated to be seven million, although to date fewer than four million have been identified.

You, as parents, know that the handicapped have been treated as a powerless minority. They have been isolated from society and often viewed as nuisances to be driven out, or as burdens to be confined.

Although our public schools have been viewed traditionally as the great equalizer, this has not been true where handicapped children are concerned; they have been consistently blocked from entering our schoolhouses. But the revolution which Dimond[1] so eloquently discusses in his journal article is upon us and professionals and parents alike have new responsibilities. This book will provide you, the parent of a child with special needs, with a new level of awareness and understanding for dealing with this Quiet Revolution.

The time has come to tell the parents of children with special needs that what now exists is what we hope will be a permanent foundation of legal rights, and that this foundation will be the basis for providing equal and appropriate educational opportunities for all children with special needs.

This book is directed primarily at parents, although we believe that it will be useful to teachers and administrators, as it clears away the tangled misconceptions about the entire special education delivery system. Parents, who are the natural advocates for their children, are often at a disadvantage when it comes to pressing for the programs and services they think are necessary for their children to be successful in school and beyond. Their role as effective advocates for their children is unclear. However, this book provides an understanding of: (1) the resource help that is available for children with special needs and how to get it; (2) legislation, litigation, and the rights of the handicapped child; (3) the entire special education process, from the formation of the parent-school relationship to the initiation of a dispute settlement; and (4) the parents' role in making the system more responsive to them and their child. Knowledge of these elements is critical if the handicapped child is to grow both mentally and emotionally.

In considering a format for this book, we reviewed a number of recent publications that addressed a similar reader population. However, none of these books presented the answers to those critical questions that we thought the parents of children with special needs had. As a result, we asked a number of these parents what their primary concerns were as they began the arduous process of insuring that their children have equal and appropriate educational opportunities. The responses we received enabled us to develop what we consider to be the primary questions parents have. Those questions were divided into the four major content areas indicated above. They are: *Resources* (Chapter 1); *Legislation, Litigation, and Rights* (Chapter 2); *The Special Education Process* (Chapters 3 through 9); and *Techniques for Changing the System* (Chapter 10).

Before we outline the contents of each of these chapters, we would like to state what this book is not, and what it does not attempt to do.

This book is not a definitive resource on all the program and service options that exist for you and your child, but it does provide direction in your quest for those programs and services. It does not define all litigation and legislation that may affect your child, but it does provide an ample overview of the litigatory and legislative rights that you do have. Nor does this book propose to make you an effective advocate overnight, but it does offer some strategies for the development of advocacy skills. It is our desire to provide you with the information and perspective necessary for you to function as a responsible and informed advocate for your child.

Additionally, this book will try to identify the education needs of handicapped children by breaking through the barrier of professional jargon, and providing parents with some understandable definitions of important terms and concepts.

This book is organized into ten chapters, nine of which are presented in a question and answer format. We selected this organizational framework because we think that these are the kinds of questions that parents are asking and that our responses provide the depth of information that parents seek.

While the chapters are designed to be read in sequence, we have tried to write each one to stand on its own. In addition, if only the answer to a specific question is sought (e.g., "Where do I go for the treatment my child needs?"), it is possible to read the response to that or other questions without reading the entire chapter. The choice is yours—read the book straight through or use it as a reference publication to get some information and advice about pressing concerns.

Chapter 1 provides a perspective on the child with special needs. It begins at the beginning: how to make it easier for the parents of the child who find out that there is something wrong with their child. It provides suggestions about where to get specific information and advice on the next steps to take. It also raises perhaps the most important issue: focusing on the facts regarding what is wrong with your child. After facing the diagnosis, you are faced with the next step—getting your child professional help.

Once your child is on his way to getting help, you must then be prepared to start that most important parent-school relationship. Practical advice on the initiation of that relationship is provided in this chapter. If you desire and/or your child requires other than a public school setting, there is a section which focuses on the function and selection of an appropriate nonpublic facility for children with special needs. Some basic issues of medical and related assistance are also discussed. The provision of care for children with special needs after parents have died is also presented clearly and sensitively. Also, when the special needs child becomes an adult, his or her family will need advice about higher education, job training, and employment. These issues are addressed, and those organizations and agencies providing help to the family are identified. Social and recreational concerns and money matters are considerable. Advice about where first to go in the system to attempt to get help is provided because those first attempts are extremely important, since the responses you receive may dictate your future interactions (positive or negative) with agencies or organizations.

Chapter 2 deals with the rights of parents and their children. These rights stem from litigation (a number of landmark law cases) and both state and federal legislation. The chapter begins with a discussion of the effect that litigation has on the educational rights of the handicapped child and proceeds to discuss the most current and most important legislative acts related to children with special needs. Additionally, a number of other pieces of federal legislation are summarized. The implications these laws have for you and your child are explained and some sources of additional information are provided.

Chapter 3 provides you with the information needed to be an advocate for your child. The chapter focuses on questions relating to the parents' role in the educational enterprise as a whole, including general strategies for interacting with the school. The next five chapters deal with specific aspects of the special education process: evaluation, individualized education program planning, placement, the provision of special education services, and program review and modification. Also considered is the parents' role in the actions that can be taken whenever the school and parent cannot agree—the due process hearing, and the final step, a court hearing.

Chapter 9 deals with some basic strategies for assisting in the creation of a system that responds to the program and service needs of your child and others like him or her. Here we turn our attention from individual advocacy to group advocacy. We explore lobbying techniques and the organizational structure of federal, state, and local government agencies.

The summary, Chapter 11, briefly recaps all that has been presented and offers a challenge for the future.

As you read the book we think you will begin to understand the complexities involved in the provision of equal and appropriate services for children with special needs. We also believe that you will begin to understand the book's limitations in addressing all the questions that you may have concerning your child and the public and private sector's responsibilities. We hope that seeking the answers to your questions provides you with the impetus to work with other parents and professionals in a joint quest for that comprehensive and quality delivery system we all so very much desire. The quest which we advocate is both exciting and frustrating. However, success will prove to be euphoric. Read on and get involved.

Notes

1. P. R. Dimond, "The Constitutional Right to an Education: The Quiet Revolution," *The Hastings Law Journal* 24 (1973): 1087–1127.

1

Resources: Persons, Places, and Things

KATHRYN A. MORTON

Are there ways of making it easier in the beginning?

Most parents of children with special needs will agree that a very difficult time was the beginning—the moment the first suspicion arose that something was wrong with their child. Then came the even more difficult task of communicating that concern to someone who would listen; confronting the family physician with the unnerving words, "I think something is wrong," then disbelieving if the doctor didn't agree, or becoming dismayed if he or she did. And, after further examinations and evaluations, the diagnosis was finally made. Most parents who have gone through this will agree that it was the longest, most painful trip of their lives into a world they did not choose and never wanted for their child.

Are there ways of making it easier? We think so. Knowing how much help is available for children with special needs, how to go about finding it, and how to use the guidelines for selecting the aids which are right for a particular child can make a large difference. For parents who have faced the fact that they have a child with a problem, finding out what to do about that problem and then doing something about it is the beginning of the climb to a purposeful way of life for their child.

As they grow up, children with handicaps may have a variety of needs and you may find yourself looking for anything from special education to a special friend, from psychotherapy to a babysitter, from vocational training to horseback riding lessons. How do parents go about finding what their child needs? Who knows about special services? Where does one start?

These are initially baffling questions with answers which vary according to the child's age, disability, and needs. But there are guidelines to follow for each stage in the child's life. This chapter will suggest various contacts to make and paths to follow to get the information you need each step of the way.

First, you will want some general sources of information about services; anyone (with or without a handicapped child) in need of information can start by going to the following:

1

Library.   Your public library has a reference librarian who tends a reference room that is rich in information about local and state services. Ask for a directory of services for handicapping conditions, and for a United Way (United Givers, Community Fund, etc.) directory of social service agencies in your community. And you won't have to rely just on books or directories. These days reference librarians are trained to do "I and R" (information and referral) and sometimes even resource counseling. So a simple request like "I'm looking for services for my child because I think he may be handicapped. Can you help me?" should get you to a person who can tell you what diagnostic or other services are available, a fair amount of information about how they work, or information about whatever it is you think you need at this point. The librarian can help you think through what you're after, and you should get a good, sound referral to the community agencies that can answer your needs.

Clergy.   As traditional "helping professionals," rabbis, ministers, and priests are good people to go to for advice. Not all of them will be acquainted with the gamut of services that are available in your community, but they should know good starting points. And, of course, they should be able to give you some supportive counseling about your concerns and anxieties. If they cannot help, and you feel the need for someone to talk to, ask them to suggest a social worker who may be able to help.

Public school system.   Almost all school systems, even the smallest, have special education departments, and the people who "do placement" there are generally well informed about diagnostic services, public or private school special education programs, residential schools, institutions, or anything else pertaining to the special needs of school–aged children.

Health department.   The health department is a good place to start if you suspect that your child has special needs. Any of its staff members should be able to direct you to a crippled children's consultation clinic, to a maternal and child health clinic, or to a special diagnostic clinic.

Medical society.   If you want to start with a pediatrician and don't have one, look up "Medical Society" in the Yellow Pages, call the society, and ask to be referred to a pediatrician. You should also ask about interdisciplinary clinics that evaluate children who may be delayed in development or have disabilities.

Yellow Pages.   You'll find some help in the Yellow Pages under such headings as "social service organizations," which will be followed by three or four columns of listings in a directory for a medium-sized city. "Clinics" will give you another three or four columns, but you'll have to wade through acupuncture, abortion, etc., listings before you get to anything that sounds like help for a handicapped child. "Child" or " children" is likely to list only child-care centers.

City telephone directory. An imaginative search might yield more results from your telephone directory's white pages, particularly if you know what handicap group you're after. You can look up "retarded" or "mental retardation" and you should find an association that can answer your questions. It's unlikely that you'll find anything under "emotionally disturbed," but "mental health" should again lead you to an association which can be helpful. "Blind" and "deaf" might yield possibilities, and so on.

Isn't there one place I can call?

Unfortunately, there isn't one central place you can call for help in any city. Most "veteran" parents of children with disabilities will tell you that there is no better training for being a sleuth than having a handicapped child. You will learn to look for clues, follow leads, fit together pieces of information gathered from various sources, and talk to all kinds of people. Sometimes you may encounter dead ends, and before your child has passed many birthdays you may feel like your home is "the place to call" for information on services for his or her problems. And that will happen for a reason: the service system for handicapped children is often so fragmented and so complex that it's highly unlikely there will be any single source of information that can tell you all you need to know at any point along the way. In rural areas information will be easier to get, largely because there will be fewer services.

For all the reasons listed above, parents have to be systematic in their search. So perhaps the first and most important piece of advice is to get a sturdy notebook and keep track of every call you make; that way you'll avoid trips back to the Yellow Pages because you left your name and number for someone to call you back who never did, and now you've lost that scrap of paper with the name and number on it (just as the person at the other end has lost the scrap of paper with *your* name and number on it). Your notebook will also serve another very important function. It will immunize you against the fear that you haven't explored all the byways.

There may be various frustrations at any point in the search for services for your child. You may encounter people who are rude, obtuse, or unhelpful. Services for handicapped children are not, sadly enough, staffed exclusively by kind and caring people. But don't let a grouchy intake worker keep you from getting what you want. Whatever the worker's mood for the day, get his or her name. Open your call with "Hello, this is Mary Jones and I'd like some information. To whom am I speaking?" "Mr. Smith," he growls/offers cheerfully, and you take down the agency, his name, and, after your conversation, a small note about how helpful he was. If Mr. Smith wasn't useful, maybe you can avoid him the next time, or at least steel yourself to deal with him. But don't let an initial bad experience turn you off to an agency that may be able to help your child.

Is more known about some handicaps than others?

It's probably generally true that people who aren't specialists in the field of handicapping conditions will know more about some handicaps than others, if only because some have been more visible than others. So, it will be easier to find information about services for children who are retarded, blind, or crippled than for those who are aphasic, autistic, or brain damaged. Associations for retarded children and Easter Seal Societies have been around for years and are probably familiar names even to the man on the street. But very few people will know that there are local chapters of the National Society for Autistic Children, or a local Association for Children with Learning Disabilities. An association for one of the older and more established disabilities can help you to learn about the "newer" ones. The newer ones may not even be listed in the phone book since there is usually no professional staff involved, and most groups formed to deal with these disabilities operate from the homes of volunteer members. After checking all these sources you will probably find all the information you need about services, and you'll get the added bonus of being in touch with experienced parents who will understand what you're going through. In recent years the National Society for Crippled Children and Adults (Easter Seal) has become increasingly involved in providing information and referral for *all* handicapping conditions.

A strong trend lately has been for all of the local organizations concerned with handicaps to band together to form coalitions to act in concert on legislative, funding, and other issues that concern all handicapped children. These people are informed and they care about each other, so chances are good that they'll care about you too, even if you are not interested in the same disabilities.

How do I find out what's wrong with my child?

The process of finding out what's wrong with your child is called diagnosis and evaluation, and it can take place in a number of ways. If the baby shows signs of a disabling condition at birth, the attending physician will call in specialists for consultation, and the parents will know there's a problem almost immediately. Just how serious the condition is may not be immediately clear, however. Certainly, in the case of children with Down's syndrome, the extent of intellectual impairment will not be known for several months, or even years. The degree of impairment of babies with spina bifida or cerebral palsy or any disability immediately recognizable is simply not known until a period of growth and observation has elapsed. So even if a child's disability is ascertained at birth, diagnosis and evaluation is not a one-time act but a process which should be continual. The hospital staff or your family doctor should be able to recommend a pediatrician or other specialist who can serve as the baby's primary physician, since a general practitioner may not have the knowledge and experience to oversee the child's case.

The primary physician is given that title because with the help of the parents he or she will coordinate referrals and visits to any other specialists who may be needed, and there could be a number of them. Aside from being medically competent, the primary physician should be a person with whom you can talk comfortably, someone who is concerned, helpful, and reasonably accessible. If the primary physician has a large practice, you might request a little extra time when scheduling appointments. If it can't be done, you may want to look elsewhere. There will be lots of questions swirling in your head, and you will want time to ask them.

Some health departments have public health nurses who visit the homes of mothers of newborn babies to see how they and their babies are doing, give advice, answer questions, and teach bathing or feeding skills if necessary. Such a visit can be especially comforting if the baby is handicapped. Give your health department a call. Such nurses may also turn out to be of great aid in helping you find other services as you need them.

But most disabilities are not identified at birth. More often something about the way the child is developing or behaving causes the parents, a relative, or a friend to be concerned. In most cases the parents will act on that concern by discussing it with the family doctor or with the physician at the child's next clinic appointment. A series of referrals to specialists might follow, and again, it is important to locate a primary physician in private practice or in a clinic to serve as the coordinator of medical information.

Who might those specialists be and what do they do?

Pediatrician. A pediatrician is a physician who specializes in the treatment of children, their development and care, and their diseases. Returning to a pediatrician for interpretation and coordination of information gathered from other specialists, as well as for general health care, is a sound practice. A continuous, cooperative, and trusting relationship with a pediatrician is the ideal to pursue, but any number of contingencies may occur to remind parents that *they* must assume the ultimate responsibility for coordinating visits, reports, and communication.

Neurologist. A neurologist is a physician who specializes in the diagnosis and treatment of problems of the nervous system and brain. A neurological examination will include a careful study of the child's history of development, an evaluation of his or her alertness and responsiveness, an examination of the sensory system (vision, hearing, and balance) and the motor system (the voluntary movement of muscles), a check for involuntary movements and a testing of reflexes, and very likely an EEG examination (electroencephalogram), which records electrical activity in the brain.

Physiatrist. A physiatrist is a physician who specializes in physical medicine—the diagnosis and treatment of disease with the aid of physical agents such as light, heat, cold, water, or mechanical apparatus (braces and other special equipment). The physiatrist helps disabled persons with mobility and with managing daily living so they are better able to deal with the environment.

Orthopedist. An orthopedist is a surgeon who specializes in preserving and restoring the function of the skeletal system, as well as muscles, joints, tendons, ligaments, nerves, and blood vessels. Some of this work overlaps that of a physiatrist, but unlike the physiatrist, all orthopedists are trained in surgery.

Psychiatrist. A psychiatrist is a physician who specializes in the diagnosis and treatment of emotional problems and mental disorders. All psychiatrists are physicians; all are trained in psychotherapy. Only a small percentage of them are psychoanalysts.

Ophthalmologist. An ophthalmologist is a physician who specializes in the diagnosis and medical and surgical treatment of defects and diseases of the eye and structures related to it.

In addition to the specialized physicians, there are qualified specialists who are not physicians but who may work under the supervision of, in cooperation with, or independently of a physician.

Psychologist. A psychologist specializes in the assessment and treatment of people with emotional, interpersonal, or behavioral problems. Clinical psychologists work in a variety of settings—clinics, schools, mental health centers, hospitals, etc. School psychologists specialize in counseling school children and their families and work with teachers and other school staff to improve the child's ability to function within the school setting. Psychological testing done in schools is conducted only by psychologists. A behavioral psychologist specializes in the purely objective observation and analysis of behavior and in developing behavior management programs.

Physical therapist. A physical therapist is skilled in the techniques of treatment to rehabilitate and restore fundamental body movements after illness or injury. Treatment may include massage or manipulation of the limbs, therapeutic exercises, hydrotherapy, electrotherapy, etc. Such a therapist always works under the supervision of a physician. The focus is on large muscle and gross motor activities.

Occupational therapist. An occupational therapist is trained to build or rehabilitate the basic skills involved in everyday living by developing treatment activities and by adapting the materials of everyday life to suit the special needs of the disabled person. These therapists focus on fine motor activities, especially the use of hands and fingers, on coordination of movement, and on self-help skills.

Speech pathologist. A speech pathologist is trained in the study of human communication, its normal development, and its disorders. He or she evaluates the reception, integration, and expression of speech and language of children or adults, and assists in treating whatever problems exist.

Audiologist. An audiologist is trained to identify and measure types and degrees of hearing loss, assess how disabling the condition is, recommend rehabilitation, fit hearing aids, and counsel parents on how to help their child adjust to his or her hearing loss.

Optometrist. An optometrist is trained and licensed to examine and test eyes and to treat defects by prescribing corrective lenses and by developing programs of eye exercise.

If you can envision a sequence of appointments—checkups scheduled at regular intervals with your primary physician, punctuated by visits as needed to specialists—you can gain some sense of the gradual unfolding of the diagnostic process. People trained in different disciplines will be looking at your child, and each examination will yield a report which will be sent to your primary physician.

Your primary physician's file on your child will grow. We suggest that you have a file that grows right along with his or hers. It is only during the past few years that professionals have come to realize that parents need to have easy access to their children's records if they are to become and stay as informed about their children as they should be. More and more physicians are agreeing to give copies of the results of their examinations or evaluations to the child's parents. However, very few will offer copies; you must ask. Discuss the question of whether or not you can have copies of your child's records with your pediatrician or primary physician early in the game. You may have to do some persuading, but we think it's very important that you try.

There may be medical terms in the reports which you don't understand. However, information in the records can be explained to you in simple, understandable terms, and having the information under your belt offers two advantages: (1) You're in a far better position to go home and explain what went on in the doctor's office to others who want and need to know and (2) you are beginning to accrue information which will help you know what questions to ask next time. If you don't understand what is going on in the early stages, you will be uninformed and at a disadvantage.

"But," your doctor may counter, "I'm your baby's primary physician and I'll be monitoring his (or her) progress." That may not be the whole truth. You can't take your physician with you when you move to another city. And the physician won't be with you when you are discussing your child with the directors of educational programs, with teachers, or with any other professionals who may work with your child.

The reality is that you, the parents, will be the chief coordinators, monitors, observers, and decision makers regarding anything that affects your handicapped child. No professional can assume that responsibility for you. And the more you know, the better you will be able to coordinate. Each professional's job, in turn, is to make you as informed as possible. However, some of them still hold the old belief that the professional is the expert, handling information so complex and so specialized that the parent could not possibly comprehend it. Many parents have come out of a professional's office as uninformed as they were when they went in. Don't let it happen to you.

After some months and a series of appointments, the primary physician's file on your child will yield a comprehensive picture of your child. But getting that picture will have entailed referrals from the primary physician to a variety of specialists in private practice, health department clinics, or hospital outpatient clinics, a great deal of appointment making and keeping, and probably a substantial period of waiting between appointments.

Is there a different route I can take to get diagnoses?

Increasingly common these days are diagnostic centers offering an interdisciplinary evaluation that is done in a relatively brief period of time, perhaps in two or three appointments scheduled in one week, or even in a single very full day of appointments. Typically, a social worker takes the family's history, a pediatrician conducts an initial medical examination, and then various specialists (usually a psychologist, child development specialist, physical therapist, speech pathologist, and audiologist, among others) make evaluations. The team then meets to share the information gained with each other and with the parents. The advantages of the team evaluation are many: less wear and tear on the parents, usually less expense, possibly a more comprehensive evaluation than would have been conducted otherwise, and the inclusion of the parents in the discussion. If the parents aren't included in the "staffing," as it's called, a social worker or another member of the team interprets what went on in the staffing to the parents. However, be sure to ask to be included in the staffing before the round of appointments begins since professionals still aren't used to involving parents in staffings, but may like it if they try it.

Many of the "one-stop" diagnostic centers also make it standard practice to give the parents a copy of each diagnostic summary completed by a professional who saw the child. If this is not standard practice, be sure to ask for a copy.

A word about communication: some professionals are friendly, relaxed communicators and others are not. The same is true of parents. It may be hard at first for some parents to feel comfortable and relaxed in discussion with a group of highly trained specialists, but time and experience make it easier. These specialists are just people, subject to the same moods, anxieties, and stresses as any other working person. It is important to remember that in this case, however, all discussion is about a child's disability and there are extra stresses involved for both the parents and the professionals. Some of them manage their emotional stress by becoming crisp and superprofessional; others are able to communicate gently, clearly, and with empathy day after day. If you are feeling too overwhelmed to deal with the situation, just ask if you might call any of them later when you've had time to digest the news and formulate the questions you know you'll have.

What are the first steps I should take after diagnosis of my child?

The process of diagnosis and evaluation gives you information about your child's handicap, but there is much that can and should go on in the life of a handicapped baby, toddler, or preschooler which has nothing to do with diagnosticians. If your private physician or clinic doesn't know of any "infant stimulation" programs, home-visiting teachers, preschools, or other early intervention programs, go back to the sources of information discussed earlier in this chapter and start calling them.

Infant programs, whether the infants are taken to a school or the teachers come to them, are becoming commonplace, and it's a good thing. Most studies on the effects of early intervention programs on handicapped children find that they have a real impact on both the infants and the parents, and often on brothers and sisters too. Everybody seems to benefit from the teaching and the learning that go on. The goal of such programs is to help the child reach his or her maximum potential, whatever that might be; there is no such thing as a child who is "too handicapped" to benefit.

More and more school systems are sponsoring infant programs, particularly for babies who are deaf or blind, since early parent training in special handling and teaching techniques is so very important. You might start with a call to the special education department of your city or county school system. Also, some health departments offer infant programs, as do private agencies, Easter Seal treatment centers, and associations for retarded citizens. There are also preschools for handicapped children.

These infant programs offer an intensive early intervention program. For instance, a program for babies with development delays might be staffed by an infant teacher, a physical therapist and/or an occupational therapist (especially helpful for feeding problems), and possibly a speech therapist. Typically, such a program would require you to bring your baby to a classroom once or twice a week for a couple of hours. The baby will be assessed to see how well he or she functions in various areas—gross motor, perceptual/fine motor, cognitive, self-care, or social and emotional development, and language. Then the teacher and other specialists figure out what activities you can do with your baby at home to help the child's development in each of these areas.

Gross motor programming would teach parents how to move their child in and out of various positions, how to hold him or her correctly, how to position the child to get the best view of the surrounding environment, and how to encourage exploration and free movement. Perceptual and fine motor programming would teach parents how to motivate their child to reach, grasp, and move toys or objects. It would also include lots of activities using materials that are stimulating to the senses, such as clay, sand, differently textured fabrics, water, and so on. Cognitive activities would include anything that helped the child understand the causes and effects of his actions, so you might be asked to help your child push a button on a toy that makes a door pop open. Your child needs to learn that even though he or she cannot see a toy, it is still there, and will need to learn about space and direction, too.

In the area of self-care you would be taught the best ways of helping your child learn to feed and dress himself or herself and to use the toilet. Probably the most important skill for a parent to learn in the area of social and emotional development is how to be comfortable in working with the baby and how to enjoy doing so. Then, as your child grows older, his or her ability to relate to other children becomes important. Finally, although "language" as an area of programming may seem premature for babies, there are any number of activities that encourage the later emergence of language.

The essential thing to remember is that babies with delays or disabilities often do not learn things in sequence or automatically as other babies do. If they cannot explore their environment, you need to bring the environment to them. If they cannot see, they must be helped to make their ears and their sense of touch compensate.

Most programs will not offer many specialists for the obvious reason of cost. But even a program staffed by only an infant teacher will accomplish what is necessary in teaching you to help your baby develop at peak rate if that teacher is experienced and well trained.

Among other advantages of infant programs is the chance such classes offer to be with other parents during the early stages of adjustment to having a handicapped child. Many of the programs include counselors who spend part of the time in group discussion with the parents as they air their feelings, learn about handicaps, hear what services will be available in later years, and share with each other solutions to the various problems that arise in rearing children with disabilities.

Another kind of infant program is the home visiting program. It offers advantages of a different sort, especially for infants who have health problems which are likely to keep them from going out regularly. The teacher and/or therapist comes to your home and teaches you there.

Costs of infant programs will vary. Some are free; others charge on a sliding scale or have flat fees. Try not to let a lack of money keep your baby out of a program. The earliest months and years are absolutely critical in terms of maximizing development; some losses suffered might never be recouped. So, if the fees are more than you can pay, be sure to inquire about the availability of scholarships from community organizations.

If you live in a small community and there are no infant programs available, ask your librarian to help you find some of the very fine books describing things parents can do at home with babies who have handicaps or who are delayed in some way. Most of them are illustrated with drawings or photographs showing you what to do. Or, contact the psychologist or child development specialist in your health department who does diagnosis and evaluation of children with disabilities and ask for suggestions. You should also call up the preschool for children like your own and ask the director to make suggestions about home-teaching activities for infants.

What about preschools for my child?

Preschools will be easier to locate. Since the federal law will be requiring public school systems to be responsible for the education and training of very young (3 years old and above) handicapped children by 1980, the special education department of your school system will know what preschool program your child should attend. You should not have to decide on your own which school is the right one. Special committees, often called screening and selection committees or preschool admission committees, will review your child's diagnostic reports, design a program for him or her, and assign your child to a school or teacher who can carry out the program. Be sure you are at those meetings and are part of that design and selection process. The school selected might be a private one or it might be operated by the public school system. Transportation may or may not be provided; if it is, it is very likely that you will be charged for it. However, as of 1980 it should be provided at no charge. Carpooling, or paying another parent to drive your child to school, are two possible solutions. Calling a parent organization, a city or county volunteer bureau, or a community organization might yield some help or suggestions for where to go next. Other church–related organizations might be helpful and come up with a volunteer.

Some preschools are cooperatives, that is, they ask parents to put in a day or two a month of work at the school. You may not work in your own child's classroom, but working with children like your own is enormously useful experience. Again, the principle holds: the more you can learn about handicapped children, the better will be your perspective on your own child and your own situation. Also, schools or programs which involve parents actively with the children and with each other serve the vital function of safeguarding those parents against what we consider a very real occupational hazard—isolation and loneliness. To be sure, every parent runs this risk to some extent; child rearing is a very demanding job and most of it has to be accomplished within the four walls of the home. But parents of very young normal children find each other at playgrounds, in grocery stores, casually walking in the neighborhood, and so on, and they find much in common to talk about. Parents of handicapped children do not find each other so easily (and they may feel they have little in common with parents of normal children), but they need each other very much.

What happens after preschool?

Graduation from a preschool program for children with special needs of any kind should lead to a review by a special committee within the public school system of the child's current strengths and weaknesses and a recommendation for an appropriate placement in a setting for school-aged children. If that setting is within the public school system, you will want to get acquainted with the child's teacher and any other school personnel, including the school bus driver, to give them some hints about how to handle aspects of your child's idiosyncratic behavior that might baffle them. The more they know about your child, the better they will understand him or her.

Well-timed information-sharing should become a habit. Some parents and teachers like to do their talking informally—whenever they're around the school, at pick-up times, etc. If a parent can't drop by the school, phone calls might work, though some teachers and parents are hard to reach. Delivering short notes via lunchbox is one way to communicate occasionally. Notes have an advantage: you can add them to your notebook. No matter how you communicate, it's a good idea to write down the essence of any discussions that you feel are important now or that might have implications for the future, especially if you have any doubts about the appropriateness of the classroom or services offered.

How do you know if the program your child is in is the right one? The answer to this very important question used to be easy. Before the advent of the individualized educational program (IEP), a teacher or principal would simply point out that Johnny either "fit" into a program or he didn't. If he didn't fit, unless he shaped himself up to do so, out he went. Now the goals and strategies for Johnny's particular style of learning are laid out in the IEP before he enters the classroom, and if he doesn't do well, different teaching strategies or approaches have to be developed. The problem is no longer the child's; it's the school's. And you, as parents, have a good tool for evaluating whether progress is really being made toward the specific goals set down in the IEP. (Chapter 3 presents a complete picture of the IEP process.)

But a word of warning: you cannot know whether strategies used to accomplish goals are working until a reasonable period of time has elapsed. So parents who think their child is in a setting or program which offers insufficient special attention must wait and watch carefully until there is evidence that change is needed.

Private special day schools

If you are persuaded that the public schools are not providing the special education and related services that your child needs, what are your alternatives? Private special day schools are a possibility. Often they have been around for a long time, antedating the time of public special education for handicapped children and founded by parents or professionals because there were no programs at all for children who could not learn in the traditional classroom setting. The reputations of these schools tend to be well established, and finding out about them should not be difficult. The people who coordinate private placements in special education departments of the public schools will be knowledgeable.

If, however, you want to do some preliminary investigating on your own, call the appropriate parent organization in your area. They're organized around specific handicaps so you should call all of those representing handicaps which seem in any way related to your child's particular problem or problems. Then call the schools in which you are interested and ask the director for an appointment to see the school and talk about your child. Explain that you're trying to get a grasp on what special services are available outside the school system as a possible alternative to your child's current placement.

It's very helpful, too, to talk to parents of children who attend the school. Often the parent associations can help you get in touch with them. Then think through the reasons you are dissatisfied with what your child's current school offers. What aspects of the program might be adapted to better suit your child's needs? What needs can't be met by making changes in the present program? What will changes mean to your child in terms of friendships, time spent on the bus, and his or her ability to adapt to the disruption of an established schedule? Remember, change is stressful; it can be *good* stress, that is, stimulating and ultimately for the best, but it can also be very difficult and unprofitable for children. You will want to approach such changes very cautiously and be as certain as possible of the advantages they offer. Be absolutely sure that when you visit the school (if not on the first visit, surely on the second) you spend time observing the teachers and the classroom where your child would be placed. The success of your child's education rests largely in that particular teacher's hands.

Keep in mind the goals you helped develop in your child's educational plan and try to take a few minutes of the director's or teacher's time to discuss specifically what they would do to help your child reach those goals. The general questions you will want to ask on any visit to a private school are similar to those you ask when evaluating any public school.

Don't rush the process of investigating your alternatives. After visiting those schools which seem likely to meet your child's needs, go back and observe his or her current school. Having gathered a lot of information and insight from your observations of the private schools, your evaluation will be more intelligent. Then make your decision as to whether or not change is needed.

Residential schools

Residential schools should be approached even more cautiously since there is a good chance that they will be some distance from your home and you will have less control of what goes on there, and less opportunity to observe and supervise your child's education and well-being. There are two main reasons children may need residential schooling: (1) such schools offer a structured setting 24 hours a day, something the family or community simply cannot provide and which is a necessary condition for some children if they are to reach their educational goals; and (2) family circumstances make it necessary for the child to be away from home. The impact of difficult children on family living can occasionally be so destructive that parents literally cannot continue to cope without disastrous consequences. Also, death, separation, or illness may make it impossible to keep a child at home.

In an effort to keep children as close to home and in the least restrictive environment possible, communities are beginning to give families in crisis the kind of support which will help them keep things together. But many communities still offer nothing, and placement in private schools or institutions, if space is available, becomes the only resort. Since school systems usually operate under laws which stipulate that reasons for private placement must be educational, a child who has family problems but whose educational progress in his local classroom is fine may have trouble getting funding for residential placement.

Under new federal and many state laws, a school system's inability to provide day programs for children with very severe, very complex handicaps is becoming the only acceptable educational reason for residential placements. It will probably become increasingly rare to find children who have mild or moderate disabilities of any kind in residential schools unless their parents are paying for their tuition, room, and board.

Where do I go to get information about private day and residential schools?

There are directories which list residential schools by state and should be available in the main branch of your public library. Call the reference librarian there to inquire. The best known directory is *The Directory for Exceptional Children,* 1979 edition, published by Porter Sargent. It lists schools for all handicapping conditions. There may be schools not listed in Sargent's directory so it is worth conducting a thorough search for possible additional listings. You may want to send away for directories if your library doesn't own any, but try your parent organizations first.

Again, the people who are in charge of private day and residential special education placements in your public school system will also be knowledgeable. And if they know your child or have his or her records in hand, they should be able to zero in on the best possibilities and recommend them to you. Also, school systems send placement staff out to visit the schools and observe children in placement there, so you will certainly want to talk to anyone who has visited a school which interests you.

Once you have the names and addresses of the schools you would like to investigate, you will want to call or write for their brochures and get as much recent information about them as possible. Some of the small ones don't have much printed information, but a call or a letter to the director will probably get you the information you need.

When you are at the point of wanting to visit the school or apply for admission for your child, make sure when you phone or write for an appointment that you explain all your reasons for wishing to investigate the possibility of admission. Many schools have long waiting lists and may discourage any of your advances because they simply don't need another student. But waiting lists can work in a curious fashion. They are often amazingly flexible and responsive to a family's or child's needs, especially if they are urgent.

If you are unable to manage the researching, calling, and visiting yourself, get help from your parent organization. If you are in a crisis, ask your school system placement people to do it for you or get help from your local social services department. If money is not a problem but time and energy are, you might be able to contract with a social worker to do the investigating for you. Parent associations, private social service agencies, and community mental health agencies should be able to suggest persons to call, or you can contact the local chapter of the National Association of Social Workers.

Where do I go for the medical and related help my child needs?

Once your child has been diagnosed, he or she may have a number of treatment needs: psychiatric treatment; behavioral management help from a psychologist; physical, occupational, or speech therapy; mobility training; or intermittent nursing or dental care. The ideal situation would be one in which your primary physician or any other professional would guide you to a reliable specialty treatment center or treatment specialist, and most of the time that's the way treatment needs are met—through referral from a physician to a treatment specialist. On the other hand, it is possible that your doctor will not know all the possible choices or locations for treatment.

A good place to start looking for a physical, occupational, or speech therapist would be your health department, an Easter Seal treatment center, or a hospital. Besides being staffed by specialists who can recommend therapists, some of the places recommended might be able to provide other needed services. Of course, the hunting you do must be, in part, dictated by your wallet; you can pay an hourly rate for a private physical therapist who will come to your home, or you can take your child to a health department, hospital outpatient clinic, or an Easter Seal treatment center and pay a sliding scale fee for treatment. Medical evaluations are free in many health departments and insurance covers most therapists prescribed by a physician.

Physical, occupational, and speech therapists have national associations which maintain listings of licensed or certified therapists in private practice. Write the national organization and ask for a local contact. The names and addresses are as follows:

American Physical Therapy Association
1156 15th Street N.W.
Washington, D.C. 20005

American Occupational Therapy Foundation
6000 Executive Boulevard
Rockville, Maryland 20852

American Speech and Hearing Association
10801 Rockville Pike
Rockville, Maryland 20852

A good place to start if you're looking for a private physician—psychiatrist, ophthalmologist, physiatrist, neurologist, etc.—is the medical society. If you're looking for a psychologist, try your mental health association or a community health center. It is important to remember that treatment can sometimes be accomplished by different kinds of professionals. For instance, psychotherapy is practiced by psychiatrists, psychologists, and psychiatric social workers. A psychiatrist is an M.D., and your child's problem may not require the attention of a physician. Determining which kinds of services you need is something your primary physician can help you do.

While the mental health association or community mental health center might be the best routes for finding a psychiatric social worker in private practice, social workers who do ordinary counseling might be available through your department of social services or through any family and child services department of a social service agency.

Your child's physician will be a source of information about whom to call and there are nursing care agencies listed in the Yellow Pages of your phone book. The visiting nurse association in your area will have nurses and home health aides on call, but be sure to inquire about hourly rates, sliding scales, insurance coverage, and the minimum number of hours required. However, you should first check with your doctor to find out the level of training and skill required to care for your child. There are registered nurses, licensed practical nurses, and home health aides, the most highly trained of whom is the registered nurse.

Where can I send for information about handicaps?

There's probably no greater asset to parents than good information about their child's handicap and about the people and places designed to help the handicapped. A good source of general information is a national information center for the handicapped called *Closer Look*. It provides information to parents on the various handicapping conditions, lists of parent organizations for each disability in each state, information about coalitions for the handicapped, the names of state–level special education personnel through whom a parent can get information on local special education offerings, helpful guidelines on getting needed services, valuable information on the rights of parents and their children, and a superb newsletter. To receive information and/or the newsletter, write to:

Closer Look
Box 1492
Washington, D.C.   20013

All items are free.

There are other national organizations which are concerned with all handicapping conditions.

The National Easter Seal Society for Crippled Children and Adults has a publications list of pamphlets, bibliographies, journals, and organizations concerned with various disabilities and all are available through its library service. Write to:

The National Easter Seal Society for Crippled Children and Adults
182023 West Ogden Avenue
Chicago, Illinois   60612

Members of the Council for Exceptional Children (CEC) can obtain a wealth of information by writing to:

The Council for Exceptional Children
1920 Association Drive
Reston, Virginia   22091

Geared primarily to the teacher of exceptional children, its information center can tell you where to write for suggestions on instructional materials and how to gain access to its bibliographies and abstracting services. It also provides information on state and federal legislation and litigation concerning the education of handicapped children. Most of what the CEC publishes is of interest to parents as well as to teachers and other professionals, and its publications lists could be very helpful.

Another good source of information, although it's designed to help all parents rather than just those with handicapped children, is the:

National Committee for Citizens in Education
410 Wilde Lake Village Green
Columbia, Maryland   21044

Besides its monthly newspaper, it has a toll-free number (800-NET-WORK) for parents to call to get advice when they're having difficulty with their school system.

For pamphlets on the causes and prevention of birth defects of all kinds write to:

The National Foundation, March of Dimes
Box 2000
White Plains, New York   10602

You should also know that the Library of Congress can provide you with a list of its regional libraries. Write to:

Library of Congress
Division for the Blind and Physically Handicapped
Washington, D.C.   20542

There you'll find talking books, tapes, and other aids for children or adults with handicaps, and the service is not limited to those who are blind or physically handicapped. Children with learning disabilities and other impairments which keep them from learning from the printed word can also borrow.

There's a *Directory of National Information Sources on Handicapping Conditions and Related Services* (1977) which you can get by writing to the following address:

Clearinghouse on the Handicapped, Office for Handicapped
   Individuals
Department of Health, Education, and Welfare
Washington, D.C.   20201

It lists all of the national organizations, indexed by disability. Each of the disabilities has national or state organizations which have publications lists, newsletters, pamphlets, journals, etc.

Besides the publications lists put out by the various agencies listed above, there is a selected and annotated listing of literature for and by parents called *A Reader's Guide for Parents of Children with Mental, Physical, or Emotional Disabilities.* The most recent edition was published in 1976, but it should be updated before too long. It lists and comments on books about handicaps (including those written for children about handicapping conditions), as well as journals, directories, organizations, and other sources of information. It is available, single copies free, by asking for DHEW Publication No. (HSA) 77-5290 at the following address:

U.S. Department of Health, Education, and Welfare
Public Health Service
Health Services Administration
Bureau of Community Health Services
Rockville, Maryland   20857

If your library doesn't have the books listed in the guide, ask the librarian to order what you want, or write the publisher for your own copy. Publishers' addresses and book prices are also listed in the guide. Your local parent organization may also have a lending library.

Who can give us moral support and practical help?

But educating yourself isn't all you must do. You should be thinking about the people you're going to lean on when you need help. Perhaps the mistake most commonly made by the mothers and fathers of handicapped children is that they rely too heavily on each other and on other family members for whatever help or support they need. Generally, it's not wise to depend on them exclusively for either emotional support or child care. It can be enormously helpful to talk with other parents of handicapped children for emotional support. Get involved in therapeutic or "rap" groups run by professionals, or get individual counseling from a professional. Family-oriented agencies, appropriate self-help organizations, community mental health centers, or departments of social services should be able to give you some options.

For a lot of reasons there is extra stress involved for the whole family in living with a child with a disability. That's not to say that there aren't extra joys, too, but more often than not, rearing a handicapped child demands time and energy far beyond that required for a nonhandicapped child, and time and energy are not unlimited commodities in any family.

Certainly, it's great when everyone pitches in and works together, but it's also important for everyone to understand that outside help can be called in and that others can be trusted to care for the child. The best reason for not relying exclusively on the family is that the handicapped child needs to develop trust in and experience with people outside the family. This is an absolutely essential part of growing up for your child just as it is for the nonhandicapped child.

Where can you find help outside the family? When the handicapped child is small, the same friends, neighbors, or local teenage sitters you would rely on for help with a nonhandicapped child can usually be asked to babysit. What you need to do is make them comfortable and secure the first few times by giving them a chance to spend time with your child before you leave and by giving them instructions for handling any specific needs the child might have. Then start by being away for just a few hours. However, as your child gets older you will find it more difficult to get sitters from the neighborhood. Check with your parent organization to see if it has listings of any trained sitters. Often workshops or training courses in caring for handicapped children are offered by parent organizations, and you can get a list of the people who have had such training. The special education department of a college or university nearby can be asked to post your name as wanting care for your handicapped child. Schools of nursing are also good sources of help.

Recently, respite care services for parents of handicapped children have appeared on the scene. The aides, or companions as they are sometimes called, have been trained to care for children and/or adults with all disabilities. Respite means relief, and the purpose of such programs is to offer parents relief from the everyday demands of constant care of a child with disabilities. Such care may be available in your home, a special respite care home, or an institution. It may be available by the hour, overnight, for weekends, or for as long as a month to allow parents to go on vacations or to help the family when someone is ill or hospitalized. If respite care is not available in your community, write to:

> Center for the Development of Community Alternative Service
>   Systems
> University of Nebraska Medical Center
> Omaha, Nebraska   68131

for information on such programs elsewhere and how to get one started in your community. Most of them have been started by small bands of parents. Respite care is a must for parents of children with handicaps, especially if the child requires considerable supervision or intensive care. And the respite should be for everyone in the family; siblings can get "burned out" and resentful if they're asked to do too much. Most of the services are reasonably priced and some programs even provide "scholarships" if you can't afford to pay anything.

It is also possible to get occasional or regular child care from professional agencies. Check "sitting services" in the Yellow Pages. They're likely to be costly, however, and you can't always be sure of getting someone who's comfortable and confident about caring for a handicapped child. You may have to do some preparing and educating, but consider it time well spent; you'll have another helper and you may have started that person out on a path of involvement with other handicapped children.

The same process of educating might have to be done if you're a working mother and need family day care. Check with your local department of social services or with your community-coordinated child care agency. Some departments of social services are involved in providing specialized day care for handicapped children, but if you cannot find such a service you will have to request care from a day care mother who is willing to learn, and then you'll have to spend the time teaching her.

Homemaker help is usually available through departments of social services or private professional agencies. Homemakers are generally reserved for situations in which the family's main provider of care is ill, hospitalized, or temporarily disabled. They take on more household responsibilities than a sitter would by preparing meals and doing light housekeeping, along with personal care duties.

Dreary as such thoughts may be, it's a good idea to think about what you would do in case of illness, hospitalization, or a crisis of another sort which might make it impossible for you to care for your child. You'll feel much more secure if you have tried some people or agencies and they know you and your child. Again, it is shortsighted to count only on your family.

What kinds of social and recreational activities are available for my child?

If your child is mildly handicapped you'll find that, as in education, more and more "regular" recreational activities programs for nonhandicapped children are opening their membership to children with handicaps. Community centers, YMCAs and YWCAs, Girl and Boy Scout troops, and local park and recreation departments are making an effort to provide extra staffing to accommodate children with disabilities.

But you need to exercise some caution and ask some questions before getting your child involved in a recreational mainstream program; you should make sure he can handle it. Is there someone on the staff who has special training and/or experience with children with disabilities? Does it look like some effort will be made to adapt the activities to match your particular child's needs and abilities? What's the ratio of staff members to children? What's the range of ages of the other children involved? How will grouping be handled? Are these planned activities competitive? Can your child compete?

On the other hand, if your child is mildly handicapped, most of his or her life will be spent in the mainstream, so you will want to give your child plenty of practice in socializing with other nonhandicapped children. You should expect the adults managing the activities to have positive attitudes about children with special needs and to communicate acceptance of differences to the other children in the program.

If your child is more seriously handicapped, you will most likely have to look for specialized programs with appropriate staffing ratios to meet the demands of supervising and teaching your child. Most city or county recreation or park departments provide special programs. Many Y's offer swim and gym programs for handicapped children. Call your parent organization and ask about special clubs or friend-to-friend programs. Check with the therapeutic recreation or adaptive physical education department at nearby universities to see if it offers an "activity clinic" for handicapped children. Or, ask if any college students might want to gain experience taking your child out for community recreational activities on weekends. Above all, keep your mind open and be receptive to all kinds of possibilities for socializing and fun. It's pretty well known by now that you don't have to be able to walk to enjoy dancing, nor do you have to be able to hear to dance. And you can bowl from a wheelchair.

What about higher education, jobs, and job training?

As your child approaches the teenage years, if not earlier, you will want to look ahead to the interests and aptitudes he or she seems to have or is likely to have in the future so that you can plan accordingly. Find out what your school system offers in the way of vocational education for handicapped children. A part of all vocational education monies is to be spent on handicapped children, so if the programs aren't there when you need them, make an appropriate fuss. It has been found that while specialized programs have been reasonably abundant for children in their early years, they have been abysmally scarce for children in their teens. The situation is improving somewhat, but complaints that there are insufficient programs addressing the vocational needs of handicapped children are still frequent and widespread.

You should also be aware of the availability of vocational rehabilitation services. These services generally become available to children 16 years of age and older and their essential function is to help handicapped people of working age prepare themselves for employment. To be eligible for services the handicapped individual must have a physical or mental disability which constitutes a substantial handicap to employment, and there must be a reasonable expectation that employment preparation will be successful. Individuals who have very severe disabilities which make them unemployable can be evaluated by vocational rehabilitation, but they're unlikely to receive services beyond that, in spite of recent efforts to extend the law to apply to persons with substantial disabilities.

After an evaluation which would include the examination of medical and education reports and an evaluation of vocational aptitude and interest, or fresh testing in any or all of these areas, the counselor recommends an individual program—perhaps specific job training or job placement. Or, if the person is less able, placement in a prevocational training program or a sheltered workshop may be recommended. There are also any number of medical services which may be provided if they are essential to achieving a specific vocational goal. Such services could include surgery, drugs, psychiatric treatment, medicine, braces, hearing aids, artificial limbs, glasses, or physical, occupational, or speech therapy. Generally, diagnosis and evaluation will be free. Counseling, job placement, and follow-up services should also be free. Medical services may or may not be paid for by the agency; this depends on the income of the client or his or her parents. Be sure to inquire about payment procedures for medical services before your child receives them.

If your child shows an unusual aptitude for academic or vocational pursuits requiring higher education, make sure he or she carefully selects course work in high school which will satisfy the admissions requirements at the school of his or her choice. You'll have to do some researching to find out if your child chose a school that provides resources and help for handicapped persons. Now that the 504 Regulations of the Rehabilitation Act of

1973 are in effect institutions of higher education are scurrying to comply with the law by making as many classes *and* buildings accessible to students with handicaps as they can, given the considerable costs involved. (This law and others will be discussed in Chapter 2.) Interpreters for deaf students, readers and tapes for blind students, resource centers and tutors for students with learning disabilities, and wheelchair ramps are among the services that schools are offering to accommodate greater numbers of handicapped students. A number of higher education accessibility guides have been developed and can be obtained by contacting the appropriate agency.

When the time comes to find a job, the Vocational Rehabilitation counselor should have suggestions. If nothing turns up through the counselor, some employment centers have rehabilitation counselors on the premises to assist handicapped people. Or, try to find out through your parent organization which local employers are hiring the handicapped. Then job hunt as you would for any person, but be realistic about your child's aptitudes, interests, and needs. Your child should apply for jobs commensurate with his skills. If your child is really qualified to do the work required, he or she should be considered favorably along with other applicants. Keep in mind that the 504 Regulations of the Rehabilitation Act forbid employment discrimination against the handicapped. So if you feel that your son or daughter has been denied employment because of a handicap, rather than a lack of qualifications to do the work, file a complaint and inform the employer you are doing so. If the employer receives any funds from the U.S. Department of Health, Education, and Welfare (HEW), file the complaint, by letter, to:

Director, Office for Civil Rights
Department of Health, Education, and Welfare
330 Independence Avenue, S.W.
Room 5400
Washington, D.C.   20201

Write or call the human relations commission of your county or state about grievance procedures.

Most handicapped people require some follow-up on the job from a counselor. There are adjustment problems for anyone in a new job; there are usually more of them for persons with handicaps. So if your child has found the job with the help of vocational rehabilitation, get back to the agency and ask for some counseling during the period of adjustment. It could make the difference between success and failure.

For general information on employment and a guide for job seekers write to:

President's Committee on Employment of the Handicapped
Washington, D.C.   20210

Does anyone help financially?

There's no doubt about it—children with handicapping conditions cost more to raise than nonhandicapped children. Some of the costs are predictable early on. There may be extraordinary medical expenses for diagnosis, therapies, or other treatment; for drugs or medicine; or for special diet supplements, special clothing needs, extra transportation costs, special schooling, and extra child care costs. But insurance plans help with medical costs, and there are some special benefits available elsewhere for people with handicapping conditions.

Paying for medical care

Almost all children with handicaps require more than the usual medical monitoring, so doctors' bills will be frequent. Any medical treatment will, of course, be expensive, so good medical coverage under an insurance plan is essential. No insurance plan will pay 100 percent of your costs, but some plans offer more assistance than others, and it's important to investigate carefully just what your group or family insurance plan covers. Look for basic benefits—ordinary hospitalization or medical care, outpatient treatment, diagnostic testing, and treatment in the doctor's office. Then you need to know what protection you have against catastrophic illness or accident expenses—long hospitalization, drugs and medications, nursing care, appliances, equipment rentals, and so on. And you need to know what psychiatric expenses are covered under your policy. All of this is important, whether there are handicapped children involved or not.

If at all possible, you should try to anticipate what those medical expenses are likely to be and budget accordingly. You will have to be ready to handle what your insurance won't cover, whether it's a whole category of expenses such as psychiatric costs, a percentage of any costs, or the "deductible" (the specific amount, usually between $50 and $200, which you must pay in entirety before the policy takes over and begins to pay all or a percentage).

Above all, make sure that your handicapped child is covered along with the rest of the family, and be aware that at age 19 most children are dropped from family policies unless they're full-time students. Find out if your dependent handicapped child can continue to be covered under the policy after 19.

A central source of information regarding private life insurance companies which will consider insuring disabled persons is the:

Health Insurance Institute
277 Park Avenue
New York, New York   10017

Tuition aid

Just how much help you will receive in paying the costs of private special schools—from preschools on up—will depend upon the reasons for the private placement and the extent to which your state, county, or city school system assumes responsibility. The federal law is pretty clear; it specifically states that handicapped children between the ages of three and twenty-one must receive a free, appropriate education. If the school system can't provide it, it must purchase it from a private school. However, the school system does not have to pay if the parents of a handicapped child decide that they prefer to send their child to a private school even though there is an appropriate program provided by the local school system.

If it's a question of private residential placement, again, the federal law is quite clear; the education should be at no cost to the parents, so long as it is not simply their preference that the child be at a residential school rather than in an appropriate program offered by the public school system. However, a few states appear to be contesting the federal law's insistence that special schooling be free and are asking parents of children in residential placements to pay some of the noneducational costs, such as food. Some states are asking other agencies, such as health or welfare departments, to bear relevant noneducational costs. Be sure to find out the situation in your state so that you are not surprised by such charges. Your state department of education should be a source of accurate information.

Some states and localities assumed responsibility for the cost of educating handicapped preschool children even though the federal law did not obligate them to do so before 1980.

Supplemental Security Income

Supplemental Security Income (SSI) is a federal program which provides monthly payments to disabled children or adults, among others, who have little or no income or resources. The amount of these payments varies from state to state. California, for instance, supplements the federal benefits. Other states don't supplement at all, in which case the federal maximum is the only payment ($208.20, July 1, 1979). Even the disabled children of wealthy families can receive SSI when they turn 18, unless they are still students, if they have no income or assets of their own.

The federal office which handles Supplementary Security Income is the Social Security Administration. Ask to be sent a brochure describing how SSI works for children or adults with disabilities and read it carefully before you go to the Social Security office. When you go, take your child with you unless it is impossible to do so. In that case, be sure to take along copies of medical records which indicate that your child is too disabled to cooperate in the application process and to sign and give consent for the release of medical or psychological reports. The new federal Privacy Act has made most Social Security Administration offices extremely cautious about allowing anyone, including parents, to provide "substitute consent." Be sure to inquire about other benefits which go along with SSI, such as Medicaid and certain social services.

To qualify for SSI, the applicant must be sufficiently disabled or blind. (There are fairly specific criteria which are matched against the evidence of disability in records gathered from your child's physician, psychologist, psychiatrist, or other professionals such as social workers, teachers, etc. Vision must be no better than 20/200, even with glasses, or a limited field of vision of 20 degrees or less for an applicant to be considered blind.) In both cases the applicant must have little or no income or assets. Bank accounts, trusts, bonds, and so on in a person's name might well disqualify him, although certain assets aren't counted. And he or she must be unable, because of the disability, to engage in substantial gainful activity. If your child is legally blind as well as handicapped, it may be advantageous for your child to apply as a blind rather than a disabled person. The income and disability criteria are less restrictive, and there may be an extra state supplement for blind persons that is not available for other disabilities.

If the applicant is a child (under 18) he or she is unlikely to qualify for SSI unless his or her parents' income is low, because their income and assets are considered available to the child and are "deemed" to the child in determining eligibility. If the person is a student between the ages of 18 and 21, parents' income and resources are also deemed to him or her unless the student's disability is severe enough to make future gainful employment improbable. For instance, the child might be a severely disabled person who is enrolled as a student in a special school which offers primarily training in self-help skills along with very limited prevocational training. If the school can prove that it is not preparing the person for competitive employment, then the child's income and not the parents' will be considered. And, presumably, the child will have little or no income, and would thus qualify for SSI benefits. You should have with you when you apply for SSI a written statement from the school presenting strong evidence that it is not preparing the student for remunerative employment. If the disabled person is not potentially employable and is enrolled in a vocational rehabilitation program, his or her counselor can help substantiate unemployability.

The disabled person can have limited assets (under $1500) and some earned or unearned income. The formulas for determining just what qualifies or disqualifies a person for SSI are complicated and often depend on particular circumstances. Where a person is living also makes a difference.

Parents of children living away from home should know about a special exception to deeming. If a disabled child is living away from home in a private, nonmedical facility, for instance a private residential school where education and training are provided in addition to residential care, and it is considered his or her permanent place of residence, deeming does not apply. If the child is otherwise eligible (in terms of disability, personal income, assets, and unemployability) he or she can receive SSI benefits. If the parents, or any third party such as a school system, are contributing to the child's support, the payments might be diminished by a fixed amount.

Medicare and Medicaid

Medicaid and Medicare are two different programs. Medicare pays some medical costs for social security recipients; Medicaid will pay most medical costs for people of low income. To be eligible for Medicaid you must be receiving public assistance, or have less than a certain monthly income and own less than a certain amount of accessible property, or have extraordinary medical expenses which you cannot pay, even though you have an income slightly above the minimum. Any handicapped person receiving Supplementary Security Income is also eligible for Medicaid, so be sure to read the preceding section on SSI to see if and when your child might qualify for those benefits. For more information on Medicaid services, call your local health department.

Are we, as the parents of handicapped children, eligible for additional income tax deducations?

Parents of handicapped children have several possibilities for claiming exemptions, deductions, and/or tax credits in addition to what any other parent can claim.

Exemptions.   You can claim the $1000 dependent exemption deduction for your child if you provided more than half of the child's support and he or she had less than $1000 gross income during the year. If the child is under 19 or a full-time student (regardless of age) in an educational institution, the $1000 income limitation does not apply.

In figuring out whether or not you contribute to more than half of your child's support, use actual expenses. You can include board, clothing, education, vacations, medical and dental care, medical insurance premiums, entertainment, etc. Keep reasonable records to document such expenses. You can also include lodging, using its fair market value for your calculations. Capital items such as furniture, appliances, and automobiles, if they are, in fact, for the individual in question, may be included in figuring the total. If your child receives Social Security benefits as the child of a deceased or disabled parent, or Supplemental Security Income, although not taxable, they do count in determining his or her share of support and must be compared to the amount which you as a parent contribute in computing who provides more than half of the support.

If your child is in a public institution or a private residential school, and even if you pay less than half or none of the cost of tuition, room, and board, you can claim the child as a dependent (regardless of his or her age) and take the exemption deduction of $1000 if the facility can qualify as an "educational institution." In such a case, tuition, room, and board are considered a scholarship and need not enter into your support calculations. (The institution must be making an effort to educate or train such persons to use their faculties to the extent that they are physically or mentally able to do so.)

Medical deductions.   In deciding whether or not you can consider your handicapped family member a dependent for purposes of medical deductions (as distinguished from exemption deductions) you can include any family member, regardless of age, even if he or she has an income of more than $1000 per year, *as long as you furnished more than half the person's support during the year.* That part of your total medical expenses paid during the year which exceeds 3 percent of your adjusted gross income can be deducted. Expenses for medical care include any amounts paid for the "diagnosis, cure, mitigation, treatment, or prevention" of a disease or a handicapping condition, or "for the purpose of affecting the structure or function of the body." Such expenses can include the following:

1. Fees paid to physicians, dentists, optometrists, psychologists, psychiatrists, nurses, therapists, hospitals, or laboratories. Drugs and medicines are also deductible but you can include only what exceeds 1 percent of your adjusted gross income. Contraceptives, over-the-counter medicines, vitamins, and special foods or beverages, if prescribed by a doctor, are deductible. The foods and beverages must be an addition to, not a substitute for, foods normally eaten by the dependent.

2. The entire cost of a residential school or institution; of a special day school; of a special class within a regular school or a special class within a parochial school; and of a sheltered workshop, special camp, or other special schooling, including the cost of meals, if provided, can be deducted *if the principal purpose of the class, school, camp, or institution is to mitigate or treat the dependent's handicapping condition.* The expense of a special community residence such as a halfway house or group home is also deductible under the same restraints.

3. Transportation expenses which are essential for obtaining medical care (diagnosis, cure, mitigation, treatment, or prevention of a handicapping condition) or are incurred in visiting a dependent at a residential facility, if the taxpayer's medical advisors consider the visits a necessary part of the dependent's treatment. You can also deduct the cost of hiring a person to accompany a handicapped child who cannot travel alone to obtain medical care as described above. Costs of meals and lodgings on long trips to get medical care, including trips to take a handicapped dependent to a special school, institution, or camp, are also deductible.

   Transportation expenses would include plane, train, bus, or taxi fares. (Be sure to keep proof of expenditures.) If you go by car, IRS allows 8 cents per mile, parking fees, and tolls. If you prefer, you can deduct gas and oil costs instead of 8 cents per mile.*

4. The entire expense of a registered or licensed nurse can be deducted. Costs of practical nurses, domestic helpers, or companions who give direct services to the disabled person are also deductible, but only that part of the wages that covers time spent in actual care of the handicapped person. If the care-giver's board is paid by the taxpayer, that is also deductible.

---

*IRS allowances change periodically. The latest IRS code should be reviewed.

5. Other special medical deductions.

   a) One-half of medical insurance premiums paid by you are deductible, up to $150 without regard to the 3 percent limitation. The rest of your medical insurance premiums are also deductible, but as an ordinary medical expense (i.e., it is subject to the 3 percent limitation).

   b) Costs of special equipment (including installation) to alleviate the person's handicap. However, this equipment must be depreciated over its useful life if its use extends beyond the tax year. Included in this equipment category are eyeglasses, crutches, braces, wheelchairs, incontinence pants (or disposable diapers if the child is well beyond the age of normal continence), artificial limbs and teeth, hearing aids, tape recorders, special mattresses, guide dogs (including their upkeep), elevators, air conditioning (if considered essential by a physician to alleviate the handicap), special equipment in automobiles, and the like. If the special equipment does not improve the value of your property, you can deduct the total cost; if it does, you can deduct the difference between the cost and the improvement in value.

Tax credits.   Be sure to check the Internal Revenue Service booklet on what credits are allowed. During recent years the tax law allowed a tax credit for child care or disabled dependent care expenses necessary to permit the taxpayer to be gainfully employed. But be careful; some of the disabled dependent care expenses may qualify as employment–related and also as medical expenses. You cannot include them in both computations.

A general word of advice: you will need documentation for any deductions or credits you claim. Be sure to keep receipts, canceled checks, bills, records of travel, records of dates of payment, amounts paid, services provided, and the names and addresses of those who provided them. If you've been conscientious about keeping the notebook discussed earlier, this won't be much of a burden. Remember, too, that tax law is sometimes subject to varying interpretations, so what passes under one auditor may not pass under another. If your medical expenses are extraordinarily high, you should be well prepared to be audited. The computer is very likely to "kick out" your return and ask for an audit. You should get the following publications from the nearest IRS office each year: Number 502, *Deductions for Medical and Dental Expenses;* 503, *Child Care and Disabled Dependent Care;* or Publication 17, which contains 502, 503, and other information as well.

How can my son or daughter be provided for after I'm gone?

One of the most difficult problems parents of seriously handicapped children have to deal with is planning how their children will be taken care of after their deaths. There are no easy answers and much depends on the kind and severity of the child's handicap. Also to be considered are the child's level of dependency, the role and responsibilities felt by the child's siblings or relatives, the type of living situation which will be best for the child—a home, a state institution, a private school, or a residence of some sort—and how much money is likely to be available as a basis for planning for your child's future.

There is a lot to think about and several decisions to make before you even contact a lawyer. When you feel you're ready to do so, you will want to make very certain that the lawyer you choose, if you don't already have one, has a good store of knowledge and experience in the application of your state laws to handicapped children. This is extremely important if your child is mentally or emotionally handicapped and could spend a period of time in an institution or state hospital. If that is the case, you will want to be very certain what claim the state would have to any funds or properties left in the child's name in the event of your death. Some states can claim all assets and use them to cover the full cost of care in an institution. Obviously, only the most enormous bequests would be sufficient.

There are ways to prevent states from claiming all assets. A knowledgeable lawyer can help you design a will that can assure you that your child will be provided for in the way you want. One of those ways is an indirect bequest by which you would leave property by will to a person other than your child with the understanding that it would be used for the benefit of your child. You run a risk, however, that unforeseen circumstances or events might cause the person to use the money for other purposes.

Another possibility is establishing a trust. A trust has the advantage of requiring the trustee to be accountable to legal authority for what he or she does with the property or money. In either case, you will need to select the receiver of the bequest or the trustee very carefully.

The wording of the trust is also important. To specify that the trustee must spend the income on the care or support of the handicapped child may make such money or property accessible to the state. However, to say that the trustee is to spend the income for comforts and luxuries for the child should be sufficient to keep the state from being able to claim the income.

The technicalities are such that they require a lawyer's assistance, yet not all lawyers are informed sufficiently about special conditions. If your child is mentally or emotionally handicapped, you will want to call your state or local association for retarded citizens or the mental health association and ask for the names of lawyers who are well versed in estate and will planning for parents of children who are retarded, mentally ill, or possess other severe disabilities. Although the following handbooks are written for parents of children who are retarded, the advice given in them holds true for parents of any handicapped child who may not gain self-sufficiency. Write to the National Association for Retarded Citizens, for *How to Provide for Their Future* at the following address:

National Association for Retarded Citizens
2709 Avenue E East
Arlington, Texas 76011

Or write the Public Affairs Committee for *Securing the Legal Rights of Retarded Persons* by Elizabeth Ogg at:

Public Affairs Committee
381 Park Avenue South
New York, New York 10016

A *guardianship* is also a possible solution. There are two kinds of guardianship: guardianship of a person and guardianship of an estate. The first type charges the person named with the supervision and personal care of a person; the second charges the guardian with management of the person's property. Either may require what is called a "declaration of incompetence," which is a legal way of saying that the person is totally incapable of self-management, including money affairs. Both kinds of guardianship require court orders. Think carefully before getting involved in a declaration of incompetence. If declared incompetent, the disabled person loses the right to vote, to buy or sell property, to have title to his or her earnings, and to write checks, among other privileges. If a person is so severely retarded that he or she could never have the skills which would allow him or her to make use of those rights, there is little lost if he is declared incompetent. But there is a lot lost if such a person is only mildly retarded. If a person who is mentally ill and declared incompetent as the prelude to commitment to a mental hospital recovers in time and wishes to exercise all of those rights, there will be problems. Fortunately, in many states guardianship no longer requires such a declaration. It involves taking away only a specified right from the disabled person.

Declarations of incompetency and the specific removal of rights through guardianship proceedings are not necessarily permanent, but they're hard to undo. If a court can determine that the disability has ceased and that the person has sufficient ability and skills to handle himself or herself and his or her income or property, guardianship can be terminated.

Now that I know a lot about resources, is there any other advice?

There are times when you will be calling or visiting an agency when you are angry because something is not happening for your child the way you had anticipated. Try not to vent that anger on an administrator. That administrator probably hears problems similar to yours all day long. Anger and hostility will not help in establishing an interpersonal relationship. Courtesy and mutual respect on the part of the agency administrator and the parent usually result in ultimate solutions to problems.

One often hears people who say, "When I have a problem I go to the top." Sometimes solutions are obtained from people at the top but the person who is generally responsible for delivering the program services is a lower level staff person. Going to the top without having dealt with the person responsible for providing the service can often result in some lingering animosity which can affect your child. The bottom–up approach is generally more successful than the top–down approach.

As was stated at the outset, knowing where to go and who to talk with is often a complex procedure. Dealing with some confusion and some possible shuffling among agencies requires some general knowledge and a great deal of patience. However, your increased knowledge, along with your improved interpersonal communication skills, will enable you to be an excellent advocate for your child.

Not every community has all it should have for children with special needs, but things are getting better all the time. The major force behind improvement is, and has always been, parents who have insisted that their children get what they need, and then work to see that they get it. Now there are laws which back many of their demands, so a parent's job today is somewhat different from what it was ten or more years ago. Then, parents' energies went toward creating educational and other services that didn't exist. Now, with so many services mandated, it is a matter of working to see that the services are as good as they should be. Monitoring one's own child's services is the basic task now, as is working to improve the system if it falls short of what's needed.

Where can I get the names and addresses of agencies, organizations, and other resources that I can refer to when seeking out information relative to my child?

Some of the most valuable resources are state and local guides to programs and services. More and more state and local agencies are producing explanatory brochures and manuals to assist parents in obtaining a more appropriate educational program for their child. Your state education department should be able to send you copies of informative materials they have developed, or they can direct you to appropriate sources. When you request materials, try to make that request as specific as possible, e.g., "May I please have your publication entitled, *Rights of Handicapped Children in the Schools.*" You may wish to enclose a stamped, self-addressed envelope with your request. This should facilitate a speedy response when looking for guidelines, manuals, directories, etc. One might frequently find that other state agencies (health, vocational rehabilitation, social services, etc.) and private sector agencies and organizations might have developed some useful materials. Ask your department of education about the availability of some of these materials.

If you wish to review copies of other publications, the following suggestions might be helpful:

See if your local public library has a copy. Don't buy a publication unless you know that it will be helpful; books are very expensive.

Check with local- or state-affiliated disability-related organizations to see if they maintain a lending library of some type.

If a publication is not available from libraries or organizations, ask the publisher if the company has a review-without-charge policy.

Some publishers have discount policies on book purchases if you are disabled or are the parent of a disabled individual.

Often, resource publications which contain the names, telephone numbers, and addresses of many organizations may be inaccurate because such information frequently changes. During the past four years, three-fifths of the state directors of special education have changed. If you call or write these or other individuals specified in this or any other publication, it is possible that you may receive a response from another person. If you don't get a response the first time, try again.

2

Legislation, Litigation, and Rights

STANLEY I. MOPSIK

Parents can serve as more effective advocates for their children if they're aware of their rights as guaranteed by federal, state, and local laws. Many of those rights have been secured by people like yourselves working through the litigatory and legislative processes.

When you visit, phone, or write your child's classroom teacher, counselor, principal, director of special education, or superintendent of schools concerning special education and related programs and services, the information obtained becomes a vital tool in securing programs and services for your child. In this chapter we provide you with some background information on the court cases and existing legislation which have greatly influenced present day programming and services for handicapped children. Additionally, we have tried to provide some capsule descriptions of the organization of government and the private sector with respect to the delivery of programs and services to the handicapped child. Some hints are also provided on the use of two communication tools: the telephone and the letter.

What effect does litigation have on the educational rights of the handicapped child?

The legality of denying public education to handicapped children by excluding them from or postponing their education is increasingly being challenged. The basis for this challenge comes from the equal protection clause of the 19th Amendment to the U.S. Constitution, which guarantees to all people equal protection under the law. What does equal protection mean? It means that *all* people must be afforded the same treatment. Thus, a state, an agency, or a legal entity cannot set up separate systems and procedures for dealing with different groups unless a compelling cause for such differential treatment can be demonstrated.

This right to equal protection under the law has caused public education to reexamine the terms "right to education" and "equal educational opportunity."

The right to education movement, as this revolution is called, is less than seven years old. It began in the summer and fall of 1971 when the state of Pennsylvania entered into a consent agreement (both parties agreed) with the plaintiff—the Pennsylvania Association for Retarded Citizens (PARC) and 13 mentally retarded children of school age (who were representing both themselves and all other retarded school children in the state). The suit was brought by PARC against the Commonwealth of Pennsylvania for failure to provide access to a free public education for all retarded children. The consent order provided the following:

> The state could not apply any law which would postpone, terminate, or deny mentally retarded children access to a publicly supported education, including a public school program, tuition or tuition maintenance, and homebound instruction.

> By October 1971, the plaintiff children were to have been reevaluated and placed in programs.

> By September 1972, all retarded children between the ages 6 and 21 were to be provided with a publicly supported education.

> Local school districts providing preschool education to any child were required to provide the same for mentally retarded children.

> It was highly desirable to educate these children in a program most like that provided to nonhandicapped children.

The three-judge panel found most convincing the testimony of a number of expert witnesses who focused on the following two major points:

> Systematic educational instruction for the mentally retarded will produce learning.

> Education cannot be defined solely as academic experiences, but it must be viewed as a continuous process in which individuals learn to cope and function within their environment. Thus, acquisition of the general self-care skills required for independence is a legitimate outcome that can be achieved through an educational program.

This landmark decision was followed by much hoopla. However, there were many doubting Thomases who said, "Well, let's see what the future brings." Later that year a more impressive ruling was handed down by the Federal District Court of the District of Columbia. In Mills v. Board of Education (1972), the parents and guardians of seven District of

Columbia children brought a class action suit against the board of education, the department of human resources, and the mayor for failure to provide *all children* (as opposed to just the mentally retarded in the PARC case) with a publicly supported education. The plaintiff children ranged in age from six to seventeen and presented varying types of handicapping conditions.

In August of 1972, U.S. District Court Judge Joseph Waddy issued a decree which provided the following:

A declaration of the constitutional right of all children, regardless of any exceptional condition or handicap, to a publicly supported education;

A declaration that the District of Columbia's rules, policies, and practices which excluded children from school without a provision for adequate and immediate alternative educational services, and the absence of prior hearing and review of placement procedures, denied the plaintiffs, and the class of individuals they represented, of their equal protection rights under the law.

The defendants claimed that they were unable to provide such services unless Congress (the funding source for District of Columbia residents) appropriated increased funds or allowed them to divert funds from other educational services. The court responded:

The District of Columbia's interest in educating the excluded children clearly must outweigh its interest in preserving its financial resources. If sufficient funds are not available to finance all of the services and programs that are needed and desirable in the system, then the available funds must be expended equitably in such a manner that no child is entirely excluded from a publicly supported education consistent with his needs and ability to benefit therefrom. The inadequacies of the District of Columbia public school system, whether occasioned by insufficient funding or administrative inefficiency, certainly cannot be permitted to bear more heavily on the "exceptional" or handicapped child than on the normal child.

Both the PARC and Mills cases were class action suits. In a class action suit a named plaintiff (or plaintiffs) brings an action for himself on behalf of all persons similarly situated. For instance, a suit may be undertaken on behalf of a class, a plaintiff, all mentally retarded persons, all residents of a single state, or all persons residing in state institutions. In order for a plaintiff to maintain a class action status, many complex procedural requirements must be satisfied.

The PARC and Mills decisions were of landmark importance and represented the beginning of special education litigation that protects the rights of all our handicapped citizens. Such litigation also presented a basis for future federal legislation and commitment to our handicapped citizenry since they both set legal precedents.

Yes, a revolution, albeit a quiet one, is occurring which will make educational opportunity a reality for all handicapped children. There are, however, pros and cons of such action and Table 2.1 gives examples of both.

Table 2.1 The Pros and Cons of Class Action Suits

PROS	CONS
Such suits can contribute positively to achieving policy change for large numbers of people.	If the plaintiffs are not fully representative of all the injustices of other members of the class, the relief granted by the court may not be sufficient to provide all members of the class with adequate remedies.
If a named plaintiff is dropped from a case, the case is not dropped because there are other individuals who are still directly affected by the outcome of a case.	
If, prior to a hearing, a temporary restraining order is issued, it applies to the group and not just a plaintiff [i.e., if mentally retarded children are being deprived of medical services and a restraining order is issued, all mentally retarded children are affected and not just the plaintiff(s)]. Therefore, all children of the class would receive medical services until the suit is settled.	
Final relief granted by the court is for all members of the class and is not limited to the named plaintiff.	If the class action suit issue is lost, it will be harder for other members of the class to bring another suit on the same issues involving the same circumstances.

I generally understand the importance of the PARC and Mills cases as decisive class action suits, but what do these "legal precedents" mean for me?

A precedent is a rule to guide or support other judges in deciding future cases. However, as a precedent, a decision will have most value in the jurisdiction where it is handed down. For example, a precedent-setting case in Idaho is more likely to be followed in Idaho than in New York, even if the same issue is being decided. Also, courts in one region of the country are more likely to follow decisions of other courts in that same region, and certain decisions of certain state, federal district, and federal appeals courts are considered more influential than others because of the recognized competence of the judges.

For instance, a decision of a circuit court of appeals has more influence than that of a federal district court. A decision by the U.S. Supreme Court establishes the greatest possible precedent because Supreme Court decisions are binding nationwide. State courts, when hearing cases relating to federal law, conform their decisions to Supreme Court rulings.

A caution, however, must be noted; when interpreting and applying Supreme Court decisions to cases with slightly different facts, lower courts may adjudicate cases differently until a Supreme Court ruling occurs that clarifies or strengthens the position. This practice accentuates the point that law does not stay static and is ever-changing over time.

In summary, a decision's importance is based upon the following five factors:

the stature of the court that issued the decision;

whether the decision is published and available;

whether the decision is being appealed;

the applicability of the decision to a specific set of facts;

the stature of the judge that issued the decision.

Now that I understand the importance of litigation, what about these new federal laws regarding services for the handicapped?

Services for handicapped children in special education programs have their beginnings in the development of state schools and institutions for the handicapped. The first ones were state schools for the deaf in Kentucky

(1823) and Ohio (1927), and schools for the blind in Boston and New York (1832). Since the establishment of these facilities, special education has made monumental advances, especially in the 1970s.

On November 29, 1975, President Gerald Ford signed into law the Education for All Handicapped Children Act, a measure of landmark dimensions which committed the federal government to the most substantial financial contribution ever made for handicapped children, while also defining and strengthening the educational rights of these children. New Jersey Senator Harrison Williams (D), the legislation's prime sponsor, has called this act, P.L. 94–142, one of the most significant education bills since the passage of the multibillion dollar Elementary and Secondary Education Act of 1965.

In addition to P.L. 94–142, Section 504 of the Rehabilitation Act of 1973 was defined by the issuance of regulations on June 3, 1977. These regulations, which apply to all recipients of Health, Education, and Welfare funds, forbid acts of discrimination against qualified handicapped persons. This act represents the first federal civil rights law protecting the rights of handicapped persons and reflects a national commitment to end discrimination against the handicapped.

Let's now find out what both of these laws are about.

What is P.L. 94–142?

Federal statistical data indicate that there are fewer than four million identified handicapped children in the United States today, and that their special education needs are not being met. Projections by the Bureau of Education for the Handicapped indicate that there may be more than seven million handicapped children in this country. In addition, Congress found that a large percentage of handicapped children in the United States do not receive appropriate educational services enabling them to have full equality of opportunity. Congress also found that many handicapping conditions go undetected, and therefore children go unserved. A lack of adequate services within school systems has also been discovered. As a result, families must often at great cost find services outside the school system. Developments in the training of teachers in diagnostic and instructional procedures have advanced to the point that, according to Congress, if state and local education agencies are given the necessary funds, they can and will provide comprehensive special education and related services to meet the needs of handicapped children.

Congress believes that state and local education agencies have a responsibility to provide education for all handicapped children but that present, and possibly future, financial resources are inadequate to meet the special educational needs of handicapped children. Therefore, it is in the national interest that the federal government assist state and local efforts to provide programs to meet the educational needs of handicapped children in order to assure equal protection under the law.

Not only was interest in providing free and appropriate services to the nation's handicapped children a mounting congressional concern, but the introduction of legislation followed some landmark court cases which established in law the right of all handicapped children to an education.

P.L. 94-142 of the Education of All Handicapped Children Act of 1975 ensures that all handicapped children have available to them a free, appropriate public education which includes special education and related services.

The term "special education" means specially designed instruction to meet the unique needs of a handicapped child and includes classroom instruction, physical education, home instruction, and instruction in hospitals and institutions. The term "related services" means transportation and such developmental, corrective, and other supportive services as may be required to assist the handicapped child so that he or she can benefit from special education. This would include speech pathology and audiology, psychological services, physical and occupational therapy, recreational activities, and medical and counseling services, except that such medical services would be for diagnostic purposes only. These services would help parents in their attempts to identify and assess their child's handicapping condition early.

Handicapped children are defined under the law. This should make it easier for you to find out quickly if your child falls in this category. Handicapped children are legally defined as those who are:

mentally retarded, hard of hearing, deaf, speech impaired, visually handicapped, seriously emotionally disturbed, orthopedically impaired, or otherwise health impaired, or children with specific learning disabilities, who by reason thereof require special education and related services.

The local education agency has a responsibility to ensure that all children within its jurisdiction who are handicapped, regardless of the severity of their handicap, and in need of special education and related services, are identified, located, and evaluated. Children evaluated must meet the criteria set forth in the preceding definition.

It is of great importance to all parents of handicapped children to know what the law says. The following are some of the key provisions of P.L. 94–142:

Highest priority must be given to handicapped children who are not now receiving an education and to the most severely handicapped children whose education is inadequate.

Strong safeguards of the due process right of parents and children must be guaranteed by states and localities. These safeguards protect parents' rights in all procedures related to the identification, evaluation, and placement of their children, and the provision of an appropriate education for their children. They also provide for the opportunity to protest education decisions made by school officials.

Strong impetus is given to educating children in the "least restrictive environment." Children must be placed in special or separate classes only when it is impossible to work out a satisfactory placement in a regular class with supplementary aids and services. This will be one of the basic considerations in designing appropriate programs for each child.

All methods used for testing and evaluation must be racially and culturally nondiscriminatory, and must be in the primary language or mode of communication of the child. No one test or procedure may be the sole means of making a decision about an educational program.

Individualized education plans are to be prepared for each child, with parents participating on the team that draws up the plan. (The child, too, is to be included, when appropriate.) These prescriptions must include short- and long-term educational goals and specific services to be provided. This provision went into effect in the school year beginning in 1977, and all individual plans must be reviewed at least annually and revised according to the child's changing needs.

When children are placed in private schools by state or local education systems in order to receive an appropriate education, this must be done at no cost to parents; private school programs must meet standards set by the law and schools must safeguard the rights of parents and children guaranteed by law.

The development of programs for preschool children is encouraged by creating a special incentive grant to states for providing services to handicapped children aged three to five.

Each state must set up an advisory board, including handicapped individuals, teachers, and parents of handicapped children. This board is to advise the state on unmet needs, comment publicly on rules and regulations, and assist in evaluating programs.

Funds can be withheld if, after reasonable notice and an opportunity for a hearing, a state is found by the U.S. Commissioner of Education to have failed to comply with the act.

Payments by the state to local school systems may also be suspended for noncompliance. If the state determines that a locality is unable or unwilling to set up or consolidate programs, or has children who can best be served by regional or statewide programs, the state will use the funds to provide services directly to those children.

You can get a copy of P.L. 94–142 (42 Federal Register 42474) by writing your congressman or ordering it from the Superintendent of Documents, U.S. Government Printing Office, Washington, D.C., 20402, for 75 cents per copy. In addition to the provisions already mentioned, each state is required to develop a state special education plan. The plan must detail how the state and each school district within the state intends to carry out the law. These documents are available to the public and can be obtained from the state's department of education or the local board of education.

P.L. 94–142, while an extremely important part of the Education of the Handicapped Act, is only a section (Part B) of the act. Synopses of the other provisions follow.

Part A—General Provisions. The general provisions section defines the disabilities covered by the act while designating the Bureau for the Education of the Handicapped within the United States Office of Education as the principal agency responsible for carrying out programs and projects related to the education and training of the handicapped.

Part B—P.L. 94–142.

Part C—Centers and Services to Meet Special Needs of the Handicapped. Part C of the act provides for the establishment of regional resource centers which would develop and apply models to appraise the special needs of the handicapped, and serve as a resource for schools, agencies, and institutions. These centers may be granted funding by the commissioner of education and they can also develop programs for handicapped children as well as provide consulting services.

Part D—Training Personnel for the Education of the Handicapped. The U.S. Commissioner of Education may also make grants to institutions of higher education and nonprofit agencies to aid in the training of the following personnel:

teachers, administrators, and other specialists engaged in the education of the handicapped;

teachers, administrators, supervisors, and related specialists engaged in or preparing to engage in providing services to the handicapped children.

This section also provides for the establishment and maintenance of stipends and scholarships for training personnel in the two areas listed above.

Part E—Research in the Education of the Handicapped. Part E of the act states that grants and contracts for research and demonstration purposes may be made to state and local agencies, institutions of higher learning, and other public or nonprofit private education or research agencies or organizations engaged in the education of the handicapped. In addition to research, new provisions to Part E support such activities as instructional development and model programs.

Part F—Instructional Media for the Handicapped. The purpose of Part F is to provide for the deaf in both cultural and educational areas and to facilitate the educational advancements of handicapped individuals through the research, production, and distribution of instructional media. The training of persons in the use of educational media and technology for instructional purposes is also authorized.

Part G—Special Programs for Children with Learning Disabilities. Special programs are authorized to support research training and model centers to meet the needs of children with specific learning disabilities. This section expired October 1, 1978, and there will be no further funding available under this provision. The new guidelines governing support for research and related purposes (new to Part E) will govern continuation projects under Part G as well as Part E. The model projects provisions under Part E will ensure the equitable allocation of funds among different disability groups and not just the learning disabled, as specified by Part G.

What is the 504 Regulation of the Rehabilitation Act of 1973?

Many individuals have said that the 504 Regulation has more power than any other piece of legislation in bringing our handicapped citizens into the mainstream of national life. This civil rights law, when fully enforced, can eliminate discrimination against disabled children and adults in education, employment, housing, health services, recreation, and eleven other areas that other citizens normally take for granted.

The 504 Regulation is actually a single sentence provision of the Rehabilitation Act, and is stated as follows:

No otherwise qualified individual shall solely by reason of his handicap be excluded from participation in, be denied the benefits of, or be subjected to discrimination under any program or activity receiving federal financial assistance.

The federal government was responsible for defining what Section 504 meant and on April 28, 1977, regulations were signed and issued by former Secretary of HEW, Joseph Califano.

The regulations of the Rehabilitation Act affect all recipients of HEW funds, and that includes states, counties, cities, colleges and universities, public and private schools, hospitals and clinics, and other agencies and organizations which provide programs and services.

Although only recipients of HEW funds are currently covered by the regulations, similar regulations are planned to cover agencies receiving any funds from the federal government. The following are some of the key provisions of the act's regulations:

All new facilities must be barrier-free, making them accessible to and usable by the handicapped.

Programs in existing facilities must be accessible. If alternatives for accomplishing this are not now possible (such as reassigning students to accessible locations, redesigning equipment, providing aides, interpreters, and appropriate materials such as braille texts and large print books), structural changes must be made within three years.

Colleges and universities may not discriminate against handicapped persons in their recruitment and admissions policies, nor in their treatment of them after admission. In addition, discrimination is prohibited in all college-related activities, including counseling, athletics, social and financial assistance, student employment, and other programs receiving federal funds.

Other provisions of the act are similar to those of the Education of All Handicapped Children Act since each school system must actively develop and implement programs to identify, locate, and evaluate unserved handicapped children; educate handicapped children in the regular classroom whenever possible; and give parents an adequate opportunity to seek a review of education decisions and challenge them, if necessary. A high priority is placed on pursuing cases in which a pattern of discriminatory placements may be involved.

Strong provisions protecting the rights of the handicapped job seeker are also part of the act. They require employers to make "reasonable accommodations" to make it possible for a disabled employee to hold a job by making facilities accessible; acquiring, modifying, or redesigning equipment or devices; providing readers or interpreters; and eliminating tests which "screen out" handicapped employees.

If you feel that you or your child has been discriminated against, you have 180 days to file a complaint. Investigatory procedures, as well as procedures for hearings, have been established.

To get more specific information about the 504 Regulation, you may write for your own copy of the Rehabilitation Act of 1973:

The U.S. Department of Health, Education, and Welfare
Office of Civil Rights
330 Independence Avenue, S.W.
Room 5400
Washington, D.C.   20201

If you have any specific questions concerning compliance which you would like to address to a nongovernmental source, you can call Mainstream Inc. (202) 833-1136. Mainstream is a Washington, D.C.-based nonprofit organization founded to encourage compliance with the Rehabilitation Act.

What other significant legislation for the handicapped has been passed at the federal level?

There are a number of federal laws which affect the handicapped person. The following are synopses of those laws:

The Economic Opportunity Act Amendments of 1972 (P.L. 92-424)

The Department of Health, Education, and Welfare was ordered to establish policies and procedures designed to assure that no less than 10 percent of the total number of enrollment opportunities in the nation's Headstart Program be available for handicapped children, and that services be provided to meet their special needs. Effective July 1, 1975, a 10 percent mandate was in effect in each state. The definition of handicapped used in these amendments is the same as that definition appearing in the Elementary and Secondary Education Act (mentally retarded, hard-of-hearing, deaf, speech impaired, visually handicapped, seriously emotionally disturbed, crippled, and otherwise health impaired).

The Vocational Education Amendments of 1968 (P.L. 90-576)

The Vocational Education Act provides that 10 percent of funds for vocational education must be spent for the handicapped, and that a national advisory council on vocational education be created, with at least one member of the council experienced in the education and training of handicapped persons. State advisory councils are also required to have a member who possesses special knowledge, experience, or qualifications with respect to the special education needs of the handicapped. Vocational education is defined as training, under public supervision, in a program designed to prepare people for gainful employment as skilled or semiskilled workers. It does not include programs which are considered to be professional or which require a college degree.

School Assistance in Federally Affected Areas (Impact Aid) P.L. 81-87 (as amended by P.L. 93-380)

The School Assistance in Federally Affected Areas Act provides aid for the maintenance and operation of the nation's school districts which have been affected by the presence of federal installations. The purpose of the act was to reduce the inequities to local school districts brought about by the presence of areas of tax exempt federal lands, coupled with a district's responsibility to provide an education to dependents of federal employees. The act also provides for one and one-half the aid for a handicapped child that is provided for the normal child under this impact aid act. However, a local education agency can only receive this aid if it is providing a program designed to meet the special education needs of the handicapped child.

An Act to Promote the Education of the Blind (P.L. 1879)

This act created the American Printing House for the Blind, a nonprofit institution located in Lexington, Kentucky, which supplies educational materials and tangible apparatus to blind and multiply handicapped persons. The act established a perpetual fund for use in manufacturing and furnishing special books and other materials adapted for the instruction of the blind. These materials are distributed among all the public institutions in the nation in which blind students are educated.

Gallaudet College (P.L. 83–420)

This act authorizes the appropriation of funds that Congress may determine appropriate for the operation of a private nonprofit educational institution in Washington, D.C. This institution, Gallaudet College, provides graduate, undergraduate, and preparatory school programs for the deaf, as well as a preschool program. There is also a graduate school program in the field of deafness and adult education for deaf persons.

Title I Elementary and Secondary Education Act (ESEA) of 1965 (P.L. 89–10)

Title I of the Elementary and Secondary Education Act provides financial assistance to local education agencies for the education of children from low–income families. Public Law 89–313 amended this title to provide grants to state agencies directly responsible for providing a free public education for handicapped children in state operated and state supported schools.

Developmental Disabilities Services and Facilities Construction Amendments of 1970 (P.L. 91–517)

The creation of the Developmental Disabilities Services and Facilities Construction Amendments of 1970 was the result of the realization that numerous services for the disabled existed but were not coordinated enough to form a comprehensive delivery system. Those who developed the program reasoned that if a structure was developed which would focus on the coordination of federal, state, and local resources, increased services to the disabled would result. The principle emphasis of this act is on planning for rather than providing services. It established grants to help with the following:

assisting nonprofit private agencies in the construction of facilities to serve the developmentally disabled;

demonstrating new or improved techniques in serving the developmentally disabled;

providing services to persons with developmental disabilities, including costs of operations, staffing, and maintenance of facilities;

training specialized personnel to assist in serving the developmentally disabled.

The Developmentally Disabled Assistance and Bill of Rights Act of 1974 (P.L. 94-103)

P.L. 94-103 maintained as developmentally disabling the conditions of mental retardation, cerebral palsy, epilepsy, and other neurological disorders, and added autism. In addition, the definition included dyslexia if it is attributable to the other specified developmental disabilities, and the provisions of the 1970 act were extended, with numerous changes made in state plan requirements. The act increased consumer participation while furthering affirmative action among developmental disabilities grantees. The following are two new important components which have been included in the law:

Special Projects and Projects of National Significance. These are developmental disabilities funds which are awarded to specific project grants to public and/or private nonprofit organizations and/or agencies.

Protection and Advocacy of Individual Rights. This provision is intended to provide a system of protection and advocacy services that can safeguard the human rights of all individuals with a developmental disability against discrimination, abuse, and neglect. To ensure that the rights of individuals are protected, each state participating in the Developmental Disabilities Program is required to have a system to protect and advocate for the rights of individuals with disabilities.

Model Secondary School for the Deaf Act (P.L. 89-694)

This act established a model secondary school for the deaf, serving primarily the residents of the District of Columbia and nearby states. This high school is to serve as a model for the development of similar schools across the country in formulating new educational methods, technology, and curriculum.

Title III Elementary and Secondary Education Act of 1965 (P.L. 89-10) (as amended by P.L. 93-380)

This act directs the commissioner of education to carry out a program for making grants for supplementary educational centers and to stimulate and assist in the development and establishment of exemplary elementary and secondary school educational programs to serve as models for regular school programs.

Now that you have read these legislative synopses, you may wish to secure further information about specific provisions of the legislation and the laws as they are being implemented in your locality. Additionally, you may wish to get the most recent version of the legislation. Table 2.2 provides you with some direction as to agencies and organizations that can provide additional information or direct you to an appropriate information source.

Table 2.2 Legislative Acts Concerning the Disabled and Information Sources

Name of Legislative Act	Probable Implementing Agency or Information Source
The Economic Opportunity Amendments of 1972 (P.L. 92–424)	Local Headstart program director
	State Department of Education, Early Childhood specialist
	Department of Human Resources or Public Welfare
Vocational Education Amendments of 1968 (P.L. 90–576)	Local Education Agency, Vocational Education supervisor
	State Department of Education, Division of Vocational/Technical Education
	State Advisory Council on Vocational Education
School Assistance in Federally Affected Areas (Impact Aid) (P.L. 81–87) (amended by P.L. 93–380)	State Department of Education
	Local Education Agency
An Act to Promote Education of the Blind (P.L. 1879)	American Printing House for the Blind, Lexington, Kentucky
	State Department of Education, State Director of Special Education
Gallaudet College (P.L. 83–240)	Gallaudet College Washington, D.C.
Title I Elementary and Secondary Education Act	State Department of Education, Federal Program Title I Administrator
	Local Education Agency, Federal Program Title I Official
The Developmentally Disabled Assistance and Bill of Rights Act of 1974 (P.L. 94–103) and the Developmental Disabilities Services and Facilities Construction Amendments of 1970 (P.L. 91–517)	Department of Health and Mental Hygiene, Developmental Disabilities Council Director or other designated agency

Table 2.2 continued

Name of Legislative Act	Probable Implementing Agency or Information Source
Model Secondary School for the Deaf Act (P.L. 89-694)	Model Secondary School for the Deaf, Washington, D.C.
Title III Elementary and Secondary Education Act of 1965 (P.L. 89-10) as amended by P.L. 93-380	State Department of Education, Title III Federal program administrator Local Education Agency, Title III Federal program project administrator
The Education for All Handicapped Children Act (P.L. 94-142) The Education of the Handicapped Act (P.L. 93-380)	State Department of Education, Director of Special Education Local Education Agency, Director of Special Education
The Rehabilitation Act of 1973 and 504 Regulations	State Department of Education, Director of Special Education, Equal Opportunity Office or Division of Vocational Rehabilitation (Note: In some states Vocational Rehabilitation may be a separate agency or located within another agency.), Office for Civil Rights, regional HEW office

What are the differences, if any, among regulations, rules, and bylaws?

It is impossible for Congress, state legislative bodies, and local governing authorities to spell out in each law exactly how it will be implemented. There are often very complex technical issues that cannot be addressed within the legislation. Therefore, the executive agency which is assigned to administer a law (e.g., P.L. 94-142 was assigned to HEW's Office of Education Bureau for the Education of the Handicapped) issues detailed regulations explaining procedures for implementation. These regulations have the force of law. In many state and governmental agencies these regulations are often called bylaws or rules.

One often sees documents entitled "departmental procedures or guidelines." Procedures or guidelines are the responsibility of the agency or department issuing them; however, they generally do not have the force of law. Procedures and guidelines are usually evolving documents which can be frequently changed.

Where can I go for help in understanding the bureaucratic writing style of regulations?

The difficulties which lay persons encounter in reading federal regulations are created by the bureaucratic jargon utilized and the complex organization of the documents. The regulations are definitely not organized like the tested James Beard recipe. To help people understand how to use these documents, the Office of the Federal Register (the organization responsible for publishing federal regulations) conducts free classes in Washington, D.C. These classes are open to the general public. Briefings are also conducted in the main cities of the ten federal regions. If you are interested in obtaining the schedule of classes you should write to the Office of the Federal Register to ask to be notified of the next class to be held in your area. Inquiries should be addressed to:

> Federal Register Classes
> Office of Federal Register
> Washington, D.C.   10408

Since some of the federal regional meetings may be inconvenient for you, assistance can always be obtained from state and local agency administrators of regulations, and state and local advocacy and interest organizations.

Spending some time in learning to understand the organization and coding of regulations as well as the jargon utilized will help you understand how to use these regulatory documents effectively.

How are government and the private sector organized to assure that programs and services get to my child?

In most cases, the federal government is not the prime deliverer of direct programs and services for handicapped children. State and local agencies are prime deliverers in most cases and, therefore, inquiries concerning delivery should be made directly to them.

The *Directory of Federal Assistance for Programs Serving the Handicapped* lists 130 programs which have provisions for handicapped individuals. Since the major focus of this book is special education we have included an organizational chart (see organizational chart, Figure 2.1) which depicts the new federal Department of Education. Programs and services related to the handicapped are lodged under an Assistant Secretary for Special Education and Rehabilitative Services (see asterisk connotation).

Figure 2-1

DEPARTMENT OF EDUCATION

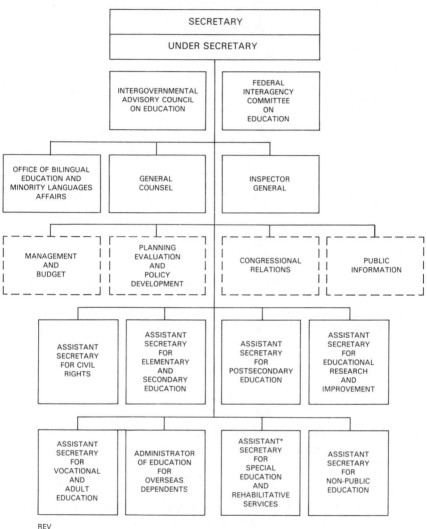

REV

_____INDICATES OFFICES STIPULATED IN LEGISLATION
― ― ―INDICATES OFFICES NOT STIPULATED IN LEGISLATION

The new Department of Education is administered by an individual in the position of secretary. Within the department are various offices, administrations, and divisions and bureaus. The bureau with the prime responsibility for special education programs is the Bureau of Education for the Handicapped (BEH). This bureau is located within the office of the Assistant Secretary for Special Education and Rehabilitative Services.

Although BEH is represented by some 200 staff members, it is just one of many agencies within the federal bureaucratic structure. BEH has the legal responsibility under its authorizing legislation to ensure that all handicapped children receive a free and appropriate educational program. The funds to be received by BEH for the purpose of state assistance amounted to more than $800 million in Fiscal Year 1980 (October 1 to September 30). The money is channeled to State Departments of Education (SEA) to provide direct services to children if the plan they develop for the delivery of such services is approved by the BEH. Once a state receives the funds under the provisions of P.L. 94-142, 75 percent of the total received by the SEA goes to the local education agency (LEA) where it is then distributed among the identified handicapped children for direct services. The remainder may be used by the SEA for model programs or projects.

As you can see from Figure 2.2 (the process is actually much more complicated) the funds that Congress approves eventually get to your child. You may now be wondering how one can be assured that the funds are being used for purposes expressly defined within law. There are a number of mechanisms which help ensure this:

Local agencies audit annually the use of federal funds.

The SEA conducts annual compliance reviews of LEA use of P.L. 94-142 funds.

BEH conducts annual program reviews in state and local education agencies to ensure the appropriate use of federal funds.

Congress, through the General Accounting Office (GAO), conducts audits and analyses of federal programs. The GAO carries out the congressional responsibility for determining whether federal agencies are complying with the law, and investigating whether the activities are being accomplished economically.

Various national organizations and interest groups closely monitor federal, state, and local agencies with respect to the administration of laws.

Figure 2-2
Special Education Funding Process

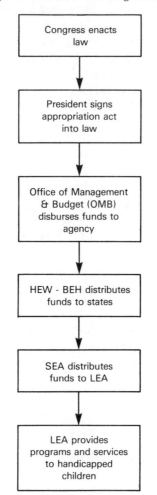

The private sector has no direct legal responsibility for assuring that handicapped children receive a free and appropriate education. An SEA or LEA, however, may contract with a private sector agency or institution to provide programs and services. The private sector then has a responsibility to the funding source agency.

Private sector agencies do provide direct services to handicapped children. Most of these agencies that operate school programs must be accredited or approved by SEAs and therefore must meet state laws with respect to the provision of appropriate special education programs and services. If state and/or federal funds are being utilized to provide for the private sector program, those agencies responsible for funding will monitor programs, as well as look at economic feasibility. (For example, does it cost more to provide the program and/or service in the private sector than it does in the public school?) Monitoring of private sector programs is likely to be more comprehensive than the monitoring of public sector programs.

Although federal law governs the delivery of programs and services to handicapped children, it must be recognized that less than 10 percent of the funds supporting special education comes from the federal government. State and local support represents the major base for the support of such programs.

Once you've added the information on litigation, legislation, and organizational structure to your store of knowledge, you're ready to use that knowledge in the verbal and written communication process.

Are there any effective methods which can be used when communicating by telephone or letter?

One of the best ways to assure answers to your questions when you want them (and not two months later) is to know how to effectively use the communication devices available to you.

Telephone

When you have a question or a problem, request to speak to a specific person; anyone in the office won't do.

Always be courteous. Many officials are constantly harrassed within and outside of their organization. Try not to increase their frustrations by beginning your phone conversation in an angry tone of voice.

Have your facts or specific questions in mind before you call; have notes if necessary.

If the individual doesn't have the answer, ask to speak to someone who does. Always request the name of the person you're talking with, or the person you need to contact. If the person you need to contact is not available, request a return call. Give notice that you will call back if a call is not received.

If answers are unsatisfactory or the official is not polite, request to talk to the individual's superior. Always be courteous even if the circumstances make that difficult.

Provide the party returning your call with options in reaching you. Give telephone numbers (home, work, friends, relatives, etc.) where you can be reached. Your willingness to be available for contact connotes the importance of your question, concern, or problem.

Keep notes of conversations; you may need these notes at a future time. (For example, our telephone conversation of 6/30/78 indicated a placement for John in a resource room at Superior Elementary School.)

If specific information or decisions are related over the phone, ask the individual to put those comments in writing. If the person is unwilling to do that you may wish to write the person a letter indicating your understanding of the information conveyed to you.

If you are still unclear about the information received via phone, ask for a face-to-face meeting.

Always end your conversation on a positive note. (For example, "I don't agree with that decision, but I appreciate your frankness and your time.")

Letter

Try to type any letter you send if it's possible, especially if your handwriting is not clearly legible.

Write your letter to a specific person, including name, title, and address of person to receive the communication.

Address your primary reason for writing early in the communication. Don't write three or four pages of history before getting to your primary issue. Remember, other people are probably writing letters similar to yours.

If your request involves a face-to-face meeting, give a number of alternate meeting dates of when you are available.

If you are writing to a local special education official with a problem or concern that he or she can directly address, do not also send copies of that communication to the state director of special education, your congressmen, the governor, and so on. Get a response directly from the official responsible before you circumvent the system and use political pressure. In many cases the responsible official will be drafting the response or providing the information for the response to their constituent.

Always convey a rational positive tone. (For example, "I know we are both interested in providing the best services for handicapped children.")

If you are requesting something which may have a price, indicate you are willing to pay for it. You may receive a free complimentary copy as evidence of good will.

Follow up communications which called for a response and did not receive one. A phone call would probably be the most expeditious way of communicating with the nonrespondent official. If it is a long distance call, ask if the person will accept the charges since you were inconvenienced by not receiving a prompt response.

In all forms of communication, the clarity with which you can define your problem, or state your concern or question will facilitate the receiver's response. Give careful thought to your call or letter.

3

The Parent-School Partnership

JUDITH ANDREWS AGARD

This chapter and those that follow will provide you with the foundation you need to be an effective advocate for your child and to work in cooperation with the educators in your community to assure that your child receives a free, appropriate public education to meet his or her needs.

In this chapter we focus on questions relating to the parents' role in the educational enterprise as a whole. The following five chapters (4 through 8) focus on each of the stages in the special education process: evaluation and determination of eligibility, development of an individual educational plan, placement in an appropriate program, delivery of special education and related services, and review of educational progress. Chapter 9 describes approaches that may be used in the event that parents and the school disagree. But first, it might help if we put these chapters into perspective for you.

First, remember that no one or two parents can accomplish all the activities suggested here and still have time to love and enjoy their child. So review our suggestions with the idea of selecting those particular activities that you can accomplish and that will be most beneficial for your child and situation.

Second, remember it is never too late to start. It is never too late (or too early) to establish a file on your child. Communicate and observe your child, visit your child's classes, and participate actively in parent/school conferences.

Third, review our ideas carefully to be sure they apply to you. We have tried to be comprehensive, making suggestions that are appropriate for all ages of children, all types and severity of handicaps, and all variations in state and local policy and practice. If what we have written doesn't seem appropriate, file it away for possible later use or share it with a friend whose situation is different from yours.

Fourth, remember school districts and states vary in their policies and practices. It is important that you know and understand your state's policies, regulations, and services pertaining to handicapped youth and adults, and your school district's practices, procedures, and programs pertaining to special education. You might use the information presented in this chapter as a guide to what might be ideal but you should always start with an understanding of what is available. Remember, however, that although a free, appropriate public education for your child does not have to be the ideal program, neither does it have to be limited to what's available.

And finally, you should recognize that the sequence presented here is delivered in this way for organization's sake and does not have to be the order in which you read or use the book. Some of the suggestions in later chapters may be just as applicable earlier. For example, many of the suggestions in Chapter 8 about how to prepare for a parent–teacher conference might also apply to a parent–teacher conference you may have prior to giving your consent for an evaluation (Chapter 4). Try to use the book as a reference; it might help to put index tabs on key topics or those questions and answers that you refer to often.

Being an advocate for your child will take some time, but it will be rewarding. The material in this chapter is intended to clarify certain procedures, to clue you in on important issues you should consider, and to assist you in your role as an advocate. Even though this book will not make you an expert on education, it should prepare you to talk with and question those who are. And no one else can provide the depth of information, the long-term perspective, and the continued commitment to securing an appropriate educational program better than you, the parent of a handicapped child, can.

We are entering an exciting period of education history. For the first time, parents are being encouraged in their efforts to become involved in the educational process of their handicapped children. Although certain school personnel in some school districts have always been open to parent participation, many school personnel, as well as some parents, have felt that parents were not well enough informed to be active participants in planning their child's school program. Recent court decisions and legislation have mandated changes, however. These changes require schools to inform parents of certain proposed actions that will affect their child and to request parental consent for these actions.

These mandates will require changes on the part of both schools and parents if a satisfactory partnership is to evolve. The questions and answers that follow are suggestive of the themes that are discussed in greater detail in later chapters. Thus, they serve as highlights of the material to follow and are a coordination of the basic ideas presented in each chapter.

What is the relationship between parents and the school?

Both you and your child's school have the same basic goal: to make sure your child has a free and appropriate education suited to your child's individual needs. The best way to assure that this goal is achieved is for you and your child's school to form a cooperative partnership—a joint endeavor built upon communication, mutual respect, and appreciation—which encourages your active involvement and participation in all major special education decisions that affect your child.

Since a partnership is the most effective way to assure that your child will receive an appropriate education, the opportunity for such a joint endeavor is mandated by federal law. Parents must be notified of any changes in their child's educational program that involve special education, and must give their consent to these changes. Parents must be invited to school conferences at which decisions related to special education eligibility, placement in special programs, and provision of special services are being discussed.

What has been the history of the parent-school relationship?

There was a time when the only messages parents received from school were report cards or written notices which called for parent conferences if a child had a serious behavior problem or was failing academically.

Traditionally, only school personnel made special education decisions because it was thought that only they and their staff possessed the professional training and experience necessary to make such important choices. Many school personnel have had unpleasant experiences in their contacts with parents of handicapped children who were angry, overdemanding, abusive, uncooperative, or apathetic. Thus, it is understandable that many school administrators and teachers have wished to avoid the difficulty and confusion which they feel may result if parents take an active role in program planning.

In addition, many school personnel are concerned about maintaining administrative efficiency and wish to minimize parental activity, which they view as interfering with internal school operations. And, despite changes in law, many of these traditional attitudes still exist.

One recent study of parent involvement[1] found that although a majority of school personnel (who were members of school placement and planning teams) agreed that parents should gather and present information on their child's development and behavior, less than half agreed that parents should be involved in planning their child's educational program.

Another recent study by Hoff et al.[2] found that school communication practices often leave parents without a clear and accurate understanding of their child's program.

And so, although the law encourages a partnership between you and your child's school, that partnership may take on different meanings in different schools. For instance, some schools may recognize that you are the following:

a vital link in the educational process;

a source of important information on the educational needs of your child;

a source of support for the school's instructional program;

the major vehicle for providing home instruction to supplement your child's school activities.

Other schools, slower to change and adapt to the spirit of the new legislation, may not yet have developed policies and practices that guarantee your involvement and facilitate your active participation. If your child is attending a school that still shows little concern about parent involvement, you will need to take more initiative and develop your own strategies in order to become recognized as a full partner in planning your child's educational future.

What is the role of parents in the parent-school partnership?

There are several different roles parents may play in the parent–school partnership.[3] They may remain outside the system, granting permission or approval when requested but remaining uninvolved in the educational decisions regarding their child. A recent study of parental involvement[4] found that about half the parents studied said they did not want to work closely with the school because they did not have the time, could not arrange their work schedules, had transportation or babysitting problems, or could not understand the jargon of or the reasons for many of the school procedures. Thus, for a variety of reasons many parents have preferred to remain "outside."

A second role parents may play is that of passive participant, providing information about their child's home behavior to school evaluation teams and attending conferences regarding their child but remaining observers, except when offering additional background information or agreeing to the action proposed. This is the role many school personnel expect and some even prefer parents to play.

The third role, and the one we recommend, is that of active participant. Parents who are active participants work closely with school personnel, raise questions regarding terms they do not understand, state the educational goals and preferences they have for their child, offer suggestions regarding possible instructional strategies, and voice their agreement or disagreement with placement and program decisions. This is the role the law anticipated parents would play, and the law places several administrative requirements on school systems to insure that parents are provided the opportunity to be active participants.

We urge you to forget any past frustrations and to overcome logistical problems of time, transportation, and child care to become a participating parent, as the law says you have the right to be. Remember, parents are the only people who remain constant forces in a child's life—you are responsible for providing a link across time to insure your child's educational progress.

Being an active participant makes you a moving force in determining the proper educational program for your child. You are your child's advocate. Ideally then, your role as a child advocate consists of the following duties:

familiarizing yourself with your rights as a parent;

understanding the special educational practices of your school district;

staying in close contact with the school through informal notes, conversations, and formal reports;

attending and contributing to parent/school conferences;

observing your child at home to find out his or her capabilities and needs;

sharing information about your child's developmental history and current capabilities and needs with school personnel;

reviewing the records the school maintains on your child to assure their timeliness and accuracy;

suggesting important educational goals and objectives for your child;

learning about the educational alternatives that might be available and helpful to your child;

evaluating the alternative educational program options available for your child according to your values and goals for your child;

contributing to the decisions that determine the educational alternatives that are appropriate for your child's needs;

giving your informed consent before evaluational and instructional services are provided;

cooperating with the school in providing your child with relevant and beneficial instructional experiences;

supporting your child's school program with worthwhile home activities;

observing the progress of your child in meeting the educational goals you and the school have selected.

Basic to all of these responsibilities, however, is the underlying need to love, accept, and respect your child as an individual, and to understand and represent his or her needs and interests. There may be times when you don't have the time or energy to play all these roles, but we hope that you will play at least some of them. And as you gain experience as your child's advocate, these roles will become easier—almost second nature.

In addition to the child advocate duties previously listed, there are certain other very important activities you should consider doing, including the following:

keeping a current file on your child's educational progress;

observing your child's progress and keeping records;

reading and collecting information related to your child's handicap;

becoming familiar with professional and technical terms;

collecting articles about special techniques and programs other schools or institutions are using with children who have the same handicap as your child;

learning about the special education services available in your school;

discovering the services and resources available for your child in the other agencies and organizations in your community;

communicating with school personnel;

understanding your child's rights;

maintaining contact with other parents and parent organizations;

establishing contact with individuals who have the same handicap as your child.

Keeping a file

Being able to keep track of your child's educational development is obviously essential. It is not enough to try and remember what your child did yesterday, last week, or last year; you should keep a file, which should include the following:

names, addresses, and phone numbers of professionals you have contacted, or to whom you have been referred;

notes on school conferences and meetings attended, including dates, persons present, topics discussed, questions asked and responses received, and decisions made;

notes on phone calls to or from school personnel, including the name of the person to whom you spoke (You may have to ask, "With whom am I speaking?");

written letters and memoranda that you received and that you sent (Make a carbon or a photocopy.);

evaluation reports from psychologists, other diagnostic personnel, and clinics, with the date, location, and results;

medical records, including dates, locations, and physicians' names;

report cards, IEPs, and other formal and informal communications from the school, including dates (Add dates to informal notes that are undated.);

requests you have made to the school (copies of letters or memoranda of telephone conversations), with the date and person contacted, the nature of the request, and action taken;

samples of your child's work, particularly writing samples and art work, with the date;

notes of activities, strategies, and other instructional changes that you are aware teachers have employed, with date started and stopped, and notes on how well they worked.

In order to maintain this file, you will need to get in the habit of keeping notes. Get a notebook—with dividers and pockets so you will not lose any small slips of paper. You can label dividers by year with subheadings for the type of item (e.g., report card). This notebook file will be very valuable when you need documentation for your child's need for special services and your reasons for recommending certain educational programs.

Observing your child

Watch your child playing with other children and doing household tasks. You might find it helpful to keep notes of your child's progress, recording the date when each new skill is mastered and when new words are learned.

Talk with and observe your child. Learn what he or she likes to do and would like to be able to do; discover what your child likes and dislikes about school and schoolwork; find out what your child's personal and vocational ambitions are; and observe what tasks or activities present difficulties for your child.

This kind of information about your child's attitudes and behavior will be very important in making decisions about an appropriate instructional program for your child.

Reading about your child's handicap

Information about your child's handicap will be helpful to you in understanding what you might expect from your child, what potential needs he or she may have, and what kinds of activities and experiences might be helpful. This information will also be useful in explaining to teachers, school administrators, and others what you think your child's needs are and how these needs may affect educational program choices.

Becoming familiar with professional and technical terms

From the first moment you realize that you are a parent of a child with special needs, you will begin to hear medical, psychological, and educational terms that have special meanings. Ask what these terms mean if they are unfamiliar to you. Write down these terms and note their meaning. (Ask how to spell them.) Some terms, particularly those used by psychologists and educators, do not have a common definition. Such terms as "minimally brain damaged," "emotionally disturbed," and "aphasic" may mean different things to different professional personnel. So do not be afraid to ask, "What exactly do you mean when you say my child is_____?" Write down the response. Educators also use imprecise terms; some examples and follow-up questions are given in Table 3.1.

Table 3.1 Educational Terms and How to Decipher Them*

Terms	Some Questions to Ask
Team teaching approach	Who is on the team? How does the team function? Does the team teach the class as a group? What is the difference between this method and the one-teacher method? Are parents part of the team? What subjects are taught by the team members? How are students grouped for instruction? Is individual instruction for certain students provided?
Interdisciplinary approach to evaluation	What professional personnel are involved? When do you use this system? What disciplines are represented? Is there one report or are there multiple reports? What is the advantage of this approach over that of using a single school psychologist or social worker?
Individualized instruction	Does the student receive individual (one-to-one) instruction? What subject areas are taught individually? Does each student have an individualized instructional plan? Are there different goals and objectives for each student? How much individual instruction does each student receive? Who provides the individual instruction—a teacher or an aide? Are materials individualized?
Parent partnership	How often are parent conferences held? What is discussed at parent conferences? Who is involved in parent conferences? Are parents encouraged to visit their child's classes? Are parents provided with activities and techniques to use with their child at home? What role are parents expected to play at parent conferences? Are there active parent advocacy groups?
Educational diagnosis	How was this diagnosis developed? What procedures were used? Who functioned as the diagnostician? What was the training of the educational diagnostician? What subjects were covered in the diagnosis? What were the results of the diagnosis?

*Developed from M. Kappelman and P. Ackerman, *Between Parent and School* (New York: The Dial Press, 1977), pp. 250-59.

Don't be afraid to question professional personnel. Because they use them so often in their own conversations, the terms seem clear and routine to them, even though they may be confusing to you. Furthermore, as you get involved in more conversations with these professionals, you will realize how many different meanings the same term may take.

Collecting articles about special techniques and programs

Information about special techniques and programs other schools and institutions are using for handicapped children will be useful to you when you are planning to make suggestions to your child's teachers about new approaches they might try with your child. You might also want to share these articles with school personnel.

Learning about the special education services available in your school

The public school is the principal institution for providing education to the handicapped child. You should learn all you can about the many different school programs and services available for your child. This information will be helpful when you are selecting an appropriate educational program for your child. If you are aware of all the available services, you can participate in the development of your child's individualized plan more effectively. You should also learn the following about the operation of the special education program in your school:

what special services are available for handicapped children;

what special education staff are available and what their roles and responsibilities are;

how the assessment or evaluation process works;

how and when individualized education programs are developed and reviewed;

how and when placement decisions are made and who makes them;

whether there are waiting lists for service.

Information on the operation of the special education program will be useful to you when you are trying to locate the person responsible for a particular aspect of the program. Knowing exactly what your school's administrative organization and regulations are will make it easier to know whom to contact and when to make a specific request or suggestion.

Discovering other services and resources available for your child

The typical public school system provides an array of educational services for handicapped students, but the following organizations also offer services that are worth investigating:

community service agencies and organizations;

mental health and mental retardation centers;

vocational rehabilitation agencies;

college- and university-sponsored clinics and facilities;

hospital and health clinics;

parent groups;

local parks and recreation departments;

private voluntary agencies such as the March of Dimes or Easter Seal Society.

These organizations support and supplement the educational services of public schools by offering programs focused upon other areas of the handicapped child's life, including recreational and social services, vocational training, counseling, medical care, and financial aid.

Communicating with school personnel

Whatever program your child is in, you will want to assist the school in whatever ways possible and especially by providing information on your child's developmental history and behavior, by reviewing your child's school progress, and by sharing information and insight on learning activities that might be effective.

You should communicate with the school early and often. Don't wait until a problem arises. Introduce yourself in the fall to your child's teachers, guidance counselor, and principal. Check to be sure that plans which were previously made for your child are being implemented. Staff may have changed special programs, and computerized class schedules may also contain errors.

Ask for a teacher conference whenever you sense that your child does not seem to be making progress. Prepare for this conference. Have the questions and the information you wish to share written down and organized into an informal agenda. Gather together and organize the material (examples of your child's work and written records) you wish to share with the teacher, talk with your child before the teacher meeting, and add to your agenda any concerns your child wishes discussed. When you meet with teachers, be specific about the reason for the meeting. Follow your informal agenda, take notes on what was said, ask questions about anything you don't understand, and summarize the decisions made regarding actions to be taken and timelines. After the conference, follow up by doing what you agreed upon, and report your results to the teacher. Ask the teacher for a report on his or her actions as well. You should also talk to your child about the meeting and explain the changes to be made and what is expected of him or her.

Understanding your child's rights

Under new legislation and judicial decrees, handicapped children and their parents have acquired important new rights. These rights include:

a free, appropriate public education;

an individualized educational plan;

opportunity to participate in critical educational decisions (evaluation, diagnosis, placement, and program changes);

access to all school programs and facilities;

instruction in the least restrictive environment;

due process procedures to handle parent–school disputes;

examination of the child's school records (including the right to ask that certain material be deleted or added).

These rights assure you that the schools must be attentive and responsive to your questions, concerns, and suggestions and must seek and obtain your consent prior to providing any special education testing or instruction.

Maintaining contact with other parents and parent organizations

Parent groups will be able to offer you information about how to cope with your child's handicap. They also provide emotional support to you when you are confronted with problems. Parents who have already gone through certain experiences with their handicapped children can offer advice and suggestions to help you prepare for similar experiences. You, organized together with other parents, can provide the school with the information and impetus to action that may help get community support for special programs.

Establishing contact with individuals who have the same handicap as your child

Other handicapped persons can provide your child with important social contacts and with role models that he or she may emulate. Successful handicapped young people and adults can offer support, encouragement, and advice to the child who is learning to cope with a handicap.

Of all the things suggested, which are the most important?

We shall try to summarize here what we believe are very important activities:

Keep careful written records with dates and names. This applies not only to documents related to your child's education, but also to conversations you have with school personnel and others about your child, as well as notes you've made about your child's progress.

Watch, talk with, and try to understand your child; this will provide you with the information you need to share with school personnel on your child's skills, accomplishments, interests, desires, and preferences and help you make decisions that conform to what your child wants and needs.

Visit your child's classes and learn all you can about his or her present program and any recommended alternative program. This will provide you with information needed to select an appropriate placement and give you a perspective on what your child does during the school day.

Attend your child's individualized educational program meetings and annual reviews; this is the time when decisions are made regarding what constitutes a free, appropriate public education for your child and you will want to participate in these decisions.

Remain in contact with the school staff. Even when you are in disagreement about a particular program or service, you will want to know what's happening and to offer your support; the parent-school partnership is a long-term relationship that should stay intact.

Most important, remember your child. The reason you and the school have formed a partnership is so that your child will receive an appropriate education. But don't get so involved with the issues and efforts of being your child's advocate that you don't have time to love, enjoy, and share with your child.

What strategies should parents use when performing their child advocacy role with the school?

Based on years of collective experience, we can offer a few words of wisdom on strategies that have been successful.

Focus on the child. You and the school system are both concerned with your child's strengths, weaknesses, and educational needs. Both you and the school system have the same goal: to provide your child with an appropriate educational program. Target your comments to your child, not to the education system as a whole.

Take a constructive approach. Instead of criticizing a particular teacher's lack of control, suggest that your child might behave better in a more structured class.

Know what will happen. Before going to a meeting with school officials, talk with someone at the school—a teacher, counselor, or principal—to find out the purpose of the meeting, what will be discussed, what the agenda will be, and what decisions will be made. Find out what your role will be, how you should prepare, and what you should bring with you.

Be prepared. If you have done your reading, maintained a notebook or file on your child, studied your child and his or her school records, and become familiar with your school system and community services, you should be able to make an agenda of all the information you wish to share and the questions you wish to ask. Prepare this list before you go to any parent-school conference, whether it be a conversation with your child's teacher or a program planning meeting.

Communicate. Communication is a two-way process; you have to listen and you have to talk. Listen carefully and be open-minded. Teachers see your child in different situations than you do; they see your child as part of a social group and coping with academic tasks.

You need to know how your child behaves in this situation. Do your share of the talking and explain:

how your child behaves at home (Give concrete examples from the notes you made when studying your child.);

what your child's interests are;

what educational activities you think might be worth trying (Share any relevant magazine articles you read.);

what you hope your child accomplishes in school;

how you feel about your child's progress.

Be persistent. You may not always find out what you need to know in the first telephone call, and your child may not get all the services you think he or she needs in the first month of his or her individualized educational program. However, as you continue to interact with school personnel, you will begin to persuade them of your reasonableness, sincerity, and concern. Furthermore, there are legal routes you can take if there is an unresolved disagreement with the school system.

Retain your self-confidence. There may be times when you feel overwhelmed by information and technical expertise, but you don't need to feel embarrassed or humiliated. If you are sincere and prepared, the school staff will respect you. You do not need to be afraid to make mistakes or to back down from a previous position if you change your mind.

Keep your cool. Be polite, respectful, and calm. There may be occasions when you feel frustrated or angry, but the last thing you want is to be branded as an irrational, obnoxious parent. Remember, the person you are talking to may be the very person you most need on your side when you go to the school board requesting a special appropriation for your child's tuition.

Will you summarize for me what my handicapped child's rights are?

Handicapped students have two basic types of rights; certain rights pertain to the nature and type of educational program handicapped students receive and others pertain to the procedures involved in planning and implementing that educational program.

Educational rights

1. Your child has *the right to a free, appropriate public education.* This means your child has the right to special education and related services that conform to his or her individualized educational program. These services must be provided at public expense and under public supervision and direction.

2. Your child has *the right to be educated in the least restrictive environment.* This means that your child has the right to be educated with nonhandicapped students, as much as possible, and that your child will not be separated from the regular education program unless the nature or severity of his or her handicap requires a different, more intensive instructional program.

3. Your child has *the right to related services.* This means your child must receive transportation and other supportive services needed to benefit from special education instruction.

4. Your child has *the right to participate in any program or service provided nonhandicapped students without being discriminated against on the basis of handicap.* This means that a school cannot deny your child access to any program or service it offers nonhandicapped students because of physical or programmatic barriers.

Procedural rights

1. As parents, you have *the right to be notified in writing before the school district evaluates your child and before the school district initiates or changes or refuses to initiate or change the identification, evaluation, or placement of your child.* This means that before your child is identified, evaluated, or placed in a special education program, or before any changes are made in his or her identification, evaluation, or placement, you must receive a written notice describing, in a language you understand, what action is proposed, why it is being proposed, the evaluation procedures, tests, or records used to support the proposed action, and your rights if you disagree with the proposed action.

2. You have *the right to grant your written consent before an initial evaluation* is conducted on your child. This means that before your child is evaluated for the first time to determine whether or not he or she is eligible for special education, you must agree in writing to that evaluation.

3. You have *the right to obtain an independent educational evaluation.* This means that if you are uncertain or dissatisfied with the results of the evaluation performed for or by the school, you may request an independent evaluation to be conducted by a qualified professional examiner or evaluation clinic. This examination will be at the public's expense unless the school district requests a due process hearing to review the appropriateness of the initial evaluation and the hearing officer concurs that the initial evaluation was appropriate and sufficient.

4. You have *the right to examine your child's school records.* This means you have the right to read, copy, and ask questions about your child's school records, including all evaluation reports. You also have the right to ask that inaccurate or misleading information be deleted or amended.

5. You have *the right to participate in the meeting where your child's individualized educational program is developed.* This means you must be invited to participate in the discussion of your child's goals and objectives, required special education and related services, and placement alternatives. You may provide information on your child's education needs, offer suggestions as to what services you believe are appropriate for meeting those needs, and participate in the selection of an appropriate program.

6. You have *the right to give your written consent to your child's initial placement in a special education program.* This means that before your child can be placed in any special education program, you must agree in writing to that placement.

7. You have *the right to a due process hearing if you disagree with your child's identification, evaluation, or placement, or any aspect related to the provision of a free, appropriate public education for your child.* This means you have the right to present your case, including documentary evidence and witnesses, to an impartial hearing officer who will listen to your and the school's arguments and render a decision. You have the right to appeal that decision to the state department of education and/or the civil court.

What are the basic components of the special education process and how do they fit together?

Planning for special education programs in most public schools takes place in the same way. Basically, there are five stages. The first stage is to locate, evaluate, and diagnose all eligible children. The second stage is to develop an individualized educational program for each child. The third stage is to place the child in an instructional setting where the educational services can be provided. The fourth stage is to provide the prescribed educational services, including special personnel (teachers, counselors, and therapists), instructional strategies, equipment, and materials, to the child. And the fifth stage is to review the child's educational program in light of his or her educational progress.

You, the parent, have an important role to perform at each of these stages: to provide information about your child, to indicate your personal goals for your child, to participate in the decision process, and to approve and authorize specific actions. In the five chapters that follow, we describe each of the stages in the educational process, indicating your parental responsibilities and answering related questions you might have. In Figure 3.1 we present an approximate sequence for how the five stages fit together.

You outlined the five stages of the special education process, but how do these stages fit together?

As you can see from Figure 3.1, you will be interacting with the school either formally or informally and either by written messages or in person at several points. Among the kinds of communication you will have are the following:

1. initial messages and conferences at which your child's educational needs are discussed and nonspecial educational interventions are suggested;

2. discussion of your child's progress without special education services;

3. written notification of referral for evaluation and request for parental consent;

4. written parental consent to an evaluation;

5. provision of information on your child as part of the evaluation;

6. evaluation team conference report;

7. IEP conference;

8. written IEP document sent or given to parents;

9. written notification of recommended placement and request for parental consent;

Figure 3-1
The Special Education Process

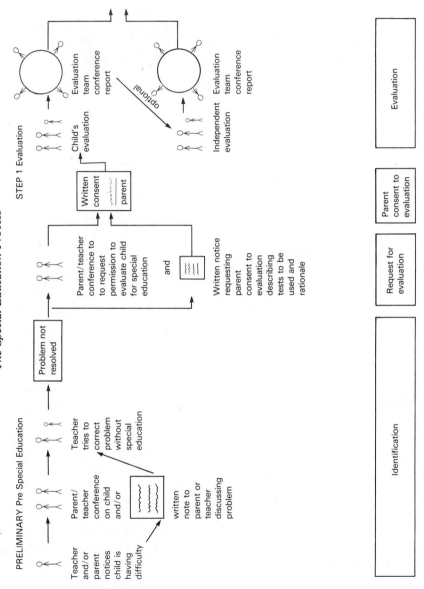

Figure 3–1
continued

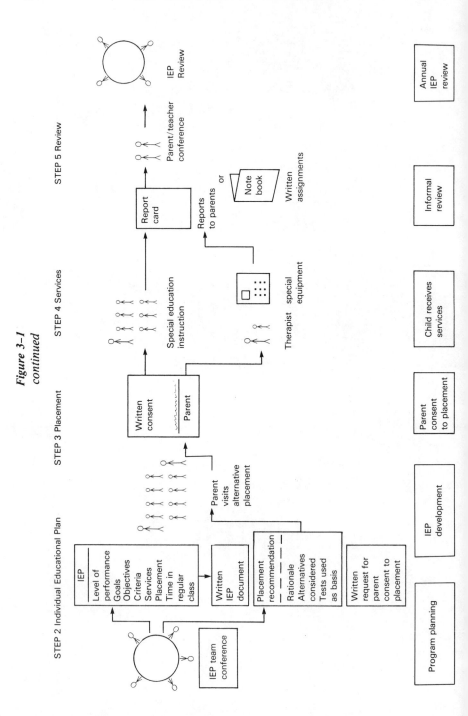

10. parent visit to alternative placement(s);

11. written parental consent to placement;

12. instructional plan developed for child based on IEP;

13. parent conversation with teachers on IEP implementation;

14. written student progress reports;

15. IEP review conference.

However, there are several possible variations in these contacts. For example, you and the school may agree not to try any interventions before a formal evaluation, thus eliminating contacts 1 and 2. You may provide background information at the evaluation conference, thus combining contacts 5 and 6. Often the evaluation results are considered along with developing an IEP, thus combining contacts 6 and 7. (We suggest that if this happens you ask for a break.) Frequently, the IEP conference serves as the mechanism for notifying parents of the recommended placement, thus collapsing contacts 7 and 9. If the parents are also asked to consent to the placement at the IEP conference, that collapses contacts 7, 9, and 11. We suggest that you don't consent to the recommended placement prior to visiting it. The important thing about these contacts is not the sequence and not whether they occur separately or independently, but whether you have time to consolidate your thoughts, consult with experienced friends, review your own records, and obtain information on various alternatives before you participate in any decision process and prior to giving your informed consent.

Notes

1. Yoshida, Roland K.; Fenton, Kathleen S; Maxwell, James P.; and Kaufman, Martin J. "Parental Involvement in the Special Education Pupil Planning Process: The School's Perspective." *Exceptional Children* 44 (1978): 531-34.

2. Hoff, Maryann K.; Fenton, Kathleen S.; Yoshida, Roland K.; and Kaufman, Martin J. "Notice and Consent: The School's Responsibility to Inform Parents." *The Journal of School Psychology* 16 (1978): 265-73.

3. Yoshida, Roland K., and Gottlieb, Jay A. "Model of Parental Participation in the Pupil Planning Process," *Mental Retardation* 15 (1977): 17-20.

4. Yoshida, Roland K.; Schensul, Jean J.; Pelto, Pertti J.; and Fenton, Kathleen S. *Parent-School Relationships in Transition: Issues in Securing Informed Consent for Special Education Placement Decisions.* Technical Report, U.S.O.E. Bureau of Education for the Handicapped, 1978.

4

The Evaluation Process

JUDITH ANDREWS AGARD

The evaluation process represents your first contact with special education. It involves the referral of your child by your school staff or some other concerned persons for a comprehensive evaluation, assessment, and a determination of eligibility for special services.

I never thought my child was having serious problems in school until the school requested an evaluation; what does it mean?

The first time many parents become aware that their child's education problems are serious is when the school requests permission to conduct an evaluation. Even though you may be surprised and distressed to learn your child needs special help, you should remember certain things:

There are many children with problems like those of your child.

You should not blame yourself or the school; the cause of your child's problem probably involves a number of factors and the important thing now is to learn exactly what the problem is and what can be done about it.

There are many special educational materials and procedures that can benefit your child.

No special evaluation or service will be provided your child without your consent, except in extreme emergencies.

It is essential to plan the best educational program possible so that your child gets the special help he or she needs and you want.

There are parent groups, private organizations, and governmental agencies that can benefit your child.

Remember, the fact that the school has requested an evaluation means that it is concerned about your child and is seeking to discover the exact nature of his or her educational difficulty so that an appropriate, uniquely tailored educational program can be devised. It does not mean your child is bad or being punished or cannot attend school or participate in all school activities, nor does it mean that your child's school program will change automatically or result in a special education classification.

What is the purpose of the evaluation?

A comprehensive evaluation is required by law [P.L. 94–142 Regulation 121a504 (a)] before a child can be considered for placement in a special education program, or be transferred or refused transfer from a special education program to a full-time regular class placement.

The purpose of the evaluation is to obtain and compile information from a variety of sources that can be used to determine:

whether a child has a physical or mental disability that substantially limits learning;

the possible causes of a child's disability;

the strengths and weaknesses of a child in the physical, emotional, social, vocational, and intellectual areas;

the educational diagnostic category that best describes a child's disability;

the special services, instructional techniques, and other interventions that the child needs;

the appropriate instructional setting (placement) for the child;

reasonable predictions of a child's academic, social, and vocational potential.

An evaluation provides basic information to determine whether a particular disability is causing a child to have difficulty in school and what is needed for him or her to be more successful; it is the process by which eligibility for special education services is established.

In most cases, you will not need to request that the school conduct an evaluation of your child. School personnel will have recognized your child's problems, recommended an evaluation, or possibly referred him or her for such an evaluation with your permission. You do not have to give your permission, although you should recognize that just because your child is evaluated does not mean he or she is handicapped or must receive special services. The purpose of the evaluation is to determine whether your child really does need help and to pinpoint the type of help needed. You also do not have to agree to all parts of the evaluation. You may, for example, request that in-depth personality tests not be given if you don't believe the tests will contribute to identifying your child's problems.

With regard to your child's evaluation, you should be sure that it is complete, that the tests to be used are suitable for your child, and that you are informed of and understand the results. Remember, the evaluation should be a joint parent-child-school endeavor. You, your child, and your child's educators need to know what your child's educational needs are before a special individualized program can be developed. A cooperative effort will assure that complete, relevant, and reliable information will be available to all concerned.

The evaluation process generates information regarding your child's strengths and weaknesses and educational needs. Based on this information, decisions can be made regarding your child's eligibility for special education, and the disability classification that best describes your child's problems.

Will the school notify me before they involve my child in a comprehensive evaluation?

Absolutely; not only will they notify you, but they will also ask for your written permission to conduct an evaluation. (See Figure 4.1.) The notice you receive should include:

the reasons why the school wishes to conduct an evaluation;

a description of the procedures, tests, records, or reports that are to be included;

an explanation of your rights with regard to granting consent.

If you do not understand exactly why your child is being recommended for a special education evaluation, you should request a conference with your child's teachers. At the conference, you should determine the following:

the problems your child is having that led to his or her referral for special education evaluation;

the educational actions which have already been undertaken to assist your child;

Figure 4-1
Sample Letter to Obtain Written Permission to Conduct an Evaluation

Greenville City Schools
P.O. Box 1009
431 West Fifth Street
Greenville, North Carolina 27834
919/752-4192

Glenn L. Cox, Superintendent

Greenville City Schools Permission for Testing

Date_____

Dear_____:

In order for the school to learn more about your child so that we can plan an appropriate educational program to meet his or her special individual needs, we would like to provide more individual testing.

If you would like to review the results of these tests, or have any questions concerning the procedures described, please feel free to contact the school.

Sincerely,

_____

Principal

_____

Counselor

Please complete the section below and return to the school.

PL 94-142 requires that this screening and/or assessment be completed within 30 days upon receiving written parental permission and that an interpretative conference be held with the parent within 15 days upon completion of the evaluation unless that right is waived by the parent.

_____I waive the right to an interpretative conference following the evaluation.

_____I would like an interpretative conference following the evaluation and would like the school to arrange a conference.

_____   _____
Date   Parent's Signature

the types of educational activities or procedures which still might be instituted but do not require a special education evaluation. (For example, your child may be eligible for remedial reading.)

Any one of a number of people may have been concerned enough about your child's educational progress to refer your child for an evaluation. Not only parents, but teachers, principals, counselors, community agencies, private professional personnel, community youth personnel (scout leaders, athletic coaches), and even other students may suggest particular students who appear to be experiencing educational, social, or emotional difficulty. Any one of these people could have contacted a teacher, counselor, principal, school psychologist, school social worker, or school nurse to initiate the evaluation process.

You have the right to know who referred your child and the circumstances which prompted the referral. If it was the result of a specific incident, you may want to add your own interpretation of what may be the cause.

In most cases, the school does not request permission to evaluate students for special services without clear indications that the student is having problems that cannot be corrected through routine minor adjustments in the regular educational program. However, sometimes students are referred for special education services because the child does not achieve in a particular type of class, or other circumstances that could be handled by simple instructional change. You owe it to your child to determine for yourself whether his or her education problems are serious enough to warrant special education services.

The school does not have to notify you or obtain your permission to administer routine achievement or aptitude tests to groups of children or to perform physical vision or hearing screening, nor are teachers required to notify you when they administer tests as part of their regular instructional program.

After your child has been admitted to a special education program, you will be notified each time he or she is to be reevaluated. The school does not have to obtain your written consent for a reevaluation.

Will some form of screening take place to determine whether my child is in need of an evaluation?

Yes; generally, school staff will conduct an informal review of existing information on the child, discuss the child's situation with his or her teachers, and observe the child's academic and social behavior in class. Occasionally, the results of this screening indicate that the child's problems are not serious, and that minor modifications in the regular instructional program are all that are needed.

In certain situations, however, the screening process confirms the initial concern, and the school staff decides an evaluation is necessary. At this point parents are contacted to begin the process.

Many schools routinely screen all students to determine whether a more thorough evaluation is necessary. Screening often occurs before students enter kindergarten, usually during a "kindergarten round-up." Schools continue to screen students by providing periodic physical examinations and eye, ear, and speech testing. Schoolwide achievement tests can be used to screen students for an evaluation, and teachers are encouraged to watch for students whose actions suggest serious enough learning or behavior problems to warrant an evaluation.

What should I do if I think my preschool child has a disability?

Many parents discover their child has special needs when the child is an infant; certain physical and mental disabilities can be diagnosed by a physician at birth.

Some parents discover their child has special needs through the gradual process of observing that their child is developing more slowly than or differently from other children. Often a physician or evaluation clinic will confirm parental observations and diagnose the particular problem more precisely.

If you have a preschool child that you believe has a disability, there are several things you should do before he or she first attends school. First, contact your school district director of special education. Even if a public preschool is not available and your child is too young to attend school, your school district staff may be able to direct you to a number of other resources that might be helpful. School personnel can do the following:

provide you with names of physicians, evaluation clinics, and other specialists who might evaluate your child or assist you in other ways;

inform you of special community preschools or other early intervention programs for which your child may be eligible; (many school districts, encouraged by the incentives provided by new legislation, are now offering preschool and even infant education programs for handicapped children);

provide you with the names of parent and other groups that can provide support and practical advice;

indicate the program alternatives available in your school district for school-aged children with a disability similar to your child's.

Second, you should get professional confirmation of your own observation of your child's disability. Your doctor should be able to recommend specialists or an evaluation clinic where your child can be tested. You may be able to locate an evaluation clinic through the telephone directory. Evaluation services are provided by hospitals, community service agencies, colleges, and universities. (See Chapter 1.)

Should I contact the public school if I have a school-aged handicapped child who is not in school?

If your child is of school age but not in public school (e.g., you may be keeping your child at home or he or she may be participating in an educational program sponsored by another public or private institution or agency), your school district director of special education should be made aware of your child's needs. Remember, each school district must maintain educational records on all handicapped children of school age in their district; they must develop an individualized education program for each handicapped child and provide him or her with an appropriate placement and necessary special services. Even if you are satisfied with the current, nonpublic school or other public agency educational program your child is receiving, you need to inform the school about your child's handicap and the educational services he or she is receiving. Furthermore, you may discover that the school district will pay for all or part of any tuition, transportation charges, health costs, and even room and board you may be paying. Or you may discover that your school district has an appropriate program for your child that you did not know about.

You should be aware that under the new federal laws all children, even the most severely handicapped, must receive a free, appropriate public education. Schools no longer can refuse to provide your child with an individualized education program and you no longer have any reason to keep your child home from school.

What should I do when I initiate contact with the school regarding my preschool or out-of-school handicapped child?

When you contact the public school, be sure you have all of your child's vital documents—birth certificate, immunization and other medical records, and evaluation reports. The school may ask you for permission to reevaluate your child; they may also ask you to sign a release form so they can have access to your child's records.

During this initial conversation, you should clearly state your child's disability and his or her special needs to the extent that you know them. You should also find out all you can about the school's special education program and the different types of special services and instructional settings available. You should establish yourself as a concerned, cooperative, and supportive advocate for your child and express your intention to be an active participant in the educational decision process.

You will have other opportunities to confer with school staff regarding your handicapped child, so you do not have to cram all your questions and concerns into this initial conversation. Be sure, though, to ask the school to notify you as to when your participation would be useful and necessary.

How often will my child be evaluated?

Your child must be formally reevaluated every three years, although some evaluation of your child's progress will take place as part of the annual review of your child's individualized education program. The school will generally take the initiative in arranging for a reevaluation but if you believe an evaluation is needed sooner, you may request one. Your child's teachers may also request a formal reevaluation if they believe it would be helpful in developing a different instructional program.

When the school requests my consent to evalute my child, what should I do?

First, read the permission form. The permission form should tell you the reasons why your child is being evaluated, the tests and other procedures that are included in the evaluation, the time and date when the evaluation will occur, the implications of the evaluation for your child, and the options open for you. If you have unanswered questions after reading the permission form, you should contact a school official (teacher, principal, school counselor or social worker, school psychologist, or director of special education) in order to obtain answers.

Second, find out about the evaluation. Before you consent to an evaluation, you should determine:

how your child will be informed about the evaluation;

who will coordinate the evaluation and administer the tests;

what tests will be given, when, and by whom;

what areas each test will cover;[1]

what information each test will provide about your child's strengths and weaknesses;

what each test will tell you about your child's educational needs and appropriate education techniques;

how long the evaluation will take, how much class time and which class activities your child will miss, and how the activities missed will be made up;

when and in what form you will receive the results of the evaluation;

when and how you will have an opportunity to provide your own input into the evaluation.

Third, grant or refuse permission. If you wish your child's educational problems to be diagnosed so that special services can be provided, then you must give your consent to some form of evaluation. Even if you do not wish your child to receive special education services, an evaluation can be very helpful to your child's teachers because it will provide information about how your child learns and what educational assistance he or she needs.

You will have an opportunity to review the results of the evaluation before you decide whether to give your consent to your child's placement in a special education program. If you are dissatisfied with the evaluation performed by the school, you have the right to request a second, independent evaluation.

If you wish, you can give provisional approval for an evaluation by designating certain tests you wish to be eliminated and/or recommending additional tests or procedures. You can suggest certain modifications in the testing program based on your own knowledge of your child (e.g., if the child cannot sit still for more than 15 minutes, the test administrator should know this and make adjustments).

In general, unless you have clear indications that the evaluation will be misused, inappropriate, or unfair, you should give consent to have your child evaluated. However, if you do not wish to have your child evaluated at this time, you should indicate this to your school in writing.

What happens if I ignore the request or refuse permission for an evaluation?

If you ignore the first request, the school will probably try to contact you again through the mail (possibly by registered letter), telephone call, or personal visit. If you never respond to any of the school's attempts to obtain your consent, the school has the right to conduct an evaluation, although it might not do so. Therefore, if you do not wish an evaluation, you should write the school denying permission. Ignoring the situation creates uncertainty.

If you refuse permission, your child will probably remain in his current educational program. However, certain educational changes may occur without an evaluation. For example, your child could be assigned to a different class or a different teacher, given remedial assistance, provided with volunteer or peer tutoring, or provided different instructional materials and/or teaching strategies. These changes do not involve special education and, hence, do not require your consent.

Even if you refuse permission it is important for you to stay in close contact with the school staff so that you are aware of how your child is doing and what educational changes were made. If your child's problems persist you may wish to change your mind about the evaluation.

If you refuse consent but the school is particularly concerned about your child, particularly if your child is causing serious difficulties to other students, the school may institute a due process hearing at which you will have to defend your position against an evaluation.

Suppose I do not think my child's problems are serious enough to warrant an evaluation, but I am concerned; what should I do?

Even if you have indicated in writing to the school that you do not wish your child to be evaluated, you might still wish to pursue the problem with your child's teachers, counselor, or principal. You might ask to visit your child's classes in order to observe your child in the school setting. Ask your child's teachers how your child's behavior and academic progress compare with that of other students. Discuss with your child's teachers what instructional changes have already been employed to help your child and what effects these changes have had. Ask your child's teachers for their suggestions on what additional steps might be taken that do not involve special education. Your child's teachers should be able to institute several changes within the regular class, such as:

class and/or teacher changes;

seating changes;

individual work assignments;

peer or volunteer tutoring;

remedial reading and/or mathematics;

work contracts;

supplemental instructional material.

Your child's teachers may already have tried some or all of these less drastic alternatives. But if they have not, these changes are worth exploring. Your child's teachers may or may not be open to making these changes; in either case, you will want to remain in close communication with them and watch for any changes in your child's attitudes or behavior. You might ask other parents (or a parent group) what suggestions they have for working with particular teachers. Also, you might want to take a friend with you when you meet with your child's teachers to get another perspective on the teacher's suggestions or to add support to your own views.

Even if you do not agree to a complete evaluation, you should arrange to have your child's vision and hearing tested by a professional aware of developmental and educational implications, and for your child to have a complete physical examination.

What is involved in an evaluation?

An evaluation is not one event but a decision process which includes three separate stages: collection, conference, and decision.

Collection

During the collection stage, information on the student is collected from existing records, observation, physical examinations, psychological tests, and interviews with teachers and parents. Often one person, usually the school psychologist or an educational diagnostician or counselor, is designated to coordinate the information collection effort. This person may prepare a summary of all the information collected.

At this stage, you may be asked to provide medical and other records on your child, to describe your child's behavior at home and in nonschool settings, and to recall your child's developmental and educational history. If you are not asked to do this, you should volunteer any information you believe is relevant.

Conference

During the conference stage, members of the evaluation or appraisal team confer as a group to discuss the information collected and to determine its relevance and appropriateness. Discrepancies in information collected from different sources, such as a student's home and school behavior, are considered and resolved. Based on this information, student educational needs are identified and decisions made.

At this stage you should be sure all relevant information is presented and discussed and that all discrepancies between your view of your child and the views of teachers, school staff, and psychologists are resolved. Be sure you understand why these discrepancies existed and what the resolution was. You may also wish to participate in discussions regarding your child's eligibility and classification.

Decision

The outcome of the conference is a group decision on the student's eligibility for special education, the student's disability classification, and special education placement and service recommendations. At this stage you are informed of the results of the evaluation and the eligibility and classification decisions that were made on the basis of the evaluation information.

The decision stage of the evaluation is often combined with the development of individualized educational plans and the selection of an instructional setting or placement. Although you may want to discuss possible programs and placements at the evaluation conference, we suggest you attend the conference without making any final decisions until you've had time to think the alternatives over. You may find that reviewing the results of the evaluation and discussing your child's disability classification and eligibility will take considerable time and thought.

Who is responsible for conducting the evaluation?

Federal law [P.L. 94–142 Regulation 121a532(e)] states that the evaluation shall be conducted by a multidisciplinary team including at least one teacher or other specialist with knowledge in the area of the suspected disability. The team usually consists of:

a special education teacher or other specialist familiar with the suspected disability;

a school psychologist or educational diagnostician;[2]

one or more regular classroom teachers, including the teacher who referred the child (requested the evaluation);

a physician and/or school nurse;

a school social worker or counselor;

other specialists (speech/language pathologists, remedial reading teachers, physical therapists).

If your child is suspected of having a specific learning disability, the evaluation team must include:[3]

your child's regular classroom teacher or a regular classroom teacher qualified to teach that age group;

a person qualified to conduct individual diagnostic examinations of children (school psychologist, speech–language pathologist, remedial reading teacher).

What areas are included in the evaluation?

The areas included in the evaluation should be determined in part by the particular problems evidenced by the child. A comprehensive evaluation may include tests or other observations in the following areas:

physical health, vision, hearing;

motor coordination, physical strength, dexterity;

adaptive behavior,[4] self-care;

communication, speech, language;

intellectual aptitude;

academic performance;

academic study skills, attention, motivation, task persistence, class participation;

social maturity, leadership, interpersonal skills;

emotional stability, psychological well-being;

school behavior, cooperation;

vocational skills, career interests, aptitudes.

In addition, the evaluation may include background information on the child, including:

educational history;

outside–of–school activities;

home background;

family relationships;

family child-rearing practice;

home support for child's educational program.

The information for an evaluation is obtained from physical examinations, psychological tests of aptitude and behavior, diagnostic techniques, school and parent records, observation of the child at home and in school, and interviews with parents and teachers.

The primary source of evaluation information is psychological and diagnostic tests. There is usually a common core of tests followed by more specialized tests in specific problem areas. Every evaluation will probably include tests of vision, hearing, physical health, intelligence, and academic achievement. Often, if a learning disability is suspected, a child will receive additional diagnostic tests and must be observed in the regular classroom; if a hearing disability is present, audiological and ontological tests may be recommended. Tests of specific abilities, aptitudes, and interests may be administered to aid in educational (particularly vocational education) planning.

Remember, if you believe that one or more of these areas is not crucial for assessing your child's problem, you may ask that tests or other assessment procedures in these areas be dropped from the assessment battery. If you believe that additional information may be useful or important, you can request that certain tests be added to the battery.

What information do I provide during the collection stage of the evaluation?

You are a valuable source of information to the evaluation because you alone have had a continuous, long-term view of your child's behavior. Furthermore, you have had an opportunity to observe your child—both in and out of school situations. Thus, the school evaluation team may request you to provide the following:

medical and psychological developmental history of your child;

information on your own personal and educational background;

descriptions of the behavior of your child at home in the areas of self care, communication, emotional stability, work habits, motivation, persistence, and cooperation;

a description of the social relationships your child has with other neighborhood children;

descriptions of your child's attitudes, aptitudes, interests, and skills in nonacademic areas.

You may provide information during any of the evaluation stages through interviews, questionnaires, or conversations. Often parents are interviewed during the information collection stage about their child's developmental history, family background, and home behavior. Then during the evaluation conference you may have an opportunity to provide additional observations of your child and to clarify any discrepancies between home and school perceptions of your child's behavior. Finally, if you do not attend the evaluation conference, you may provide information related to the results of the evaluation, clarifying particular findings and expressing agreement or disagreement with evaluation recommendations.

The important thing is not when or how information is collected from you but that you have an opportunity to share your insights into your child's problems with the evaluation team before the important evaluation decisions are made. If you feel you have important input that is not being considered adequately, mention this to a school official or the person coordinating the evaluation, or both.

What will be my role at the evaluation conference or consultation session?

Your role is to be an active participant in the evaluation decision process, to learn all you can about your child's problems, to provide whatever additional perspectives you have on your child, and to contribute to the discussion of the decisions and recommendations considered during the conference. To fulfill your role you must do the following:

Listen attentively and take notes or tape record (if permissible).

Obtain, if possible, copies of the results of all tests and examinations.

Ask for explanations of all medical, psychological, and educational terms you do not understand.

Obtain clear, complete interpretations of all test results in terms of your child's strengths, weaknesses, and educational needs.

Ask for suggestions about the probable causes of the child's disability.

Be sure you understand the implications of the test results in terms of your child's current educational needs and long-term outlook or potential.

Provide your own insights into your child's problems and needs based on your observations and conversations with your child.

Assist in resolving inconsistencies between school and home reports of your child's behavior.

Offer alternative explanations to suggestions and conclusions with which you disagree.

Participate in discussions regarding the education decisions affecting your child by sharing information and asking questions.

Another function you should be prepared to perform at the conference or consultation is to clarify differences between your child's behavior at home and at school. For example, you may be able to explain, based on conversations with your child, why he or she is shy with classmates but plays happily with friends in the neighborhood. To perform this clarification function, you should try to relate specific instances rather than general remarks.

Many critical decisions may be made during the evaluation team conference—decisions on eligibility, diagnosis, recommended placement, suggested educational goals, and needed services. You should be prepared to contribute to the discussion of these decisions based on your own hopes and expectations for your child and what you believe will be in your child's best interests.

Although the evaluation reporting conference or consultation may seem technical, you should remember that you are an important component in a cooperative venture designed to provide your child with an appropriate educational program. You have a definite right to know any and all information about your child's special needs (this right includes having access to all information in his or her file), a right to provide the school with your perspective of what you believe is an appropriate education program, and a right to institute due process procedures whenever you believe a decision to be detrimental to your child.

Who pays for the evaluation?

The evaluation should be provided free of charge, and you have the right to ask for a complete examination of your child if you believe it is necessary to determine his or her precise educational needs. If required, the school will pay for diagnostic evaluations by neurologists, orthopedic specialists, ophthalmologists, and psychiatrists, among others.

You also have the right to a second independent evaluation, although if the school contests the need for it through a due process hearing, you may have to pay for that evaluation.

Is it possible for me to review my child's records prior to the evaluation?

Yes; not only is it possible for you to review your child's records but it is very important that you do so, and at regular intervals.

The Family Educational Rights and Privacy Act of 1974 (Buckley Amendment) states that parents have the right to view, take notes from, obtain copies of, correct, and control access to their child's records. This covers all records, files, and documents maintained by the school and includes discipline folders, health records, grade reports and special education evaluation reports, IEPs, and annual reviews. It does not include teacher or counselor personal notes or records of security police.

With regard to your child's records, you have two important rights: the right to request that the records be corrected, and the right to restrict those who see your child's records.

To view your child's school records, you should follow whatever procedure has been established by your school. If you don't know what the procedure is, call or write the school principal. The school must let you see the records although they have up to 45 days to grant your request.

When you go to the school to view your child's records you may:

take notes from the records;

obtain photocopies of the records (at a reasonable cost);

ask for explanations or interpretations from a school staff person;

bring a friend or your child with you to help you understand the records or provide explanations.

After you have reviewed your child's records, you may decide that certain material should be removed. This is one of your important rights—the right to correct your child's records. Items that you might want removed include:

old test results (3 years or more unless being used to show progress over time);

teacher's and other informal anecdotal comments;

notes on your child's behavior;

information you believe is no longer accurate;

information you believe is inappropriate to educational decisions;

subjective or personal interpretive material.

If you find information that you believe is outdated, irrelevant, inappropriate, and/or inaccurate, explain your reasons to the principal and ask that it be removed. If the principal refuses, you may request a due process hearing at which an impartial hearing officer will determine, after listening to both you and the school, whether or not to remove the material. Even if the material is not removed, you may add your own written statement to your child's records explaining why you think a particular piece of information is inappropriate, irrelevant, or inaccurate.

The second important right you have with regard to your child's records is to restrict the number of persons who may review your child's records. There are, however, several persons who can see your child's records without your consent:

school officials in the same district with a legitimate educational interest;

school officials in the school district to which your child intends to transfer (but only after you have had a chance to request a copy of the records and to challenge their contents);

various state and national education agencies, when enforcing federal laws;

anyone to whom the school must report information as required by state statute;

accreditation and research organizations helping the school;

student financial aid officials;

those with court orders.[5]

However, for all other persons (including in many states[6] police, probation officers, and employers), the school must contact you each time that someone requests to see your child's files, and tell you who has made the request, why the request was made, which records were requested, and how the records will be used.

Many requests for access to your child's records will come from individuals who are preparing to assist your child in some way. If you wish this assistance, you will need to grant access. Other requests will come from organizations doing educational research, particularly research on changes in special education laws, policies, and programs. In these cases, your child's records will be aggregated with other records and your child's identity will remain confidential. It is important for those organizations that must evaluate new laws and programs to obtain information on all types of students. However, before you grant consent for research organizations to use your child's records, you should be sure your child's identity will remain private.

An important free publication on your rights regarding school records is entitled *Your School Records* and is available from:

Children's Defense Fund
1520 New Hampshire Avenue, N.W.
Washington, D.C.   20036

What should I do to prepare my child for an evaluation?

You want your child to participate in the evaluation testing without fear, anxiety, or tension. For this to happen, you must emphasize the positive outcome—development of a better school program—and deemphasize the problems leading to the evaluation.

You should find out from the evaluation coordinator the dates of the evaluation, the number of sessions, the approximate length of each session, and the individuals involved. Share that information with your child, as well as the fact that the tests will not hurt. Explain that the evaluator(s) will help both of you to learn more about your child's school problems and to find out what can be done to make school a better place to be. Tell your child that this person will ask many questions and may give a few tests. Also explain that even though some questions may seem difficult, there is no cause for worry; just do the best he or she can.

Be sure your child understands that the results of the evaluation will not be used to put your child in an unhappy classroom or school situation, that the nonmedical parts of the evaluation are not a physical exam, and that there are no shots.

The evaluation testing will be conducted by individuals trained in assessment procedures including how to motivate students and encourage their best response. The testing sessions are usually private with only the student and examiner present. For these reasons most students do not have negative or unpleasant reactions to the testing experience.

It is important to talk to your child after the evaluation is over. Find out what happened, what your child thought about the tests, and what problems occurred. Find out whether your child had trouble understanding any of the evaluators or doing what was expected. This information may be useful in explaining why certain unexpected results were obtained. During this time you should be supportive and assure your child once again that there is no such thing as failing the examination.

Will the evaluation be fair?

Federal law (P.L. 94–142, Regulation 121a.532) specifies that certain conditions be followed when an evaluation is conducted, namely that:

tests be administered in the child's native language or other mode of communication (e.g., sign language);

tests be validated for the purpose for which they are to be used;

tests be administered by trained examiners according to test instructions;

tests be administered in a manner that takes account of the child's disability (e.g., an intelligence test requiring manual dexterity would not be given to a child with cerebral palsy to test intelligence);

tests be designed to assess specific educational concerns and not just to provide a general intelligence quotient measure.

Although school systems are required to satisfy these provisions when conducting an evaluation you may wish to share your particular concerns with the person coordinating your child's evaluation. The following are some questions you might ask:

Will the testing and interviewing be conducted by someone familiar with my child's cultural background?

Are the test items (particularly intelligence test items) fair to my child's cultural background?

Will the testing or interviewing take into account my child's handicap?

   If the child has a reading disability, will there be tests for skills other than reading?

   If the child has a short attention span, will the length of test sessions reflect this?

   If the child has fine motor coordination problems, will the tests involve writing?

Many tests, even those not intended to test academic achievement, depend on certain language, reading, and writing skills and require attention and concentration. You should verify with the coordinator of the evaluation team that the tests and procedures your child engages in will take into account his or her particular disability. Nothing is more unfair to a child than to be evaluated as poor in mathematical ability, for example, because of an inability to read the instructions or write the answers. This is not to say that there won't be tests directly related to your child's disability, but that tests in other areas take that disability into account.

One final word about fairness. There may be areas of your child's life that you believe are not properly part of the school's concern. Questions regarding your child's personality and home and family life need to be asked (and answered) only if the questions have a bearing on your child's school life. Although information about your child—early development; home behavior; interactions with parents, siblings, and neighbors; your child rearing and discipline practices—may assist the evaluation team in understanding your child, you do not have to respond to questions on these topics if you believe they are too personal or inappropriate.

What happens while my child waits for an evaluation and its results?

Your child will stay in his or her present setting unless the school agrees to provide a temporary placement for your child or to make some modification in your child's program that does not involve the special education program. Schools are generally reluctant to do that, however, and you have no legal right to insist on this type of change.

Often delays in evaluation reflect the lack of an appropriate placement. If all the classes for young, moderately or severely retarded students are full, then some schools, rather than have a waiting list for service, just slow down on the evaluation and subsequent planning process. This is, of course, against federal regulations. If you suspect this might be causing the delay in evaluating your child, you should contact your school's director of special education. Gentle pressure may speed up the process and continued pressure may force the school system to open up or expand its programs. Remember, the school must provide you with an evaluation of your child within 30 days after referral.

You should stay in contact with your child's teacher while your child is waiting for an evaluation. Encourage the teacher to continue to work with your child, and find out what you can do at home to reinforce the teaching efforts during this interim period.

What are the outcomes of the evaluation process?

The direct product of the evaluation process is a set of information—test scores, observations and perceptions of parents and teachers—on the educational strengths and weaknesses and educational needs of the student. This set of information is used in the process of making decisions related to:

eligibility for special services (i.e., the student possesses some disability that substantially affects his or her learning and requires special instruction and related services);

designation of specific handicapping condition (classification);

recommended placement;

suggested instructional goals and objectives;

recommended special education services.

Remember, in many school systems not all these decisions will be made at the same conference. Some school systems have appraisal teams that collect and examine information on the child and determine eligibility and handicap designation, while a second team—a placement team—makes placement and instructional programming decisions. You should find out before going to the evaluation conference if the conference is also going to discuss and make decisions about your child's placement and individualized educational program. If it is, you should read those chapters which discuss placement and the IEP.

How will I find out the outcomes of the evaluation?

When you give your consent to the evaluation, you should be informed when and by what method you will learn the results of the evaluation. You could be briefed on the evaluation results either by attending the appraisal team conference at which your child's evaluation is discussed, or you could be briefed at an individual consultation session with a member of the appraisal team after the team has discussed your child.

If your school system has invited you to attend the appraisal team conference (often called a case review or staffing) and to contribute your knowledge, understanding, and insights to the evaluation decisions concerning your child, we encourage you to attend. If your school system prefers to use individual consultation sessions to inform you of the evaluation results, you may request permission to attend the appraisal team conference instead.

You may feel that the appraisal conference will be too technical, too time-consuming, and possibly too difficult emotionally for you. Or, you might want to observe the appraisal team conference and save your questions for an individual consultation session.

What specific sorts of questions should I be prepared to ask about the test results?

The principal goal of the evaluation team conference or consultation session is to consider the information collected on your child during the evaluation and to use this information to make decisions and recommendations about your child's educational program.

Thus, you should examine the scores of each test or procedure used with your child to be sure you understand what those scores mean in terms of the educational needs of your child. You might ask the following questions:

What specific characteristics or behaviors were measured by the tests or procedures used?[7]

How are the scores interrelated? What patterns were detected?

How accurate are the scores? How confident can I be that the scores are accurate?

Why might my child have received these scores?

What circumstances in the testing situation (anxiety, personality factors, motivation) might have affected my child's performance?

How do my child's scores compare with those of other children in the same grade or class? Of the same ethnic group? With the same disability?

How do my child's test scores compare with scores he or she received on similar tests given at an earlier time?

What do the scores mean in terms of predicting future behavior or long–term potential?

How will the scores be used in educational planning?

This may seem like a very long laundry list of questions. You do not have to ask all or even any of them, but you should listen carefully and be sure you thoroughly understand all that was learned during the evaluation of your child. You should learn the following:

your child's educational strengths and limitations;

unique aspects of your child's personality;

the situations that cause your child difficulty;

beneficial activities you can provide at home;

recommendations for an appropriate individualized educational program;

the rate at which your child could be expected to progress in his or her psychological and educational development;

reasonable predictions and expectations you might have for your child's future.

In addition to learning all about what your child's test scores mean, you also should learn what happens to these scores and all the other information presented at the evaluation conference or consultation. You will want to know which scores or other information become part of your child's permanent record, where that record is housed, who has access to it, under what circumstances, and for what purposes.

Does my child have to take an I.Q. test as part of the evaluation?

In most cases an individual intelligence test is an important part of a comprehensive evaluation, but it is by no means the principal component.

Until recently, certain items on intelligence tests were thought to be culturally biased since the scores for intelligence tests were standardized on the basis of results obtained only from white children. However, revisions have been made in the commonly used intelligence tests to eliminate or modify the scoring of culturally biased items and nonwhite children have been added to the sample on which the norms are based.

More important, intelligence tests scores, while still useful for diagnostic purposes, must be considered along with other information such as the child's adaptive behavior, language skills, academic achievement, school experiences, cultural background, motivation, and other factors which may affect measured intelligence. Thus, no child can be granted or denied eligibility for special education on the basis of an I.Q. score.

If properly administered and interpreted, intelligence tests can provide useful, predictive diagnostic information, when used in conjunction with other tests and assessment procedures. Careful interpretation of intelligence tests can offer useful insight into a child's personality, creativity, test-taking ability (attention, concentration, anxiety), and emotional stability. However, these interpretations should be considered only as insights; rarely do the subtests or other subscales developed on the basis of personality or educational theory possess adequate reliability and validity to be used as quantitative measures of personality disorders or emotional disturbances.

If an eligibility, classification, or placement decision that you disagree with has been determined primarily on the basis of intelligence test results, you should try to get copies of the actual test protocol and find out how your child's responses to particular items were interpreted and scored.

The psychologist administering the I.Q. test exercises considerable professional judgment in scoring, and you must be aware of what these scores mean in order to defend your position.

What are the definitions used by the federal government for defining the various handicapping conditions?

It is important that you understand in which federal disability category your child will be included since that is how your child will be counted in your school district statistical reports to the state and any special education program evaluation reports prepared for the school board or community. Furthermore, many services and organizations that provide services and financial resources are organized around and sometimes limited to certain disabilities.

The following are the federal definitions (P.L. 94–142 Regulations Section 121a.5):

Deaf—a hearing impairment which is so severe that the child is impaired in processing linguistic information through hearing, with or without amplification, and which adversely affects educational performance.

Deaf-blind—concomitant hearing and visual impairments, the combination of which causes such severe communication and other developmental and educational problems that they cannot be accommodated in special education programs solely for deaf or blind children.

Hard-of-hearing—a hearing impairment, whether permanent or fluctuating, which adversely affects a child's performance but which is not included under the definition of "deaf" in this section.

Mentally retarded—significantly subaverage general intellectual functioning existing concurrently with deficits in adaptive behavior and manifested during the developmental period, which adversely affects a child's educational performance.

Multihandicapped—concomitant impairments (such as mentally retarded-blind, mentally retarded-orthopedically impaired, etc.), the combination of which causes such severe educational problems that they cannot be accommodated in special education programs solely for one of the impairments. The term does not include deaf-blind children.

Orthopedically impaired—a severe orthopedic impairment which adversely affects a child's educational performance. The term includes impairments caused by congenital anomaly (e.g., clubfoot, absence of some member, etc.), impairments caused by disease (e.g., poliomyelitis, bone tuberculosis, etc.), and impairments from other causes (e.g., cerebral palsy, amputations, and fractures or burns which cause contractures).

Other health impaired—limited strength, vitality, or alertness due to chronic or acute health problems such as a heart condition, tuberculosis, rheumatic fever, nephritis, asthma, sickle cell anemia, hemophilia, epilepsy, lead poisoning, leukemia, or diabetes, which adversely affects a child's educational performance.

Seriously emotionally disturbed—a condition exhibiting one or more of the following characteristics over a long period of time, and to a marked degree, which adversely affects educational performance:

an inability to learn which cannot be explained by intellectual, sensory, or health factors;

an inability to build or maintain satisfactory interpersonal relationships with peers and teachers;

inappropriate types of behavior or feelings under normal circumstances;

a general pervasive mode of unhappiness or depression;

a tendency to develop physical symptoms or fears associated with personal or school problems.

The term includes children who are schizophrenic or autistic, it does not include children who are socially maladjusted, unless it is determined that they are seriously emotionally disturbed.

Specific learning disability—a disorder in one or more of the basic psychological processes involved in understanding or in using language, spoken or written, which may manifest itself in an imperfect ability to listen, think, speak, read, write, spell, or do mathematical calculations. The term includes such conditions as perceptual handicaps, brain injury, minimal brain disfunction, dyslexia, and developmental aphasia. The term does not include children who have learning problems which are primarily the result of visual, hearing, or motor handicaps, of mental retardation, of emotional disturbance, or of environmental, cultural, or economic disadvantage.

The specific learning disability child does not achieve commensurate with his or her age or ability level when provided with learning experiences appropriate for the child's age and ability level such that there exists a severe discrepancy between achievement and intellectual ability in one or more of the following areas:

oral expression;

listening comprehension;

written expression;

basic reading skill;

reading comprehension;

mathematical calculation;

mathematical reasoning.

What does the diagnostic label given my child mean?

One outcome of the evaluation process is to determine the disability classification that best describes your child's problems. During the evaluation conference or consultation session you should ask the following questions about that classification:

What evaluation results (test scores, observations, etc.) led the appraisal team to suggest that classification?

How does the classification translate into federal definitions required by P.L. 94-142?[8]

Does the classification fall within the legal definition of "developmental disabilities" (which may determine my eligibility for certain other support services)?

What does the classification mean in terms of making my child eligible or ineligible for certain financial, legal, and other community support programs?

The classification given your child will be relatively permanent so be sure you know why your child was diagnosed as possessing a certain disability and what it means medically, legally (in terms of state and federal law and eligibility for specific services), and educationally. And most important, be certain you agree with the classification. There are tremendous gray areas in classification, particularly in the area of distinguishing whether an individual is mentally retarded or learning disabled, autistic or severely mentally retarded. Furthermore, there are a variety of terms that may be used in different school districts or states and by different evaluation clinic staff, school psychologists, and physicians. Your child may be called minimally brain damaged, language disabled, learning disabled, hyperactive, neurologically impaired, mentally retarded, or severely maladjusted by different people at different times.

Why does my child have to be classified or labelled into a specific handicapping designation?

No one issue in special education has consistently aroused as much argument as the classification or "labelling" of handicapped students, particularly those with mild cognitive impairments. For this reason, many states and/or local school districts have abandoned classifying students by disability and instead classify them by service needs or placement (Level I, Level II, etc.).

Classification systems are designed to cluster configurations of similar physical and psychological behavior patterns. The name or label given a particular pattern (e.g., autistic, aphasic, cerebral palsied) makes it easier to communicate in a general way the particular type of disability a student has. Knowing the classification or diagnostic category that includes your child will make it easier for you to locate professional specialists who work with your child's disability, parent and consumer groups concerned with that disability, literature (books, magazine articles) that discusses your child's disability, and physical equipment, toys, games, and learning materials designed for children or young adults with similar disabilities.

Classification is also important for recordkeeping and program accountability purposes. The federal government, for example, requires that states report the number of students served by type of handicap. In many cases, a particular classification is required for eligibility for specific services.

However, you should be aware that within each diagnostic classification there are tremendous variations in the type and severity of the particular problems evidenced by the student and the specific educational assistance the student may require. For example, visually impaired children vary in the degree to which they have residual sight; for some students, large print books are a useful instructional strategy; for others they are not.

The dangers of classification are twofold: first, children with certain designations may be stigmatized by other students (and even some adults); and second, children with similar designations may be provided similar instruction despite the fact that they may have very different instructional needs.

There is ample evidence that children and young adults can be abusive to their handicapped classmates, refusing to work or play with them, teasing them, and calling them names. This abuse is usually generated not so much by the label itself as by the behavior of the child, and not labeling the child will not change the child's behavior.

Stigmatization can be corrected by strong, consistent social instruction on the part of the schools and parents emphasizing that disabilities can happen to anyone, that individuals with disabilities are to be welcomed members of any group, and that verbal or other abuse is not to be tolerated. Under the impetus of recent legislation, more and more handicapped individuals are becoming equal participants in our schools and communities so that the presence of a handicapped student in school no longer seems strange and should not arouse stigmatizing behavior on the part of fellow students.

The second danger—that of using diagnostic classification to make instructional decisions—has been a pervasive problem. Traditionally, school systems have offered programs for the deaf, for example, without considering the particular communication skills of each individual deaf child. As a result of the strong language of P.L. 94–142 concerning individualized educational planning, the general assignment of students to a particular educational program based on diagnostic classifications is being replaced by placement according to the unique education needs of the student. You should be wary, however, of the tendency to make education decisions based solely upon the diagnostic classifications. Just because your child has Down's syndrome, does not necessarily mean he or she should be in a program for trainable mentally retarded students. Your child may be functioning higher or lower than other Down's syndrome children and the instructional program should be individually determined.

Is it possible for my child to receive special education services without being designated as having a disability?

Technically, no, it is not; although some school systems provide for extra instructional support through programs like remedial reading, Title I, and parent volunteers, which do not involve special education. Some school systems provide for limited special education teacher assistance for the regular class teacher in the form of routine student diagnostic testing, recommendations, and the provision of special materials or short-term crisis intervention. But if you want your child to receive the benefits of an intensive, continuing special education program, he or she must be evaluated and defined as having some qualifying disability.

What are some signs that suggest a child might need special help?

Many parents first become aware of their child's special needs when their child begins attending school. At this point, identification of a child's special needs becomes a joint parent–child–school effort. There may be several clues to your child's needs for special help:

You observe that your child is slower and less mature than his or her classmates; that he or she cannot do things other children the same age are able to do.

Your child tells you that school work is too difficult and that he or she does not like school.

Your child receives poor grades on report cards and/or is not promoted to the next grade.

Your child tells you that he or she does not like his or her classmates; that he or she has no friends, gets into fights, or is lonely.

Your child's teacher suggests that your child is having difficulty with schoolwork, that the child's school behavior is inappropriate, or that he or she does not get along with other children and is lonely and rejected.

The school discovers learning problems as a result of schoolwide intelligence or achievement tests.

The school discovers physical problems as a result of schoolwide vision or hearing screening or physical examinations.

If you have received one or more of these clues, you may wish to request that the school conduct an assessment of your child's educational problems and need for special assistance. This assessment must be provided at no cost to you. Even if you do not request an assessment, if your child continues to have serious problems coping with school experiences, the school may request permission to evaluate your child for special services.

What should I do if I wish to have the school conduct an evaluation of my child but the school has not yet requested one?

Contact your child's teacher to discuss your concerns about your child. It might help if you visited the classroom to observe your child. In your conversation with the teacher you should discuss the following:

evidence of your child's problem (report card grades, class test results, homework);

your child's views about school problems;

difficulties you observe your child to be having that the teacher may not have noticed;

possible ways your child might be helped (e.g., different materials, more individualized instruction, greater teacher attention, possible incentives, or motivating strategies).

Your child's teacher may already have noticed your child's problem and may be doing things for your child that you are not aware of. In some cases, your child's teacher may suggest changes in the instructional program, such as class and/or teacher changes, individual work assignments, tutoring, remedial reading and/or mathematics, and work contracts. Or, something as simple as a seating change may correct the problem. Certain behavior management strategies may be all that is needed to correct discipline problems or a poor attention span.

You should consider these suggestions and, if you agree, set a date when you and the teacher will review your child's progress. If you do not agree with the teacher's suggestions you can still request an evaluation. If your child's teacher does not agree to refer your child, you may request an evaluation yourself by writing the school principal and the school district director of special education.[9] In this request, you should explain in full all your reasons for wanting your child evaluated (all that evidence you have collected) and you should describe the actions already taken to help your child and why you think these actions have been unsuccessful. (See Figure 4.2 for an example of such a letter.) Once you have requested an evaluation of your child, you should not have to wait longer than one month for it to take place.

In some school districts, there are more children needing an evaluation than can be accommodated. Your child may have to undergo preliminary screening procedures before receiving a comprehensive evaluation. These procedures are designed to insure that only children who would benefit from a comprehensive evaluation receive one. However, you will want to keep careful records of the dates of the communications you have with school personnel to avoid delays in the assessment of your child.

During the time you are waiting for an evaluation, try to maintain contact with your child's teachers. Try to encourage them to continue to help your child in whatever ways possible until an alternative placement is selected and an individualized education plan developed.

If your child still has problems even after the teacher's intervention, you and your child's teacher should set a time when you can discuss together the progress your child has made. During this discussion, you should explain that you think your child's school-related problems have persisted in spite of changes instituted by your child's teacher, and that it is time for your child to be evaluated for special services.

Usually at this point your child's teacher will agree to refer your child for special education services and will begin the necessary administrative procedures.

What should I do if I want an evaluation but the principal or special education director does not agree to provide a comprehensive evaluation of my child?

Assuming you have made formal requests to the principal and director of special education without success, there are two things you may do. First, you may obtain your own evaluation through your physician and/or an out-

Figure 4-2
Example of Letter to Request a Comprehensive Evaluation

2542 Winding Way
Austria, Virginia 23270

October 15, 1979

Dr. Burton Dunn, Principal
James Monroe Elementary School
1721 Schoolhouse Drive
Austria, Virginia 23270

Identification   Re: David Ajar, Age 9
Information   Ms. Murphy's 3rd Grade Class

Dear Dr. Dunn:

Purpose
We wish to request that our son, David Ajar, be given a comprehensive evaluation for the purpose of determining his eligibility for special education services.

Past
History &
Present
Problem
Last year, David's report cards from second grade (Ms. Sweaning's class) indicated he was not doing well in reading, spelling or writing. This year, his reading has not improved and Ms. Murphy has called us twice regarding David's lack of attention in class and disruptive behavior particularly during his reading group activities.

Activities
Attempted
Last year, David was in a remedial reading program one hour a week with Mr. Richards. This year, Ms. Murphy has tried using work contracts and other behavior management activities. Although his behavior seems to have improved a bit, his reading level is still way below that of the other children in his class.

Action
Requested
We believe David should be evaluated to determine what is causing his reading problems and what special materials or teaching might help him improve his reading.

We shall be happy to cooperate in this evaluation in any way we can.

Sincerely yours,
Judith Swerdna, Mother
Robert Ajar, Father

Copy to:
Dr. Elizabeth Filbert
Director of Special Education

side evaluation clinic. You should indicate in writing to the principal and the director of special education that you intend to obtain an outside evaluation and that you will request the school to pay for it. (See Figure 4.3.) However, you may initially have to pay for this evaluation yourself, although you may later be able to convince school officials that this expen-

Figure 4-3
Example of Letter to Request a Comprehensive Evaluation to be Paid for by the
School (after the school has refused to conduct an evaluation)

2542 Winding Road
Austria, Virginia 23270

October 30, 1979

Dr. Elizabeth Filbert
Director of Special Education
Austria Public Schools
7920 Municipal Road
Austria, Viginia 23270

	Re: David Ajar, Age 9
Identification	James Monroe Elementary School
	Ms. Murphy's 3rd grade school

Dear Dr. Filbert:

On October 25, we received a letter from Dr. Dunn, Principal of James Monroe Elementary School denying our request for
an evaluation of our son, David Ajar, dated October 15, 1979.

Dr. Dunn suggested that before conducting an evaluation, he
wants David to receive remedial reading one hour a week with
the remedial reading teacher, Mr. Richards. However, David had
remedial reading instruction last year and it was not effective.

Because the school has refused to conduct an evaluation of
David, we are taking him to the High Point Psychological
Assessment Clinic (recommended by our physician) in Austria for
a comprehensive evaluation. The clinic has told us the assessment
will cost $350 and we are requesting the school district to pay
for this evaluation.

We have scheduled an appointment for David on November
12, 1979. If we do not hear from you before that time, we will
assume that you are agreeing to this course of action and are
willing to pay for this evaluation.

After the evaluation, we will call Dr. Dunn to arrange a
conference when we can discuss the evaluation results and
consider David's situation.

Please feel free to call us or the clinic if you wish more
information about their procedures and costs.

Sincerely yours,

Judith Swerdna

Robert Ajar

Copy to Dr. Burton Dunn, Principal
James Monroe Elementary School

Margin labels:
Prior Action
Rationale for Prior Action
Action to Be Taken and Request for School Assistance

diture should be borne by the school. The school, in turn, may ask for an impartial hearing to contest the need for, and hence the school's obligation, to pay for this evaluation. Should the hearing officer agree with the school, then you must pay for the outside evaluation.

The school staff must consider this outside evaluation when making educational decisions regarding your child, although the school may wish to conduct its own evaluation to confirm the findings obtained from the outside evaluation.

Second, you may request a due process hearing at which you present to an impartial hearing officer your reasons and supporting evidence for wanting an evaluation. The school personnel will present their reasons for believing an evaluation is unnecessary and the hearing officer will make a determination.

Obtaining an independent evaluation may be faster but you run certain financial risks. A due process hearing might take more time, may require an attorney, and may be psychologically stressful. On the other hand, confronting the school officials with a written notice of intent to either charge them for an outside evaluation or force a due process hearing may be enough to convince them of your persistence and force them to reconsider the need for an evaluation.

What can I do if my child is found ineligible for special education?

First, find out all you can about the evaluation the school performed. Second, review the evaluation procedures used to be sure they were comprehensive, appropriate, and fair (as discussed in previous sections). Third, find out why your child was determined ineligible, which people were involved in the decision, and what evidence provided the basis for the decision. It may be a good idea to talk with each person on the evaluation team to determine what specific factors influenced each person's decision. Try to determine if your child was denied eligibility for administrative reasons (e.g., because appropriate services are not available).

You should find out which tests results were weighed most heavily, and have the results of these tests explained to you. If you still believe that your child is eligible for and needs special education, you may request an independent evaluation.

Under what circumstances should I request an independent evaluation?

You may request an independent evaluation whenever you disagree with the result of the school's evaluation. The following are examples of such reasons for disagreement:

your child was determined ineligible for special services (perhaps because the school has no program or limited space in a program that would assist your child) but you believe he or she needs special help.

Your child was determined eligible for special services (perhaps because he or she is having trouble with a particular teacher) but you believe he or she could "make it" without special education with just a few minor changes (e.g., a different teacher, more discipline, more individualized attention).

Your child was designated as having a particular disability classification that you believe is not appropriate; for example, you believe your child's problems are a result of factors other than those considered in the evaluation. (Other outcomes, particularly IEP goals and objectives, placement decisions, and service needs, are discussed separately in other chapters.)

You should consider all the benefits and drawbacks before requesting a second evaluation. It will take as much or more of your child's time and psychic energy as the first evaluation, and you may end up having to pay for it yourself. Furthermore, certain decisions, particularly those related to classification, may be based on state law so that a second evaluation would not produce a change. For example, you may believe your child is aphasic but the evaluation designated him or her as specific learning disabled. However, aphasia may not be a recognized disability category in your state. A second evaluation, even if it supported your position, would not assist the school since it must classify and report all special education students according to state definitions.

However, if you do desire a second evaluation, the school staff should be able to recommend physicians, psychologists, and evaluation clinics that provide them. Other sources of information about evaluations may be obtained from public health officials, community mental health centers, psychology or special education departments of local colleges and universities and from parent and other organizations (e.g., the Easter Seal Society). When selecting a person or persons to evaluate your child, remember you want to use the results of the second evaluation to augment and challenge the original school–provided evaluation. Thus, the independent evaluation should be conducted by persons as qualified as those who conducted the school's evaluation and, if possible, by individuals or a clinic that is independent of the school.

When you have selected a person or clinic to conduct the evaluation, inform school officials in writing that you intend to get a second evaluation.

Your letter should also tell them who will perform the evaluation, what skill or behavior areas will be evaluated, and what it will cost. Explain why you want a second evaluation and request that the school pay for it. (See Figure 4.4.)

The report of the second evaluation should include, in addition to an assessment of your child's educational strengths and weaknesses, a discussion of how and why the second evaluation differs from the school's, as well as an assessment of your child's educational needs and appropriate placement.

After you have received this second evaluation, you should request (in writing) that the school's evaluation team review its decision in light of these findings. Ask that the person(s) who performed the second evaluation be invited to meet with the school's team to contribute to the decision process.

If, after considering the results of the second evaluation, the school still considers your child ineligible for special education, you can request a

Figure 4-4
Example of Letter to Request an Independent Evaluation (when there is a disagreement with the results of the school's evaluation)

2542 Winding Road
Austria, Virginia 23270

November 10, 1979

Dr. Elizabeth Filbert
Director of Special Education
Austria Public Schools
7920 Municipal Road
Austria, Virginia 23270

Re: David Ajar, Age 9

Identification   James Monroe Elementary School
Ms. Murphy's 3rd Grade Class

Dear Dr. Filbert:
On October 25, our son David was examined by Dr. Stephen Lorton, the School Psychologist, regarding his reading problems. On November 3, 1979, we participated in a confer-

Past action   ence with Dr. Lorton, Dr. Dunn, Ms. Murphy and Mr. Garcia
and   (a special education teacher) regarding the results of that
School's   evaluation.
Position   The evaluation indicated that David has a mild learning disability compounded by serious hypertension and aggression. Mr. Garcia suggested that David be placed all day in his special class for students who require structure and discipline.

Figure 4-4
continued

Parent's Disagreement	We do not believe that David's behavior is so disruptive that it requires him to be separated from his friends and put into a separate class. We also believe that David's reading problems are serious and that the examination conducted by Dr. Lorton was insufficient to detect the real causes of David's reading problem.
Proposed Action	We would like to have a second independent evaluation of David conducted by the High Point Psychological Assessment Clinic, a clinic recommended by the President of the Austria ACLD. This clinic specializes in diagnosing reading problems. The clinic has told us this evaluation will cost $350. We are requesting the school district to pay for this evaluation.
Request for School Assistance	We have scheduled an appointment for David on November 20, 1979. If we do not hear from you before that time, we will assume that you are agreeing to this independent evaluation.

After the evaluation, we will call Dr. Dunn to arrange a conference when we can discuss the evaluation results and reconsider the placement for David.

If you want more information about the evaluation clinic, please feel free to call us or the clinic.

Sincerely yours,

Judith Swerdna

Robert Ajar

due process hearing. Before doing this, however, you should reflect on your position and discuss your feelings with other experienced parents. Your child's school problems may not require special education, although some other action or program changes may be needed.

What can I do to make certain that the results of the independent evaluation will support my position?

An independent evaluation is supposed to be just that—independent—so there is nothing you can or should do to make sure the evaluation results concur with your beliefs. However, there are some things you can do in order to get a truly independent evaluation.

If you request a second evaluation at the school's expense, they will probably recommend a clinic or psychologist whose charges are reasonable.

Furthermore, it is only reasonable to expect school staff to recommend evaluation clinics or psychologists with whom the school has good working relationships and who share a similar educational philosophy with regard to the provisions of special services.

It might be a good strategy, therefore, to locate an evaluation clinic on your own. Friends, parent advocate groups, your attorney, or a local university special education department may be able to recommend one. You may be able to discover one or more clinics that have a philosophy of special education that is similar to yours (e.g., believing that intensive, structured instruction in a more restrictive setting is often appropriate).

You should remember, however, that if you select an evaluation clinic or other diagnostic specialists that the school does not usually recommend and that are much more expensive than the typical clinic, you may end up paying for the evaluation yourself.

Also, when you select an evaluation clinic or clinical psychologist, you should remember that you will most likely want to use this evaluation to counter the results of the school evaluation. Therefore, you should be sure that the evaluation clinic or clinical psychologist has equal or better qualifications than the school evaluation team and that the evaluation includes all the components and meets the requirements of the school evaluation. An incomplete evaluation done by individuals with credentials considered inadequate by the school will not provide you with credible evidence even if the evaluation results support your opinion. Remember, too, that a hearing officer presented with two widely divergent evaluations may well request a third evaluation.

Notes

1. One very useful and readable book describing evaluation tests and test procedures is Stanley Klein, *Psychological Testing of Children: A Consumer's Guide,* Boston: The Exceptional Parent Press, 1977.

2. An educational diagnostician is an educator qualified to administer and interpret diagnostic tests.

3. From the Procedure for Evaluating Specific Learning Disabilities P.L. 94–142 regulations as amended in Section 121a.540.

4. Adaptive behavior refers to an individual's ability to perform the activities of daily living, including socialization skills.

5. From the Children's Defense Fund booklet, *Your School Records.*

6. States which did not have a law granting access to records for these individuals in effect prior to November 19, 1974.

7. A useful reference for understanding some technical terms used in testing is Stuart M. Losen and Bert Diament, *Parent Conferencing in the Schools,* Boston: Allyn and Bacon, 1978, pages 111–133.

8. Even if your district or state does not classify students, you should find out what category your child will be counted in for federal reporting purposes.

9. Some teachers are under pressure from administrators to reduce the number of referrals they make. Thus, they may welcome parent-initiated requests.

5

The Individualized Educational Program

JUDITH ANDREWS AGARD

After your child has been evaluated and designated as eligible for special education, the next step involves developing his or her educational program.

Each handicapped child must have an individualized educational program (IEP) which is developed after one or two conferences that include the child's teachers, parents, other school staff, and possibly the child. At this conference (or conferences) the child's evaluation results are reviewed; educational needs, goals, and objectives are selected; procedures for reviewing progress are established; a tentative placement is selected; and the necessary instructional and supportive services are designated. These decisions are incorporated into a written IEP document that serves to guide your child's instructional program.

As the advocate for your child, you will want to participate actively in the IEP conference, obtain and study the resulting IEP document, and use it as a basis for determining your child's progress.

The IEP is the most important document related to your child's education because it defines what constitutes a free, appropriate public education for your child. The school must do everything reasonable to assure that your child receives the services listed on his or her IEP, that he or she is placed in the instructional settings described in his or her IEP, and that your child achieves the goals and objectives specified in the IEP.

Some school systems, in an effort to save time, combine the meeting in which the results of the evaluation are discussed with the IEP development conference. This is a logically sound idea since the results of your child's evaluation should form the basis for the IEP. However, you may wish to separate the discussion on the evaluation results and the discussion on the IEP so that you are able to prepare for and function effectively when making decisions in each area.

Remember, if you believe that any aspect of your child's IEP is inappropriate, you have the right to a due process hearing. *The IEP is the key to your child's program.* You should actively participate in its initial development and its review.

What is the purpose of the IEP?

The IEP should clarify for you the educational program and services your child will be receiving, how the program and services provided will assist your child, and the changes in behavior and developmental growth you might expect your child to make under the particular program offered.

Because parents are invited to participate in the development of their child's IEP, the IEP provides an important opportunity for parent–school cooperation. It also provides an opportunity for you to have an influence on the selection of the educational goals and the program and services that you view as most important for your child. The IEP provides a bridge between home and school activities; because you are involved in and aware of the instructional program your child receives in school, you can encourage your child to work on related and supportive activities at home.

It is important to remember what the IEP is not. It is not a daily or weekly lesson plan for your child's instruction, although your child's teachers should develop lesson plans based on the IEP. It is not a contract or guarantee that your child will achieve the goals described; there are always factors that affect your child's progress over which the school has little control. It is not a system for monitoring teacher behavior or determining teacher effectiveness.

Special educators have long been encouraged to develop individualized instructional programs based on student needs, so the concept of individual planning is not new. However, the use of the IEP as the major coordinating mechanism for the planning and monitoring of a handicapped student's instructional program extends the concept of individualized instruction far beyond its original scope. Educators have not, to date, developed anything analogous to IEPs for nonhandicapped students, perhaps because curriculum guides and textbook outlines are expected to serve a similar function, and the instructional services needs of nonhandicapped students are not as complex. On the other hand, handicapped students have unique and multifaceted instructional needs that require an individualized, coordinated approach to instructional planning if an appropriate educational program is to be provided.

The federal legislation refers to the IEP as a written document, but the spirit of the law goes beyond that. The IEP is considered a planning system including, in addition to the preparation of the IEP document, the planning conferences and subsequent implementation, review, revision, and evaluation activities.

Despite its potential usefulness, there are many barriers preventing successful implementation of the IEP. For example, both regular and special education programs have, until recently, focused on a group approach to instruction—in the regular class through the design of curriculum and organizational strategies, and in special classes through the clustering of similarly diagnosed handicapped students. In addition, there have been few service options available other than self-contained special classes. Teachers are generally not trained in the task analysis needed for developing sequenced instructional objectives, and few districts provide administrative mechanisms to facilitate cooperative planning. Models of individualized programs or even of IEP documents have not been generally available.

Developing an IEP demands teacher, parent, and administrator time and skills. Additional staff are often required to manage the record-keeping, meeting scheduling, and other clerical tasks. Limited evidence from various investigators suggests that regular teachers often do not receive, do not use, and do not value the IEPs that have been developed.[1]

In sum, the IEP is a key concept in the provision of appropriate education to handicapped students, but it is a new educational procedure and its implementation may be creating problems.

What will happen to my child during the time between the evaluation and the IEP conference?

Your child will remain in the program or class where he or she is currently placed. Occasionally, modifications may be made that do not involve special education; for example, your child may be transferred to a different (but not special education) teacher or receive remedial instruction, or be assigned a peer or volunteer tutor. Because no special education services can be provided to your child until an IEP is established, it is important that there be as little delay as possible in the scheduling of the first IEP conference. You will want to stay in touch with your child's teacher during the interim to be sure your child's needs are not forgotten.

Some school districts develop IEPs in two stages. The first stage outlines basic goals and objectives and determines the placement. The second stage develops specific instructional objectives and special services needed. At least the first stage must occur before service can be provided, although the second stage can take place a few weeks after placement when teachers have had an opportunity to observe and work with your child.

How long after the evaluation does my child have to wait before the IEP is developed and put into effect?

The law requires that an IEP meeting be held within 30 calendar days of the determination that a students needs special education or related services [Regulations Section 121a.343(c)], and that the IEP must be implemented immediately after the meeting, except in circumstances where making arrangements such as transportation requires a short delay [Regulations Section 121a.342(b)].

This means that there can be no such thing as a waiting list for services. However, many schools are under pressure to provide services to more students than they originally expected. This means that schools are initiating new programs and expanding old ones to accommodate the increasing need for special education and related services. This uneven match of services to student needs may create hidden waiting lists. The following are examples:

Your child may have waited a long time for an evaluation—some school systems are not evaluating students unless they are certain they have space in the program the child needs.

Your child may be recommended for a particular program where there is space on a trial, temporary, or diagnostic basis.

The class size of your child's designated placement or the case load of the specialists who will provide special services may be increased beyond what is reasonable for providing appropriate instruction.

Your school system may deliberately establish a waiting list to bring pressure on the community and school board to allocate funds for developing a new program.

Some school systems extend a short delay beyond what might be considered reasonable to make arrangements permitted by the law.

It is important that you investigate any delay in the implementation of your child's IEP and be firm in your role as advocate for your child. Make sure the IEP developed for your child is appropriately implemented, if necessary through a due process hearing procedure or an administrative complaint to the school district or state.

Will I be notified about the IEP conference?

Yes, you should be contacted, although it may be by phone or a personal visit rather than in writing, and it may be termed something other than an IEP conference. The development of the IEP may be included as part of the evaluation conference or it may be called a placement team meeting because the educational placement is a major component of the student's educational program.

The regulations of P.L. 94–142 (Section 121a.345) state that the public school must take steps to insure that one or both parents of the handicapped child are present. This means that:

You should be notified of the meeting early enough so you can make preparations to attend.

You should be informed of the purpose of the meeting and who will participate.

The meeting should be scheduled at a time and place agreeable to you and the school.

The meeting should be conducted in a manner that facilitates your understanding, including arrangements for an interpreter for parents who are deaf or speak a language other than English.

The school must show good faith in its efforts to notify you of the IEP meeting. If there are two IEPs, the school must notify you about both. If you do not respond to their initial notification, school staff may call you, send registered letters, or attempt to contact you personally.

If you cannot attend the meeting at the scheduled time, you should try to get this time changed. Or, you can ask to meet with a school staff person at a different time to discuss the contents of the IEP. Even if you don't meet with the school about your child's IEP, you should arrange to get a copy of the IEP and to review it carefully.

Should I attend my child's IEP conference?

You should definitely attend your child's IEP conference(s). Even if you attend only to observe, it will be a worthwhile experience for you to see how the school staff view your child and the time and consideration they give to developing his or her educational program. Furthermore, even if you do not participate actively, you may be able to provide information about your child's interests, attitudes, social maturity, emotional reactions, and practical daily living skills.

We urge you to be an active participant in designing your child's educational program by engaging in the discussion of alternatives and the final selection of appropriate goals, objectives, placements, and services.

Since the IEP is the key to your child's educational program, you will need to be an active participant in its development to assure that your child receives appropriate services, is placed in an appropriate setting, and receives instruction targeted toward the attainment of appropriate objectives.

As an active participant you may encounter some resistance. However, with the implementation of P.L. 94–142 school personnel have become more receptive to active parent involvement in the educational planning process than they were previously, and your cooperative and concerned attitude should reduce any remaining doubts about the value of full parental participation.

What is the role of the parent at the IEP conference?

The three major roles you will perform at the IEP conference are to:

provide information;

share in the decision process;

learn about your child's educational program.

Provide information. Although the results of the evaluation will be the principal basis for developing your child's IEP, there is still a need for you to provide the following information about your child:

your view of your child's social and academic abilities, interests, and needs;

your realistic expectations for your child;

educational goals you believe are most important;

services you believe your child needs;

methods you have used successfully to help your child or manage his or her behavior.

Share in the decision process. Decisions will be made at the IEP conference related to the major educational goals and objectives that will guide your child's educational program and the special education program and related services that are required to assist your child in meeting those goals and objectives. You will want to contribute to the discussions related to these decisions. In this discussion, you might want to raise the following concerns:

Are the goals and objectives practical; that is, are they directed toward assisting your child to become a socially contributing citizen?

Do the goals and objectives represent a realistic and appropriate balance of academic, social, and vocational areas?

Are the goals and objectives progressive rather than recycled?[2]

Are the goals and objectives going to restrict your child's later choices (e.g., prevent him or her from being able to enter a particular occupation or post secondary educational program)?

What services will be needed to facilitate progress in each of the educational objectives selected?

Are the services to be provided sufficient to accomplish the goals and objectives selected?

Which of the program alternatives are most appropriate for delivering the instructional services required by your child?

What instructional activities can you provide your child at home to support or extend the school's program?

One particular responsibility you have is to make sure the IEP is specific and complete. Be sure that all the services your child needs are included and described in detail: who is responsible for providing each service, at what time, for how long, exactly what the instruction will consist of, and who will coordinate the service with the basic instructional program.

During the discussions you should feel free to express your own views and values and to reflect as best you can what you believe is in the best interest of your child. You should ask for an explanation of any terms and expressions you do not understand and question any proposed alternatives that do not seem appropriate. You should offer suggestions on the services you believe your child needs to achieve the goals and objectives specified for him or her.

What should I do to prepare for the IEP conference?

Much of what you should do to prepare for the IEP conference is similar to what you did to prepare for the evaluation conference. Ideally, you and/or your spouse should do the following:

Talk with a school staff person about the IEP conference; find out what will happen, what you should do to prepare, who you should bring, and whether your child should attend.

Find out the agenda of the meeting, particularly the critical decisions that will be made and the actions that will require your consent.

Be sure the school is aware of special needs you may have for an interpreter, babysitter, or transportation.

Talk with other parents who have attended IEP meetings at your school; find out about their experiences, the things they did or wished they had done to prepare, how they felt about the process, and the questions they asked or wished they had asked. Your school should be able to provide you with names of parents or parent groups who might help you.

Seek advice from individuals knowledgeable about the IEP conference. This would include parent advocates, psychologists, physicians, and attorneys, among others.

Obtain a description of the special education programs and services offered by your school district and a copy of the IEP document form (if any) used in your district. You should also learn what additional placements and services might be appropriate. Don't limit your horizons to what's available in your district.[3]

Review your files of interesting programs, materials, and techniques that others have used with children with problems similar to those of your child.

Discuss career goals with your child, the knowledge and skills he or she wants to acquire, and the classes and courses he or she wishes to take.

In establishing educational goals for my child, are there certain things I should be concerned about?

During the process of developing your child's IEP you should ask yourself the following questions:

Are the school's goals realistic? Are they challenging or just frustrating my child?

Is the school forcing my child into a vocational or general program when he or she could, with a little assistance, be in an academic or college preparatory program?

Why is it necessary for my child to be separated from friends in order to get needed services?

Shouldn't preparation for a productive adult life be given priority over academic skills (e.g., why are you teaching my child to read when he can't even dress alone?)

You should ask these questions, not only of school personnel, but also of your friends, your family, your child, and other professionals outside the school. Times and cultural mores change; students once considered unable to attend college have graduated and gone on to complete graduate school, and students once thought unable to work productively have full-time employment. Help your child to develop goals and strategies for achieving those goals which will realize his or her full potential.

Can I request specific instructional approaches, equipment, and materials or teachers to be part of my child's IEP?

You definitely can suggest particular instructional approaches, including teaching methods, special materials, and equipment. Naturally, different teachers will have different reactions to your suggestions. Some teachers will welcome your suggestions because they have been searching for new ideas on how to instruct your child. Others, who believe that their approach is having the desired effect, will tell you that they appreciate your interest, but feel there is no reason to change their style. If you really believe your suggested approach is a necessary part of an appropriate instructional program, be firm and ask for a teacher who will use this approach.

Special equipment or materials is another area in which your suggestions may not be well received because such things are expensive and often fail to live up to expectations. However, again, if you believe this equipment or material is a critical component of an appropriate program, press for it.

Asking for specific teachers is often a problem. One tactic is to request a placement where a specific approach you believe is appropriate for your child (e.g., a very structured class) is offered, and suggest that the alternative placement is inappropriate because of the lack of structure available. That tactic depersonalizes the request; instead of criticizing the teacher, you are merely pointing out how his or her instructional approach is inappropriate for your child.

More difficult (and unfortunately quite common) is the situation in which your child, prior to special education placement, was receiving and greatly benefitting from services (such as remedial reading instruction) that were discontinued when he or she began a new placement program. You want to know why your child can't still receive the other services and the school says the service or services are only for students who are not eligible for the more intensive instruction provided by a resource teacher. We have no answer to this problem. Your child should have access to, say, the remedial reading program, and if you insist, arrangements may be made to continue remedial reading instruction, at least during a transitionary period.

Who will attend the IEP conference?

The regulations of P.L. 94–142 (Section 121a.344) state that the following persons may attend:

a representative of the school who is qualified to provide or supervise the provision of special education (this could be the director of special education, a special education supervisor, or a special education teacher);

the student's teacher (this may be the student's current special education teacher, his or her current regular education teacher, or a teacher qualified to provide instruction in the program in which the student may be placed);

the student's parents;

the student, if appropriate, and if you make arrangements;

a member of the evaluation team or other person knowledgeable about the evaluation (if the student has just been evaluated for the first time);

a person knowledgeable about learning disabilities (if the student has been designated as having specific learning disabilities);

a person from a parochial, private, or public setting (if a student might be placed in such an institution or agency);

other individuals invited by the school or parents;

a vocational education teacher, counselor, or coordinator (if the student is in a vocational education program);

representatives from other agencies (if the student receives services from them, particularly vocational rehabilitation services).

Many state and local school systems have regulations about who is required or requested to attend IEP conferences, so the list could be expanded to include the following:

school principal or assistant principal;

school psychologist or educational diagnostician;

therapists (speech, physical, occupational);

guidance counselor, social worker;

physician, nurse, other medical specialists;

vocational rehabilitation counselor;

curriculum and/or learning material and equipment specialists; remedial reading or mathematics instructors.

Although this list sounds as if it contains a cast of thousands (and in some cases all or most of these persons are present), most often those who attend the IEP conference are two or three school staff plus you, the parents. In two-level IEP conferences the second level may include only your child's teacher and you.

You have the right to invite other individuals to attend and participate. These might include:

your family physician (if your child has medical needs);

a personal friend who knows your child;

a representative from a parent advocacy group;

another parent of a handicapped child who has gone through the IEP process;

an attorney (if you expect the school to disagree with some of your suggestions).

These individuals could be helpful by explaining to you what's happening, taking notes so you can concentrate on the discussion, providing additional observations of your child, supporting your position in the discussion, and recalling and interpreting the major points discussed. It should be noted that the number of conferences scheduled is likely to affect the number of persons who participate at one time.

If you have any reason to suspect that you and the school will seriously disagree about any element of your child's IEP (particularly an element with financial implications) to the extent that a due process hearing will be required, you may want an attorney present. An attorney will assist you in clarifying certain issues and asking important questions. The presence of an attorney adds a dimension of seriousness and careful deliberation to the discussion. Unfortunately, it may also turn a cooperative relationship into an adversarial one (the parents against rather than alongside the school). Try to avoid this result by discussing beforehand the strategies your attorney might use that will not antagonize or intimidate school staff.

You should find out the names, backgrounds, roles, and responsibilities of each person present at the IEP conference. This is important since you may want to contact these persons later to discuss a particular issue or problem.

There are, however, some restrictions regarding the types of persons who can attend. Persons who are not directly involved with the student should not be invited to attend because this would violate the laws related to confidentiality of student records. (Often, confidential information from student records is discussed at IEP meetings.) Thus, you have the right to question the presence of individuals who you feel are inappropriate (teacher union representatives, for example).

Although it would be ideal if all of a student's teachers could participate in educational planning for a handicapped student, this becomes impractical at the junior high or high school level. Typically, the special education teacher rather than a regular teacher attends the IEP conferences. Guidance counselors may also attend to represent the regular teacher perspective.

You might request a particular teacher—one who has shown special concern for your child, one who has worked successfully with your child, or one who teaches a particularly critical subject area for your child. If your child is to be enrolled in a vocational education or other special program, you should request that the vocational education teacher or coordinator be present.

If you think that some key individuals are not present at the IEP, ask what arrangements have been made to relay the contents of the IEP to them. You might want to contact these individuals later to be sure they share your understanding of the IEP.

Should my child attend the IEP conference?

That depends on a number of factors: the age and maturity of your child, the nature and degree of the handicap, your child's emotional stability, and his or her ability to understand the event and not be bored, frightened, embarrassed, or upset.

Children of all ages and with all types of handicapping conditions have attended IEP conferences, contributed their ideas, and been interested and attentive during the proceedings. Students who attend their IEP conferences have an opportunity to see the level of care and concern the school and their parents have for them. As they participate in setting their own goals, they begin to realize that they are responsible for their own actions and decisions.

You should discuss whether your child should attend the IEP conference with school personnel. Even if you decide that your child should not attend the IEP conference, you should request a second, smaller, more personal conference attended by you, your child, and his or her teachers during which you discuss the IEP with your child.

In general, most high school age students should be able to benefit from participating in the development of their IEPs, and most younger students can understand the meaning and importance of their IEP goals and objectives if they are explained to them. If your district has a two-level IEP process, the smaller second-level discussion of particular short-term objectives and relevant services may interest your child more, although attendance at both levels may be desirable.

What will happen at the IEP conference?

Two of the things you should have done to prepare for the IEP conference are to obtain an agenda from the school staff and to discuss the IEP conference with other parents who have participated in one.

Basically, the IEP conference will be a discussion of each of the major areas required in the IEP. An example agenda and the role you should play at each stage is presented in Table 5.1. Many IEP conferences will not follow this outline, but all these points should be discussed.

During the opening remarks and introductions you might find it helpful to note the name, position, and location in the room of each person at the conference. For example:

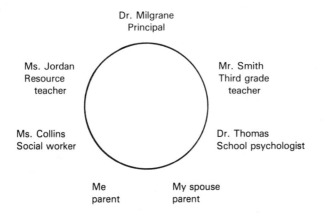

The discussion at an IEP conference may seem to wander or jump from topic to topic. It might help you to note what you think were the major points raised, the alternatives presented, the decisions reached, and

Table 5.1   Agenda for IEP Conference

Opening remarks (Levels 1 and 2)
  Purpose of meeting
  Identification of student whose IEP is being considered
  Introduction of persons present and their roles

  [Be sure you write down the names and roles.]

Student's current status (Level 1)
  Academic achievement
  Social adaptation
  Psychomotor skills*
  Self-help adaptive behavior
  Vocational skills

  [Be sure to share your view of your child's behavior at home.]

Summary of evaluation findings** (Level 1)
  Psychological tests
  Observation in school
  Educational experience
  Medical and developmental history
  Parent/family information

  [Be sure you understand all of the tests and observation results and that you agree with their interpretation.]

Identification of education strengths and weaknesses (Level 1)

  [Offer your own comments on what you believe are your child's strengths and weaknesses.]

Review of previous services and progress (Levels 1 and 2)

  [Offer your own comments on whether your child's progress was adequate.]

Identification of long-range (one year) priority educational goals (Level 1)
  Academic goals
  Practical daily living skills goals
  Career and vocational goals
  Social goals

  [Many goals may be suggested for your child; be sure to express your own concerns for your child—what you think are of highest priority—and be sure the goals selected as high priority are realistic and important for your child.]

---

*Coordination, agility, and mobility.

**You should already know this information from the evaluation conference, but be sure any new information agrees with previous information.

Table 5.1 continued

Short-term instructional objectives (Level 2)

[Be sure you understand the sequence of objectives and how the objectives will lead to the target goal, as well as the time by which each objective is to be achieved.]

Criteria for determining student progress (Level 2)

[Be sure you understand and agree with the methods and time schedule proposed to determine if your child is making progress.]

Services required to meet goals (Level 2)

(Be sure *all* the services you feel your child needs are identified and completely described and that you know the person responsible for each service, as well as exactly what will be done, and when the service will start and end. Remember, *all* the services your child requires should be indicated in the IEP.)

Materials, strategies, motivation, and techniques used (Optional, Level 2)

[Be sure you discover what activities, materials, and strategies can be used with your child at home to supplement the school program.]

Placement alternatives (Level 1)
Appropriate alternatives
Advantages and disadvantages of each
Placement(s) selected (teachers, room numbers, subjects taught)
Hours per day or week spent in each placement
Percentage of time to be spent in regular school program for academic and non-academic programs

[Be sure to share your thoughts on the appropriate placement for your child. If you are not offered alternatives, ask what other placements could be considered. Ask for time to visit alternative placements, if you haven't already. Be sure the placement decision is based on the needs of the child, not on the basis of handicap designation.]

Meeting summary (Levels 1 and 2)
Goals selected
Services to be delivered
Placement
Timelines for progress
Person responsible for coordinating the implementation
Major education goals and timelines
Placement alternative selected
Nature and extent of the needed services
Role you are to play at home
Contact person
Time when the IEP will be reviewed

[This recapitulation will insure that everyone at the IEP conference share the same understanding about the major decisions that were made.]

the rationale for the decisions offered. If you allow separate sheets of note paper for each agenda area, it might help you organize your note taking. At the end of the meeting you should ask someone to recapitulate the major decisions made.

Remember, the IEP conference is intended to be an open forum in which the program and placement alternatives for your child are explored. Then the persons present, including you, make an educational judgment regarding what constitutes an appropriate educational program for your child. You have a right to participate actively in this forum, to suggest the goals, placements, and services you believe are appropriate, and to have your views considered.

There are some school systems that have instituted a practice of conducting preconference staff meetings in which decisions are made and/or an IEP is developed without the parents being present. The decisions and/or preliminary IEP are then presented to the parents at an IEP conference for their approval. This practice violates the intent of the law and if you believe this has happened in your child's case, you should complain to the principal and then to the director of special education and/or parent advocate group in your school district. If you are presented with a complete IEP, you still have an opportunity to review it carefully, and to request that certain changes be made. Remember, even though you do not think you have much to offer to the discussions about various educational objectives, services, and placement alternatives, you should have the opportunity to listen to the discussion and to offer whatever insights or opinions you may have.

It will be very helpful to you and your child if there is one person designated as the principal person for assuring that the IEP gets implemented. This person could be a teacher, counselor, or principal, and will serve as your principal contact when you review your child's progress. If no such person is indicated, ask that someone be designated as a contact for you.

Are there any special things I should be concerned about if my school conducts a two-level IEP conference?

A two-level IEP conference has a number of advantages. Different individuals are involved at different levels, thus optimizing the accuracy and usefulness of the document and the efficient use of professional staff time. This will, of course, be time-consuming for parents, and there is the danger that you will not be able to attend both meetings. If it is impossible for you to attend both meetings, be sure to obtain copies of the decisions made at both levels so that you can review them carefully.

Many districts develop the first part of the IEP at the evaluation or placement meeting and obtain parental consent for their placement decision. Then, after the child has been in the program for one or two weeks, the instructional staff develop the second part of the IEP. This procedure puts parents in the awkward position of approving the placement without knowing exactly what services will be provided, since decisions regarding additional instruction and related services will be made as part of the second level.

Try to avoid signing a consent to placement until you are sure you know exactly what services your child will receive in that placement. Knowing that a speech therapist is available is not the same as knowing your child will receive one hour a day of one-to-one speech therapy from a trained speech therapist. Your child's evaluation should provide enough information (including the observations of teachers) to develop a complete IEP before your child is placed, and your child's teacher can request an IEP review if he or she thinks that certain aspects are inappropriate.

What is the content of the IEP document?

The federal regulations for P.L. 94–142 (Section 121a.346) require the IEP to include the following:

a statement of the child's present level of educational performance;

a statement of annual goals;

a statement of short-term instructional objectives;

appropriate procedures for determining (at least annually) whether the short-term objectives are being achieved;

a statement of specific special education and related services to be provided to the child and providers of services;

dates for initiation and duration of services;

a statement of time to be spent in the regular educational program;

date of IEP review.

The format of an IEP varies from district to district. We have included some sample IEP forms so that you can get a feel for their format and content. (See Figures 5.1 through 5.3.)

School districts that use a two-level form consider both levels as comprising the student's IEP. You should receive copies of both the general program plan (level 1) and the instructional unit plans (level 2).

Figure 5-1
Sample IEP Form

INDIVIDUAL EDUCATION PROGRAM
GREENVILLE CITY SCHOOLS
19_____ to 19_____

Complete this section in pencil

I. Name: Age:
   Address: Date of Birth: Business Phone:
   School: Home Phone:
                   Grade Placement:

II. Level of Functioning (Complete only sections that are relevant at this time. Please date comments.)

AREA (Give name of test)   GENERAL NEEDS

	19_____	19_____	19_____
A. Academic Reading			
Spelling			
Math			
B. Behavior			
C. Motor			

D. Pre-vocational or Vocational

_____ (Date Taken)

State Competency Test Score

F. Pertinent Medical Information
   (ie: glasses, hearing aid, medication)

E. Learning Style (Check ONLY if appropriate)
1. Student appears to best remember when:
   ____ he sees information
   ____ he hears information
   ____ concrete objects are used to teach
   ____ learning is reinforced through activities
   ____ frequent check-ups are provided
   ____ work is slowly paced
   ____ work is frequently reviewed

2. Student appears to best express what he knows through:
   ____ speaking   ____ writing   ____ activity

3. Student works best:
   ____ alone   ____ with a partner   ____ in a small group
   ____ away from (visual) (auditory) (tactile) ____ stimuli
4. ____ Student has no apparent learning preference
5. ____ Student appears to be ____ an auditory learner ____ a visual learner

Figure 5-1
continued

III. Annual Goals: Put date in blank space by each goal selected.

19 _____   19 _____   19 _____

A. Academic

1. to improve use of acceptable language forms and patterns
2. to improve ability to accurately describe person, places, feelings
3. to improve listening comprehension
4. to improve oral communication
5. to improve reading skills (refer to specific skill chart)
6. to improve math skills (refer to specific skill chart)
7. to maintain work level of regular class
8. to improve background of general information
9. to improve written expression
10. _____

B. Behavior

1. to respond appropriately to stimuli
2. to improve "time on task" behavior
3. to improve ability to listen and follow directions
4. to improve ability to relate to another person
5. to improve ability to function appropriately in a group
6. to increase positive classroom behaviors
7. to increase ability to handle frustration (wait, change routine, etc.)
8. to express feelings appropriately
9. to increase ability to work toward long-range goal
10. to improve school attendance
11. to increase ability to select appropriate leisure activities

C. Motor

_____ 1. to improve self-help skills
_____ 2. to improve gross motor skills
_____ 3. to improve eye-hand coordination
_____ 4. to improve ability to reproduce symbols accurately
_____ 5. to improve handwriting
_____ 6. to improve mobility and dexterity
_____ 7. to improve sensory-motor integration
_____ 8. to improve articulatory skills appropriately
_____ 9. to improve vocal production
_____ 10. to improve speech fluency
_____ 11. to provide follow-up for hearing impaired

D. Pre-Vocational or Vocational

_____ 1. to increase awareness of the world of work
_____ 2. to increase awareness of appropriate occupations in community
_____ 3. to increase awareness of community resources
_____ 4. to develop pre-employment skills
_____ 5. to develop job survival skills (application, tax forms, etc.)
_____ 6. to develop realistic career goals based on strengths
_____ 7. to become employable
_____ 8. to improve on-job performance
_____ 9. to develop specific competencies as specified on:
_____ G.V.C.T. (P-VAC)
_____ General Skills Test-Reading-Math
_____ Pre-Vocational and Social Information Battery
_____ Other: State Competency Test Mastery
_____ 10.

Figure 5-1
continued

IV. Instructional Objectives and Evaluative Criteria

_____ to _____

Short range objectives to be used to meet each goal selected.	Evaluative Criteria How will objective be measured? (Name specific tests to be used)	Responsible Person	Review Date
A. Academic			
B. Behavior/Social	_____ Observation _____ Parent Conference _____ Time Sampling _____ Anecdotal Record _____ Rating Scale		
C. Motor	_____ Standardized Tests _____ Observational Reports _____ Work Samples		
D. Pre-Vocational or Vocational	_____ Norm References Tests _____ Criterion Reference Tests _____ Conference		

V. Specific Special Education and/or Related Service
_____ to _____

Specific Special Education and/or Related Service	Extent of time in regular program		Additional support services
	Regular	Special	
Regular class w/consultation services			
_____ speech/hearing			
_____ O.T. or P.T. program planning			
_____ adjustment counseling—behavior management			
_____ visual mobility planning			
_____ enrichment			
_____ academic (individualization)			
_____ vocational planning (V.R.)			
Regular class W/direct resource			
_____ language development			
_____ sensory-motor development			
_____ gifted enrichment			
_____ tutorial services			
_____ learning disability services			
_____ remedial reading—math			
_____ speech therapy			
Part-Time special class/program			
_____ transition class (primary) (intermediate)			
_____ block resource			
_____ pre-vocational activities (P.VAC)			
_____ work-study program			
_____ vocational class			
_____ research and independent study			
_____ advanced academic class_____			
_____ community-based (_____)			

Figure 5-1
continued

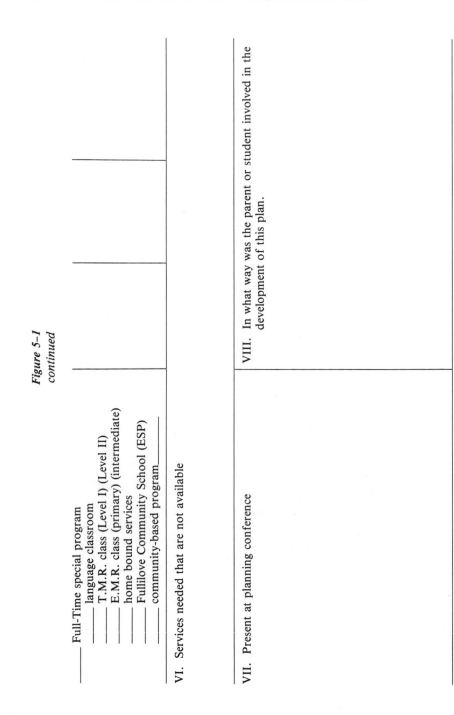

_____ Full-Time special program
  _____ language classroom
  _____ T.M.R. class (Level I) (Level II)
  _____ E.M.R. class (primary) (intermediate)
  _____ home bound services
  _____ Fullilove Community School (ESP)
  _____ community-based program

VI. Services needed that are not available

VII. Present at planning conference

VIII. In what way was the parent or student involved in the development of this plan.

Figure 5-2
Sample IEP Form

GASTON COUNTY SCHOOLS
PROGRAMS FOR EXCEPTIONAL CHILDREN
INDIVIDUAL EDUCATION PROGRAM

NAME _____
    Last   First   Middle

ADDRESS _____

GRADE or _____ AGE _____
SUBJECTS

DATE of BIRTH _____

PARENTS' NAME _____

HOME PHONE _____ BUS. PHONE _____

IEP   FROM _____ TO _____

_____ SCHOOL

COMMITTEE

NAME   POSITION

Have Problem Identification
Procedures Been Followed?

yes _____ No _____

PRESENT LEVEL OF EDUCATIONAL FUNCTIONING:

STRENGTHS: NEEDS:

EDUCATIONAL AND OTHER SERVICES TO BE PROVIDED:

A. SERVICES REQUIRED	B. DATE INITIATED	C. DURATION OF SERVICE	D. INDIVIDUAL RESPONSIBLE FOR SERVICE

DAILY SCHEDULE

Extent of time in regular class:
Justification of the Individual Education Program:

I have had the opportunity to participate in the development of
the Individual Education Plan.
I agree with the Individual Education Program _____
I disagree with the Individual Education Program _____

_____ Parent's signature
_____ Date

Figure 5-2
continued

ANNUAL GOAL STATEMENTS	INSTRUCTIONAL OBJECTIVES	OBJECTIVE CRITERIA AND EVALUATION

Figure 5-3
Sample of Two-Stage IEP Form

Individual Education Program: Total Service Plan

Child's Name _____

School _____

Date of Program Entry _____

Prioritized Long-term Goals:

Summary of
Present Levels of Performance:
_____
_____
_____
_____

Short-Term Objectives	Specific Educational and/or Support Services	Person(s) Responsible	Percent of Time	Beginning and Ending Date	Review Date

Percent of Time in Regular Classroom _____

Committee Members Present _____

Placement Recommendation _____

Dates of Meeting _____

Committee Recommendations for
Specific Procedures/Techniques, Materials, Etc. (include information about learning style)

Objective Evaluation Criteria for each Annual Goal Statement

From: National Association of State Directors of Special Education
Functions of the Placement Committee in Special Education
1201 Sixteenth St. N.W.
Washington, D.C. 20036

Figure 5-3
continued

Individual Education Program: Individual Implementation Plan

(Complete one of these for each goal statement specified on Total Service Plan)

Child's Name _____   Goal Statement: _____

School _____

Date of Program Entry _____   Short Term Instructional Objectives: _____

Projected Ending Date _____   _____

Person(s) Completing Form _____   _____

Behavioral Objectives	Task Analysis of Objectives	Strategies and/or Techniques	Materials and/or Resources	Date Started	Date Ended	Comments

Some school districts have attempted to streamline the development of the IEPs. For example, some districts may be using a computerized management information system that is programmed to match student characteristics to particular IEP content. Thus, a teacher or staff person places general diagnostic facts about the student into the computer system and the computer then generates goals, objectives, instructional material, and evaluation criteria to match the student. While this might be a useful technique for suggesting what some goals and objectives might be, the IEP developed for your child should involve a closer matching of student needs and characteristics to goals, objectives, services, and placements than can, at present, be done through a computer process.

Some school systems are using computerized and noncomputerized sequenced objective banks that provide sets of instructional objectives ordered by subject matter and difficulty level and that have corresponding evaluation criteria and in some cases are cross-referenced to instructional materials. These objective banks have been found particularly useful in developing the second level of the IEP—the more specific instructional unit plans.[4]

Many school systems are using diagnostic assessment instruments that translate directly into a measure of the child's level of functioning and into specific instructional objectives. This process short-circuits the need for an interpretation of test results—the tests interpret themselves. However, these interpretations, like all test results, should be confirmed by other tests or observations.

Many districts and some states have computer management information systems in which IEP data on each student are stored. You should definitely find out what information from your child's IEP is maintained in a computer data bank, who has access to it, and under what circumstances. Get the name of the person who is responsible for maintaining and releasing the information and find out the procedure for managing this data base.

If involved in a vocational education or vocational rehabilitation program, your child will have individualized vocational or rehabilitative plans for those programs. These plans should be consistent with and may even be incorporated into your child's IEP. Now, we will give a more detailed description of the IEP document.

Child's present level of performance

This section of the IEP provides a summary of the information gathered during the evaluation process. If you disagree with any of the evaluation findings or their interpretations, you should raise questions. However, you should be familiar with most of this information and have discussed it at the evaluation conference. Be sure you understand any new, additional evaluation information that is presented. The information from the evaluation often is considered in terms of the student's strengths and weaknesses. Evaluation information and related strengths and weaknesses should be considered for several areas:

academic achievement;

social adaptation;

physical and motor skills;

adaptive behavior (or self-help skills);

communication skills.

Annual goals

This section of the IEP discusses the goals expected to be achieved by the end of the school year. The annual goals should be based on the results of the evaluation and directed toward meeting the student's educational needs. The goals should be realistic yet challenging. Although several goals may have been suggested at the IEP conference, these suggestions should have been discussed and priorities established so that certain goals on the IEP document have top priority.

Annual goals are general directions that describe what needs to be learned by the student. These should be translated into more detailed and concrete statements about specific skills and knowledge the student should have at the end of the school year.

Short-term objectives

For each of the long-term or annual goals, there should be several short-term objectives—statements that describe the specific steps that will lead to the accomplishment of the annual goal. These objectives form the basis for the instructional activities that will occur and provide a framework for parent-school discussions of the student's progress. The time frames for the short-term objectives will vary; some may be weekly, some monthly, and some based on a marking or reporting period.

Often, short-term objectives are not fully discussed at the IEP conference; rather they are developed in detail by each teacher or therapist as he or she develops the instructional plans for the student.

Objective criteria

For each annual goal and short-term objective, the procedures and criteria to be used to determine whether the student has achieved that objective should be specified. These are usually statements such as:

By the end of the marking period, the student will be able to spell correctly at least 75 percent of the spelling words in Unit 2.

These evaluation criteria may also not be discussed in detail at the IEP conference. Instead, individual teachers may formulate specific criteria as they develop and refine the short-term objectives. However, the evaluation criteria should be part of the complete IEP document you receive to enable you to determine whether your child's progress is satisfactory.

Services to be provided

During the IEP conference you should have discussed and agreed upon the services your child is to receive. This should include such areas as:

regular academic instruction (including music and art);

special education instruction;

career education (including vocational and prevocational education);

physical education;

speech therapy;

physical therapy;

special media, materials, and equipment;

transportation.

In addition to listing *all* the services to be provided, the IEP should indicate the name of the person who provides each service, the place where the service will be rendered, the duration and frequency of sessions, and whether the service is provided on a one-to-one basis or in group sessions. Bear in mind that the IEP must include *all* services that the IEP conference team (and that includes you) has developed.

Dates when services begin and length of time they continue

During the IEP conference the date when each service is to begin and its duration should be discussed and you should have an understanding of the intensity and timing of all services to be provided as specified.

Placement alternatives

You should discuss possible placement alternatives and you may agree upon an appropriate placement or the placements you wish to consider.

Extent to which child will be in a regular program

This figure may be expressed in terms of hours per day or week, or a percentage of time that your child will spend with nonhandicapped students. Discussion on this issue should have taken place at the IEP conference. However, what may seem like enough contact with nonhandicapped students when considered in terms of class periods may not seem like much in terms of hours a day, so you should take a close look at the figures given on the IEP to be sure of the time your child will be in a regular program.

Schedule for review

There should be a date on your child's IEP which indicates when the program will be reviewed. The review procedure, as well as the contact person or IEP coordinator, should also be indicated.

You should mark the review date on your calendar so that you will be ready with your own observations of your child's progress.

Note the name and telephone number of the contact person and communicate with him or her regarding any important changes you think are necessary in your child's IEP. Keep the IEP in your file or notebook; it is an important document and vital for assuring a consistent, continuing educational program for your child.

In sum, an IEP is a comprehensive, complicated reference document that should help you in several ways:

It serves as the basis for your child's instructional program.

It details the top priority educational goals selected for your child and indicates the objectives that will lead to those goals.

It specifies the services the school district is to provide at no cost to you.

It provides a time schedule for monitoring your child's progress.

It provides a way to measure the educational growth achieved by your child.

When will the IEP be reviewed?

Your child's IEP can be reviewed any time you or the school requests. (See Figure 5.4) However, it must be reviewed at least annually, and you should be invited to participate in the review conference.

Since the IEP contains short-term objectives, your child's progress is actually being reviewed frequently and you should ask how your child is

Figure 5-4
Example of a Letter to Request an IEP Review

2542 Winding Road
Austria, Virginia 23270

October 15, 1979

Mr. Jose Garcia
James Monroe Elem. School
1721 Schoolhouse Drive
Austria, Virginia 23270

Re: David Ajar, Age 9,
Mr. Garcia's Special Class

Dear Mr. Garcia:

Reason for
requesting
conference

Support of
teacher's
efforts

Logistics
Persons
attending

This is to confirm our telephone conversation yesterday, in which we requested to review the program developed for David in his IEP. Specifically, we wish to discuss whether David should remain in your class since his reading is not improving and his behavior at home is getting worse. In our opinion, David seems to be copying the poor behavior of the other students in the class. We know you are trying hard to teach David, but we believe that your class is not an appropriate place for David to be.

We are looking forward to meeting with you, as we agreed, on February 19th at 4:00 p.m. Accompanying my husband and me will be Ms. Maryann Hobb, a friend and parent of a learning disabled student who attends Walden Intermediate School.

Sincerely yours,

Judith Swerdna

Robert Ajar

Copy to:
Dr. Dunn, Principal

doing. Many school systems have timed the short-term objectives to correspond to parent reporting schedules (report cards or parent conferences).

You should review the progress of your child carefully, and if that progress is not what you expected, you should discuss your child's program with his or her teacher to determine the reasons for the lack of progress. If necessary, you can request that your child's IEP be revised to include the additional services you feel are necessary to assure that your child makes the expected progress.

Is the IEP a legally binding document?

No, the IEP document is not a contract for services or for educational growth, nor is it a formal mechanism for monitoring or evaluating teacher competence. School districts and teachers cannot be held liable if a student does not make the progress expected, but the school staff must make every effort to assist the child in achieving the goals specified in the IEP.

Many teachers, however, fear that they may be sued or terminated if a student does not progress according to IEP goals. These fears sometimes result in teachers selecting educational goals they are almost positive a child can attain rather than attempting more challenging goals. You may, therefore, want to assure teachers that you want your child challenged and will not blame them if the progress made is less than expected.

Although the IEP is not a contract for services, the school must attempt to provide the services indicated. If certain services are not available, the school must state when they will be available and what will be done in the meantime. If you believe that the school is not providing the services stipulated in the IEP, your recourse is a due process hearing.

If the IEP is not a legal document, how will it be used?

Unfortunately, some IEP documents are filed away and not used by either the parents or the school. However, the IEP document should be used to:

form the basis of a review of your child's educational development;

record the priorities given to the educational goals selected for your child;

indicate the special education and related services your child is entitled to at public expense;

coordinate the instructional services provided your child by several teachers, therapists, and other specialists including those in other community agencies such as vocational rehabilitation;

communicate to all those concerned exactly what your child's educational needs are and what services each person is to perform, when, and for how long;

establish the instructional activities to be performed in the home;

serve as a basis for developing vocational rehabilitation, vocational education, and career education programs for your child;

provide evidence of educational progress that can be considered in pupil progress reports (report cards) and in awarding a diploma.

The IEP is a relatively new procedure in education and no one is sure how many functions it is destined to perform. Recently, educators have suggested that the continued record of student progress documented in the set of IEPs might replace the competency tests now being required in certain states.[5] One might also argue that handicapped students who have met the objectives framed in their IEPs should be eligible to graduate and receive a diploma. Successful completion of IEP goals and objectives could form the basis for recommendations for post high school training and/or employment. Parents may wish to use the IEP to document their child's need for continued education, training, and support.

What should I do if I disagree with the IEP document?

The law specifies that your child must receive a free, appropriate public education. What constitutes appropriate is defined in your child's IEP. Therefore, the IEP is a key document and it is important that you agree that the goals, objectives, services, and placement are appropriate for your child. If you disagree with any aspect of your child's IEP you have the right to a due process hearing.

Although the federal law does not require your written consent to any IEP element except placement, many school districts and states are requesting written parental consent to the entire IEP document.[6] If you disagree with any component of the IEP document, you should first share that fact with the school principal and director of special education. Many times the school staff is not aware that parents are dissatisfied and are willing to make modifications in a student's IEP.

If you and the school still disagree on your child's IEP, you have several options:

Give your consent to certain IEP sections but not others (e.g., "I consent to the IEP, except I believe three hours of speech therapy a week is not appropriate; five hours is appropriate").

Give your consent, but only for a limited time period (e.g., "I consent to the IEP as appropriate for the next three months, but I wish to review its appropriateness at that time").

Refuse to consent and request a second independent evaluation (if your child has not already had one).

Refuse to consent and request a due process hearing.

Remember, if you withhold your consent to the IEP your child will remain in his or her current placement, receiving only those special education services which both you and the school agree are needed.

Most parents and school staff try to avoid the formal, stressful, and expensive due process hearing as a means of getting appropriate educational services for their child. In many instances, continued expression of concern and requests for review of the student's progress and services provided will be a more effective means of getting changes in the IEP.

Furthermore, a second evaluation may help to clarify what goals and objectives are realistic and appropriate, what services are needed, and what expectations of child progress are legitimate. If you think a second evaluation would help you, you should request one.

If you have serious disagreements with certain provisions of your child's IEP and if these are supported by an independent evaluation and/or lack of child progress, and if continued requests to school staff for modifications have been unfruitful, your only recourse may be to request a due process hearing.

Do handicapped children in private schools have to have an IEP?

All handicapped students who are eligible to receive special education services and who are enrolled in a public school or other public agency (e.g., mental health agency) must have an IEP. In addition, all eligible handicapped students who are placed in a private or nonpublic facility by the public school or other public agency or who have been enrolled in private or parochial schools by their parents but who receive special education or related services from the public school or other public agency must have an IEP (P.L. 94–142 Regulations Section 121a. 341). Thus all handicapped students receiving special education or related services either directly or indirectly (through a contract with a nonpublic school) from the public school must have an IEP.

Furthermore, the local public school system or other local public agency is responsible for developing the IEPs, monitoring their implementation, and reviewing their appropriateness for all students including those placed or enrolled in private facilities. If your child is in a private placement you should find out what arrangements for overseeing the implementation of his or her IEP have been made. Find out the dates established for any monitoring or review and learn what actions resulted from these activities.

What should I do after the IEP conference?

The goal of the IEP conference is to produce a written document. In some school systems the IEP document is completed at the conference and a copy will be given to you immediately after the conference, if you attend. In other school systems, the IEP document is completed after the conference, and the recorder's notes taken at the conference are used. You should receive a copy of the completed IEP document within a reasonable time after the meeting. If you do not receive a copy of the IEP document within a week, you should request one.

After you have received your copy of your child's IEP document (or documents if there was a two–level conference) you should review it carefully to make sure you agree with it and it agrees with your notes and memory of the decisions made at the IEP conference. You should ask yourself the following questions:

Are the goals for my child the ones I believe are of highest priority?

Are all the services I believe my child needs identified?

Is my child placed in the right instructional setting?

Will my child be with nonhandicapped students for a long enough period of time each day?

If you were not at the IEP conference you should study the IEP document with special care. In many instances, time runs out at the conference before some issues can be thoroughly discussed. For example, you may have agreed that your child needed speech therapy but the extent of speech therapy was not discussed. On the IEP document you find that your child will get speech therapy every day and you think this will mean your child will miss too much class instruction. If you have questions or concerns, get in touch with a school staff member.

After you have reviewed the IEP document, and especially if you did not attend the IEP meeting, you might find it helpful to discuss the IEP document with a school staff member—the designated contact person or your child's teacher, counselor, or school psychologist. Many parents feel overwhelmed at the IEP conference and when they get home have second thoughts about some of the decisions that were made. If you feel that way, you should definitely ask for a smaller, more informal meeting for review and clarification.

If you are satisfied with the IEP document, you may want to discuss it informally with your child's teachers, particularly those teachers with major responsibility for implementing it. Occasionally teachers who are not at the IEP conference, and even some who are, do not receive copies for the students they instruct. While it is not your responsibility to provide teachers and others with copies of your child's IEP document, it might be very helpful if you discussed particular IEP goals and objectives with the teacher responsible to determine how he or she plans to approach that goal—what materials, strategies, techniques, activities, assignments, and tests are involved. This conversation should put you, your child, and your child's teacher on the same wavelength. This same procedure holds true for persons other than teachers who will be providing services to your child.

If your child's IEP involves services provided by persons outside the public school, you should find out the name of the person responsible for coordinating services provided by outside agencies. You will want to be sure that all outside agencies are aware of the provisions of the IEP and the appropriate public school contact person.

You will want to discuss the IEP conference with your child if he or she did not attend. You might also want to arrange a parent/student/teacher conference so that everyone involved understands the three-way educational process involving school, parents, and child.

Notes

1. Kaufman, Martin J.; Agard, Judith A.; and Vlasak, Jerry W. *Current Issues in Appraisal, Project Prime.* Technical Report, U.S.O.E. Bureau of Education for the Handicapped, Washington D.C., 1973. Weatherly, R., and Lipsky, M. "Street-level Bureaucrats and Institutional Innovation: Implementing Special Education Reform." *Harvard Educational Review* 47 (1977): 171–197.

2. All too often with handicapped students, educators start students in the beginning of a new program, curriculum, or set of learning material that repeats (although in a new way) knowledge and skills the student has already mastered.

3. Seek advice from individuals knowledgeable about the IEP conference. This would include parent advocates, psychologists, physicians, and attorneys, among others. It might help you to review the range of special education and related services discussed in Chapter 7. This will expand your frame of reference.

4. Safer, Nancy D.; Morrissey, Patricia A.; Kaufman, Martin J.; and Lewis, Linda. "Implementation of IEPs: New Teacher Roles and Requisite Support Systems." *Focus on Exceptional Children* 10 (1978): 1–20. Morrissey, Patricia A., and Safer, Nancy. "The Individualized Educational Program." *Viewpoints* (Bulletin of the School of Education, Indiana University) 53 (1977): 31–38.

5. McClung, Merle Steven, and Pullin, Diana. "Competency Testing and Handicapped Students." *Clearinghouse Review,* March 1978, pp. 922–927.

6. Because parents have the right to initiate a due process hearing about any aspect of the IEP with which they disagree, many school districts require written parental consent to the IEP as a procedural safeguard.

6

Placement Procedures and Alternatives

JUDITH ANDREWS AGARD

One component of the individualized educational program involves place-ment—designation of the setting for the special instructional and supportive services received by your child. You must be notified and give your in-formed consent to this placement. The placement alternatives available and the procedures used to determine the appropriate placement for your child vary from school system to school system. As the advocate for your child you will need to become familiar with the placement alternatives available and give your consent only if you feel completely informed and in agree-ment with the placement proposed.

Placement refers to the educational settings in which a student re-ceives instruction. For example, Mr. Fisk's third grade class is a placement as are the Group A team teaching unit, the seventh grade gifted program, and Mr. Sanchez's total communication class for young deaf children. A placement involves any number of classes and settings in which a student re-ceives instruction, and is similar to a class schedule. For junior high and high school students and those students with multiple teachers, placement is, in fact, a class schedule. All students, including nonhandicapped ones, have placements, but the concept of placement has special significance for handicapped students.

In this section we describe the placement decision process and suggest certain activities you, the parents, should do before giving your informed consent to a placement decision.

What is the general process involved in making a placement decision?

The general process involves the following five steps:

1. identifying the educational needs of the student;

2. determining the special services required to meet those needs;

3. proposing alternative placements (classes, programs, special facilities) where these services may be delivered;

4. assessing the appropriateness and restrictiveness of proposed placements;

5. selecting an appropriate, least restrictive alternative.

The general process may be implemented in several ways depending on state policy and regulations and on school system practices.

There are several methods that might be used by a school system:[1]

Administrative fiat.   A school administrator decides that all students with a particular handicap will be instructed in a particular placement.

Expert or professional judgment.   A school psychologist reviews all information about a student and available placements and makes a recommendation.

Group negotiations.   Interested parties to the decision (school staff, parents, and perhaps the student) participate in a group conference that makes a joint placement decision.

Quasi-judicial procedures.   A designated impartial party conducts a due process hearing, evaluates the evidence presented, and makes a placement decision.

Each of the preceding decision-making methods is probably being used in some school districts at one stage or another in the LRE decision process. For example, a given school may recommend that all learning disabled students spend part of the day in class with nonhandicapped students (administrative fiat). A school psychologist then recommends for a particular student the extent and location of this integration (expert judgment). A group consisting of parents, teachers, and support staff review and agree to this recommendation (group decision). If there is no agreement on this placement, the parents or school may request a hearing (quasi-judicial procedure). Of course, not every district will use all of these procedures or use them in this order.

The actual procedure followed in your child's situation might be one of the following:

The placement decision is discussed with you at the evaluation conference and your written consent is requested at that time or at some date shortly thereafter.

The placement decision is discussed with you at the IEP conference and your written consent is requested at that time or soon thereafter.

The placement decision is discussed at a placement team conference (with or without you) and your written consent is requested at that time (if you are present) or soon thereafter.

The placement decision is discussed with you at an IEP planning and placement conference and your written consent is requested at that time or shortly thereafter.

What are the federal legal requirements regarding the placement decision process?

The regulations of P.L. 94–142 require that the placement decision (P.L. 94–142 Regulations 121a.533, 551, 552) be the following:

based upon carefully documented and considered information from a variety of sources, including aptitude and achievement tests, teacher observations, physical examination, social or cultural background, and adaptive behavior;

determined by a group of persons, including persons who are knowledgeable about the child, the meaning of the evaluation information, and the placement alternatives;

based upon the students' individualized educational program;

as close to the student's home as possible;

selected from a continuum of alternatives that includes instruction in regular classes with supplementary services (such as resource classes or itinerant instruction, special classes, special schools, home instruction, and instruction in hospitals and institutions);

in conformity with requirements related to the least restrictive environment, yet with consideration given to any potentially harmful effects on the student or on the quality of services which he or she needs.

Note that although the law says the placement decision must be made by a group, one of whom is knowledgeable about your child, it does not require that you, the child's parents, be a part of that group. We urge you to request that you be involved in the placement team deliberations. We believe that you will have a clearer understanding of the alternatives recommended for your child and be able to make a more informed choice among these alternatives if you are present and can participate in this discussion.

Who will participate in the placement team conference?

The people who may be involved on the placement team are most of the same individuals who participated in the evaluation and IEP conference. Many school systems have a hierarchical placement decision procedure. The first level considers the placement of all students within the school building and the placement team consists of building personnel (teachers, principal, counselor, educational diagnostician assigned to that building). The second level considers the placement of any students recommended for programs outside the building (a special class in another building, special school, private and/or residential placements) or placements with which the parents disagree. Members of this second level placement team include district personnel (school psychologist, director of special education, superintendent of schools, district specialists).

What factors need to be considered when choosing a placement?

The selection of an appropriate placement for a handicapped student is guided by two broad principles and some practical considerations. The two principles are that the placement must be appropriate and that it must be in the least restrictive environment.

Deciding exactly what constitutes an "appropriate" and a "least restrictive" placement involves complex questions of judgment. Answers to these questions will depend heavily on the individual student and the particular placement under consideration since a placement that might be non-restrictive and appropriate for one handicapped student might be totally inappropriate for another. And a placement that is appropriate one year might be inappropriate the next. Let's look at the factors that must be considered.

Appropriateness.   The federal laws do not define what is appropriate. Instead, an appropriate placement or program is to be determined by the child's individualized educational program. An appropriate setting could be considered one in which the student's educational goals and objectives are addressed, where the student's educational needs are provided for, where the services prescribed in the student's IEP are made available, and where the student can function happily and make satisfactory educational progress.

The questions that you need to consider when determining whether placement is appropriate for your child are:

Will this placement address my child's particular educational needs?

Are the teaching methods, curriculum, instructional materials, and activities used in that placement appropriate for my child?

Will my child receive the intensive, individual, or small group instruction needed?

Is the environment too noisy and distractive?

Are there adequate structure and organization in the class?

Will extensive modification of the current program be required to accommodate my child?

Is there time or support provided the teacher so that these modifications can be made?

Is the teacher in that class trained or experienced in instructing children with needs similar to my child's?

What educational goals and objectives are emphasized in this placement?

What are the academic demands of the placement? What is the relative balance between academic achievement and social adjustment?

Will my child receive an appropriate career education program in this setting (work/skill training, career awareness, career planning, job placement)?

What are the staff expectations for my child in this placement? Are they challenging yet realistic?

Will this placement offer the special supportive services my child requires?

Will my child have access to the specialized materials, equipment, and facilities needed?

Are the services of therapists, counselors, and other specialists available?

Will there be supportive services available (interpreters, attendants, special equipment, materials)?

Will my child be able to maintain the physical pace required and be able to move around the building with other students?

What is the climate of the placement? Is the class a warm, supportive, tolerant, cooperative place? Will the teachers and other children accept my child?

What is the danger that my child will be ignored, rejected, or isolated socially and frustrated and pressured academically?

Are there other students in this placement who will be appropriate models for my child?

Does this placement have a stigma or negative connotation associated with it?

Will my child be happy, self-confident and feel positive about school in this placement?

What are the recreational and social opportunities for my child in this placement?

Restrictiveness.   The federal laws are very clear that to the maximum extent appropriate, handicapped students (including students in public or private institutions or other facilities) must be educated with students who are not handicapped, and that special classes, separate schooling, or other methods of removing handicapped students from the regular educational environment should occur only when the nature or severity of the handicap is such that education in regular classes or school buildings with the use of supplementary services cannot be achieved satisfactorily (P.L. 94–142 Regulations Section 121a.550). Furthermore, this law requires that in non-academic and extracurricular activities (meals, recreation and recess periods, school clubs, organizations and interest groups, vocational education, athletics, and student employment and job placement services), handicapped students should participate with nonhandicapped students to the maximum extent appropriate to the needs of the child (P.L. 94–142 Regulation 121a.553). Thus, even handicapped students whose instructional needs preclude their participation in the regular program must be permitted to participate in other regular school activities with nonhandicapped students.

The least restrictive environment (LRE) provisions cited above are intended to assure that handicapped students are in contact with nonhandicapped students to the maximum extent possible. The LRE provisions do not prohibit the use of more restrictive environments (special classes, special schools or centers, residential facilities) when the student's educational needs cannot be met in any other less restrictive placement. However, students who are placed in more restrictive environments still should have recreational and other nonacademic opportunities to be in contact with nonhandicapped students.

An important component of the LRE provisions is accessibility. Handicapped students have the right to participate in all aspects of an educational program without architectural, physical, financial, or attitudinal barriers.

The following questions need to be considered when determining whether a placement is restrictive for your child:

Are the classrooms, auditorium, cafeteria, laboratories, industrial arts shops, music rooms, art studios, and gymnasium accessible to my child?

What are the architectural or physical barriers that will restrict my child's access to particular services or activities (stairs, narrow doorways, inaccessible bathrooms)?

What can be done to eliminate these barriers (ramps, elevators, relocation of activities, assistance of attendants)?

How much time will my child spend with nonhandicapped students, when, and for what activities?

How physically close will my child be to nonhandicapped students?

What will be the ratio of handicapped to nonhandicapped students in the class placement and in the building?

What are the social behaviors expected of my child in that placement?

To what extent will my child be able to participate actively in the instructional activities and projects of the class?

Will my child be ridiculed, ignored, isolated, or rejected by nonhandicapped students?

Will my child make friends, have fun, and feel welcomed in that setting? Will he or she be assimilated into the group activities and accepted as a valued member?

The process of selecting an appropriate, least restrictive environment obviously involves careful evaluation. There are also serious practical considerations to evaluate. A placement must be practical from the perspective of parents, child, and school. Although ideally such elements as cost, convenience, timing, and availability should not affect the selection of a placement, they often become overriding considerations. For example, you should understand that the following practical placement issues must be considered:

Logistics.   How far away from your home is the placement? How will your child get there, and how long will it take?

Transportation.   What means of transportation will be used and how comfortable is it? What supervision will be provided?

Living arrangements.   If your child is not going to live at home, what are the living arrangements—dormitories, foster homes, group homes, half-way houses, hospital wards?

Availability of space.   Can alternative placements accommodate your child, or is there overcrowding or underutilization in a particular placement?

Costs.   How much will alternative placements cost the school district? What are the financial implications for you (spending money, visitation costs, etc.)?

Critical numbers.   Are there enough students with educational needs similar to your child's to support the existence of a designated placement targeted specifically toward those needs?

Management.   Will the placement involve more than one instructional staff person or teacher? How will these staffs be coordinated, and by whom? Who has ultimate responsibility for your child's program?

Movement.   How much movement in and out of one class is involved. in the placement? Will this movement be disruptive? Will your child miss important instruction?

In sum, considerations of practicality, as well as appropriateness and restrictiveness, constitute the major factors in the selection of a placement.

Remember, the selection of a placement will almost always be a matter of balancing pros and cons. The most important thing is that your child be in a situation where he or she is happy and progressing. You should not consent to any placement that you feel will be detrimental to your child.

What are some possible placements for handicapped students?

The federal law specifies that a continuum of alternative placements be available to meet the varied needs of handicapped children (P.L. 94–142 Regulations Section 121a.551). Included in this continuum must be instruction in regular classes (with supplementary services such as a resource class or itinerant teacher), special classes, special schools, home instruction, and instruction in hospitals and institutions. These alternatives may be expanded to include other settings as well.[2] Some of the more common types of placements available are presented in Table 6.1.

Table 6.1   Examples of Alternative Placements

↑ MORE INTEGRATED	Regular class with special consultative assistance, materials, and aides for the regular teacher, but no direct instructional service to handicapped student
	Regular class with direct instructional services to handicapped students provided by itinerant teacher, aide, attendant, or interpreter
	Regular class with limited resource class instruction (1 to 1½ hours a day)
	Regular class with substantial resource class instruction (1½ to 3 hours a day)
	Special class with academic and nonacademic instruction in regular classes
	Special class with nonacademic instruction in regular classes
	Special class in regular school building offering noninstructional activities (e.g., lunch, assembly) with nonhandicapped students
	Special class in a special education center with some classes or activities in a regular school building
	Special classes in a special education center without regular program contact
	Residential school program (public or private) with some classes or activities in regular education programs or in the community
	Residential school program (public or private) with no contact with regular education programs or the community
MORE INTENSIVE ↓	Home and/or hospital instruction

The placements differ in two dimensions: the degree of integration with nonhandicapped peers and the intensity of the instruction offered. Although the placement alternatives listed in Table 6.1 seem to offer considerable variation, there may be important differences within each category. For example, resource classes may differ in terms of their academic focus (reading, basic learning skills, mathematics), special classes may differ in terms of a student's handicapping condition, and special centers and residential schools may differ in terms of their organizational structure (public or private) and program focus. Thus, in considering alternative placements you must consider not only on what step of the continuum ladder you think your child should be placed but also, within that step, what particular placement is appropriate to your child's needs.

In addition to the basic placements indicated in the continuum ladder, other special programs and placements may be available in your school district or community. For example, there may be parent/child instruction programs available for handicapped preschoolers. Many nursery schools, preschools, and day care centers include handicapped children as part of their regular program. Head Start programs are mandated to serve handicapped children since federal law requires that ten percent of all enrollment opportunities in each state must be available to handicapped children (Community Services Act of 1974, P.L. 94-644).

Some school systems offer a short-term (less than three months) diagnostic placement during which time a complete educational assessment of your child will occur. The additional time available permits a thorough investigation of the particular learning materials, instructional activities, motivational techniques, and behavior management (discipline) strategies that may be effective with your child.

For older, more severely handicapped students, placements in such settings as supervised work-study programs, sheltered workshops, group halfway houses, foster homes, and adult day care centers are possibilities.

Thus, the number and variety of placements are extensive. It is well worth your time to investigate thoroughly the programs available for your child, and not only those offered by the public school but also those offered by other community agencies and private institutions. And don't ignore programs and placements that appear to be open only to nonhandicapped children (e.g., private cooperative nursery schools). As the mainstreaming philosophy becomes more widespread, and as the regulations for Section 504 of the Rehabilitation Act of 1973 become widely known, these organizations will be making their programs accessible to handicapped children. Your child, if you investigate and press, could be one of the first to gain admittance to such programs.

One placement alternative that is not acceptable, however, is for your child to be out of school and not enrolled in any educational program. At a minimum, the school must provide homebound instructional programs, and you might be surprised to learn how much your child can learn and develop. The school may request that you keep your child at home for disciplinary reasons, which should be only for short periods, but you should be clear about what the reasons for such a request are, and how long your child must remain at home.

Occasionally, schools have issued long-term suspensions or even expelled students because of their disruptive behavior. However, disruptive behavior in and of itself does not necessarily mean a student needs special education services. Such behavior is often associated with a handicap that does require special education, however; and an appropriate alternative to continued suspension or expulsion might be a special education evaluation referral.

A school cannot expel a special education student for disruptive behavior without denying his right to a free, appropriate public education. An appropriate education program must be provided these students, a program that the parents have either consented to or can appeal through a due process hearing. Thus, although under certain circumstances short-term, clearly defined suspensions may be used with disruptive handicapped students, long-term suspensions or expulsions deny them their right to an appropriate education. Instead, the student should be placed in a special program where appropriate behavior control techniques can be used to modify or prevent disruptive behavior from occurring. Remember that if your school system cannot provide an appropriate placement, then it must arrange and pay for your child to be placed in a program in another school district, intermediate unit, or private or other public agency, facility, or state residential school.

What should I do before discussing or agreeing to the proposed placement for my child?

Much of what you should do prior to discussing the placement alternatives or consenting to a placement decision is similar to what you did to prepare for the evaluation and/or IEP conference:

Talk with a school staff person about the way the placement decision will be made, when it will be discussed, and whether you can attend that discussion.

Make arrangements for you and/or your spouse to attend that discussion.

Review all the school's and your own records and reports on your child; review your notes on your child's evaluation and IEP.

Talk with your child about school preferences, the classes he or she likes, the courses your child wants to take, the activities he or she enjoys doing.

Discuss career goals with your child and determine the vocational skills needed to pursue those goals.

Determine what alternative placements are being considered for your child.

Contact other parents, parent groups, and community agencies to determine what other placement alternatives may be available.

Discuss alternative placements with friends, parents of children with educational problems similar to those of your child, and other professionals.

Visit any placement alternatives that seem potentially appropriate for your child including placements suggested by the school, other parents, or your own research.

If you have visited one or more of the proposed placement alternatives, you may also want to do the following:

Share your perceptions of your visit to the alternative placements, and raise any unanswered questions about any of the programs you visited.

Discuss the appropriateness and restrictiveness of each placement alternative in terms of providing your child with the services needed.

Determine which of the alternative placements you think is appropriate for your child; if more than one is appropriate, you must decide which one is most appropriate and least restrictive.

Remember, the placement decision is an educational judgment that must be made with your informed consent. As the advocate for your child, you should listen and contribute your views and concerns to the discussion about the appropriateness and restrictiveness of each placement in terms of how it will affect your child.

The discussion of a placement should include a discussion of alternatives. Research has suggested[3] that in some instances school personnel may present only one placement option to parents and then attempt to convince them that this one placement is the only appropriate alternative. Don't let this happen to you. Even if you have no objections to the proposed placement, you should understand what alternatives were available and why they were rejected and you should visit the recommended placement to be sure you agree with the school that it is appropriate for your child.

When will I have an opportunity to discuss the placement alternatives for my child?

The context within which the discussion of placement alternatives occurs will vary and the discussion may be separated into two different periods. For example, the discussion of possible placements may begin at the evaluation conference and end with a placement alternative selected at the IEP conference, or the discussion may begin at the placement team or the IEP conference and end with the selection of a placement alternative in an informal meeting between you and a school representative.

Another possibility is that placement alternatives are suggested and discussed at either the evaluation, placement team, or IEP conference with no opportunity for further discussion before you receive a written notice requesting your informed consent. Often this placement decision and request for written consent will be part of the conference proceedings. If this happens, you may want to delay giving your consent until you have arranged to visit the proposed placements. After your visit you can request a meeting with a school staff person with whom you can discuss the results of your visit.

If you are part of the placement discussion, you should, as with the IEP conference, offer all the information you can about what you think your child's educational needs are. However, you should also do the following:

Offer additional placement alternatives (in addition to those proposed by the school) you believe might be appropriate for your child.

Be sure you understand what each alternative placement represents (who the teachers will be, how much time your child will be in that class, and what the instructional approach is).

If you have not visited at least the recommended placement, ask if you might do so before consenting to the decision.

What should I be looking for when I visit alternative placements?

We cannot urge strongly enough that you take time to visit the alternative placements suggested by your school and any others you think might be equally or more appropriate. Both regular and special education teachers and programs vary tremendously and what may seem appropriate when described in a brochure or discussed in conversations with a school administrator or counselor may be quite different and perhaps inappropriate in practice. It might help you sort out your thoughts if two people visit—both parents or one parent and a close friend or experienced parent.

You should make some arrangements about the day and time with school staff (a principal, special education director, or counselor) before your visit. When you arrive you should talk first with one or more individuals knowledgeable about the special education program as it operates generally in that school, agency, or institution. This is especially important if the placement alternative is not in your own neighborhood school. You should find out the following:

the program's general philosophy and approach;

the curriculum orientation of the program;

other special features of the program;

the frequency and type of contact with nonhandicapped students;

the number and type of program staff including specialists and paraprofessionals (aides);

the special facilities, equipment, and materials available.

Next, you should visit the class or classes in which your child might be placed. During your visit you should observe the composition of the class, which would include the location and physical features of the building, its accessibility, the number and characteristics of the students, and the number and roles (teacher, therapist, aide, volunteer) of adults present. The atmosphere of the class should also be considered. This would include activity level, degree of cooperation and support shown, emotional tone exhibited, and social patterns. In addition to class composition and atmosphere, a third consideration, instructional conditions, should be evaluated. They include curriculum, course organization, teaching methods, grouping practices, cognitive stimulation provided, special equipment and materials available, and the organization and structure of the class and class activities. We have provided an outline of the specific features you should consider during your observation in Table 6.2. However, in no one visit, even a long one, can you get precise information on all of these placement considerations. You will also have to make allowances for the fact that the day you visited may not have been a typical one. But this table should still provide you with a guide and help you organize your notes.

Table 6.2   Characteristics of Placement Alternatives (to be determined during visit)

I. *Composition of the Class—Teachers and Students*

Location in building (distance from other classes)

Accessibility (doorways, bathrooms, desks, tables, laboratory benches)

Physical features
  special equipment and materials
  neatness and attractiveness
  lighting and temperature
  adequate space for students to move around freely

Students
  number present
  ratio of handicapped to nonhandicapped
  age range
  types of handicap represented
  severity of handicap represented
  diversity in skill level

Teaching staff available
  number of teachers, aides, other assistants present

II. *Atmosphere*

Tone
  cheerfulness
  absence of pressure
  enthusiasm
  warmth
  friendliness

Activity level
  level and direction of activity
  level of student attention
  extent to which activity is directed toward useful purpose
  level of disruptive behavior
  discipline techniques used
  noise level

Support/Cooperation
  degree of cooperation among students
  extent and nature of competition

Social patterns
  level of communication or conversation among students
  opportunities for cooperative play, joint projects, group discussion
  degree and type of contact between handicapped and nonhandicapped
    students
  level of involvement of handicapped students in social activities
  level of acceptance and friendship offered handicapped students

Table 6.2   continued

III. *Instruction*

Curriculum areas covered
  daily living skills
  academic skills
  social and interpersonal skills
  career awareness and preparation for work
  vocational skill areas taught

Equipment and materials
  text books and supplementary materials
  audiovisual materials
  special equipment and materials
  learning aids and games
  special adaptations provided handicapped students

Teaching methods
  activities, projects used
  types of assignments
  teaching style
  specific approaches (e.g., total communication, behavior modification)

Grouping practices
  use of one-to-one and small group instruction
  size of learning groups
  methods for grouping students
  participation of handicapped students in groups with nonhandicapped
  use of learning centers, work stations

Individualization
  individual assignments
  flexibility in assignments of students to learning groups
  modification of assignments and activities to fit individual student needs

Organization and structure
  lessons and assignments coordinated and sequenced
  degree of disruption in transition from one activity to another
  length of time students must wait for assistance
  degree of teacher direction and control provided

Cognitive stimulation
  level of student's interest, attention
  degree of challenge offered
  motivation strategies used
  student feedback system (grades, stars, individual progress charts, work
    diaries)

Try to find an opportunity to talk with the teachers in classes you visit. In these conversations, find out how much training and experience they have, particularly with students with needs similar to your child's; their educational orientation and approach; their feelings about teaching handicapped students like yours; and resources they receive from the school's central special education office.

During the visit take written notes of what you observed and were told. Sometimes it helps to talk these notes into a tape recorder and then take written notes from the tape recording. Another good idea is to discuss your visit with another person and tape record that discussion.

Will I be notified about the placement decision if I am not at the meeting when it is discussed?

The law requires that you receive written notification a reasonable time before the school makes any changes in your child's placement (P.L. 94–142 Regulations Section 121a.504). In addition, if this placement will be the first special education placement for your child, you will be asked to give your written consent. (See Figure 6.1.)

The notification you receive must include all of the following:

a description of the proposed placement;

an explanation of why that placement is being proposed;

a description of the alternative placements considered and why those placements were rejected;

a description of the evaluation procedures, tests, records, or reports used as a basis for the proposed placement;

a description of other factors relevant to the proposed placement (e.g., the date the placement would start);

a description of the procedural safeguards available (e.g., right to access to your child's records, right to a second evaluation, right to a due process hearing).

The notification must be written in language you can understand—that means in your native language or other mode of communication.

Under what circumstances do I give my consent to the proposed placement?

The most important action you must take regarding your child's placement is to decide whether to give your informed consent or to withhold it and request a due process hearing, or place your child outside of the public school program, or both.

Figure 6-1
Sample Parental Consent Form for Special Services

ONSLOW COUNTY SCHOOLS
DEPARTMENT OF PUPIL PERSONNEL SERVICES
P.O. BOX 99, JACKSONVILLE, N. C. 28540

PARENTAL CONSENT FOR SPECIAL SERVICES

Name_____School _____ Date _____

This permission is based on my understanding from the principal that my child has been evaluated by an appropriate staff member(s) of the Onslow County Schools, that a Placement Committee has recommended this special placement as being in the best educational interest of my child.

I understand that my child's enrollment status will be reviewed annually each school year by a Placement Committee and that a recommendation regarding placement for the next year will be made at that time. I understand, also, that my permission to place my child remains in effect until such time as I either withdraw my permission by written notice or the Placement Committee recommends a change in program status. I have been advised of my rights to appeal this placement and understand that I may obtain additional evaluations of my child by persons outside of the school system. The special programs or services listed below have been described to me.

Category:_____Type:_____
     (LD, EMH, etc.)   (Contained, Resource, etc.)

_____I give my permission for my child to receive the special services described on this form.	_____I *do not* give my permission for my child to receive the special services described on this form.
_____ Signature	_____ Signature
_____ Relationship to Student	_____ Relationship to Student
_____ Address	_____ Address
_____	_____

If this is to be your child's first special education placement, then your consent must be written. Although school staff are not required to obtain your written consent to subsequent placements, you do have to be notified about any placement change and you have the right to a due process hearing if you disagree with the proposed change. Thus, even for subsequent placement changes, you must provide at least tacit consent.

Before you give your consent, you should:

Visit the placement (if you haven't already).

Be sure you understand what the placement means in terms of:

teachers and other persons involved;

subject areas covered;

amount of time to be spent with nonhandicapped students and for what activities.

Agree that the placement is appropriate for providing your child the services he or she needs.

Be sure the placement is complete, that it includes all essential services required by your child, and that it includes all courses or activities you feel are important.

Determine the person who will be responsible for assuring that your child is placed according to this decision.

If you are informed and satisfied on all these points, you should give your informed consent.

There are, however, circumstances under which you might not want to consent to a placement. You should not give your consent if you believe the placement is inappropriate or harmful or if you feel an essential part of your child's placement is missing (e.g., placement in physical therapy). Too often school systems recommend certain placements because of practical factors (cost, space, accessibility, transportation, efficiency). School systems do have certain constraints under which they operate, but remember your child has only one life and cannot wait too long for the school system to obtain funds, hire and/or train staff, make building modifications, or get new equipment. If you think that practical considerations are restricting the placement alternatives the school has available for your child to those that you believe are inappropriate, you should discuss your concerns with school personnel. For example:

If you believe that your severely retarded child will suffer if removed from family contact and placed in a residential program then press the school to develop a local program.

If you believe your physically handicapped child would learn more in regular classes if those were physically accessible, then insist that elevators or ramps be installed or that class locations be moved to the first floor.

If you know your deaf child is capable of and wants to study auto mechanics in the regular vocational education program, insist that an interpreter be provided.

If you think your learning disabled child needs to be in a specific reading instruction program that cannot take any more students, press the district to hire additional staff to expand the program.

When considering alternative placements, remember that the law says the placement *must be appropriate, not ideal* and *not the most appropriate.* There is probably no such thing as a perfect placement; every placement decision involves trade–offs and is constrained by practical factors. There will always be honest disagreements between parents and school about what constitutes an appropriate placement.

You must decide whether the placement alternative recommended by the school is appropriate for your child. If you are not in complete disagreement, you can consent to a temporary placement. Then you can request a review at a later time if you think your child is not making adequate progress. If you believe the recommended placement is not appropriate, you should withhold your consent and request a due process hearing. At the due process hearing you and the school will have an opportunity to recommend different placement alternatives and to offer evidence and argument in support of those recommendations. You can, of course, place your child in a private school at your own expense without a due process hearing.

Before you decide to withhold your consent, you should discuss your child's needs and the placement options available with other people you trust and who know your child—your physician, friends and relatives, individuals who have worked with your child (athletic team leaders, music teachers, religious instructors), and other specialists. Speak with an attorney, parent advocates, and other persons who have been involved in due process hearings to find out whether your reasons for rejecting the suggested placements are sound and how likely you are to be supported by a due process hearing officer or panel.

Your child will remain in the program he or she is currently in until you give your consent for placement. If this is a first special education placement, your child will remain in the regular class without any special assistance. If enrolled in a private school, your child will remain there.

The fact that no initial placement change can be made without parental consent puts some pressure on you to decide quickly. However, you should not let that pressure force you to decide before you have fully explored each alternative and have informed and satisfied yourself that you agree with the recommended placement.

Are there special factors to consider if the placement involves a work assignment?

There are several possible placements for students that involve a vocational or job placement:

regular education vocational training programs with special supportive services;

special education vocational development programs;

supervised part-time work placement in regular employment (work/study arrangements);

work placement in a sheltered workshop;

placement in a community activity center.

You should do some investigating to determine what potentially appropriate vocational or work-related programs or placements are available in your area. Be sure to investigate the programs available for non-handicapped students, too, since these programs will offer training in a wide variety of vocational areas.

Remember vocational placements, like other special education placements, are subject to the least restrictive environment provision of P.L. 94-142. So, handicapped students, to the maximum extent possible, must receive vocational education in regular vocational classes, laboratories, technical centers, or job training and work/study programs with supportive services and materials provided as needed. Don't let your child be closed out of a vocational program or technical center because of such barriers as the following:

restrictive eligibility requirements (e.g., high level reading or mathematics requirements for skill areas that don't require that level of proficiency);

standardized testing programs that discriminate against handicapped students;

discouraging advice from guidance counselors;

physical inaccessibility of the room or building where the classes are held;

inappropriate, narrow stereotypes about what handicapped persons can do or the skills they can acquire.

As your child's advocate, you are in a position to support your child's right to participate in the vocational education program in which he or she is interested and has some aptitude. Under the new laws the school system is required to provide the supportive service your child needs to succeed in that program (interpreters, taped or brailled materials, adaptive equipment, tools, work areas, supportive instruction in basic academic skills.

If you don't think the regular vocational education program is appropriate and yet you still want your child to receive vocational training, a more restrictive special vocational development program might be appropriate. However, these programs are few in number and often have unofficial waiting lists, so you may have to do some strong convincing to obtain the desired alternative placement. For those students who need extra supervision and who cannot cope with the requirements of a regular job or need a work placement where they can improve their skills, a sheltered workshop may be an appropriate placement. For severely handicapped students, activities centers provide a placement alternative where they can work at special tasks, have social contacts, and achieve some independence.

Regardless of what vocational training placement you and your child select, you want it to be a pleasant, worthwhile, and rewarding experience. Therefore, you should consider the following factors in making your selection:

Are the individuals who will supervise and/or train your child understanding of your child's capabilities and special needs?

Are the facilities and equipment where your child will be working adaptable to your child's special requirements?

Is there a variety in the tasks and activities your child will be doing?

Will the tasks your child will be doing develop his or her full potential?

Will your child be learning a variety of different vocational skills?

Are the skills your child will be learning and practicing usable in other employment situations and appropriate to the current labor market in your area?

Will your child be learning positive work habits and attitudes as well as specific technical skills?

Will your child have an opportunity to be trained and/or work with nonhandicapped individuals?

Will the experiences your child has in this placement assist him or her in gaining other employment?

Are there special factors to consider when one of the placement alternatives is a special day or residential school?

As handicapped individuals become more and more integrated into the mainstream of life, and as school buildings and programs become more accessible to handicapped students, there will be fewer and fewer students who will require instruction in separate special schools or residential facilities. Whether your child is one of those for whom a special school or residential setting is appropriate depends on several factors:

the nature and severity of your child's handicap;

your child's need for intensive long-term care, specially designed facilities and equipment, or certain numbers and types of special instructional staff, therapists, and other specialists to be involved in your child's educational program;

the resources available within your local neighborhood school to meet your child's educational needs;

the resources available within your community to assist you in caring for your child at home;

the social companionship available for your child within your community and neighborhood school;

the effect of providing for your child's daily care on your family life and family relationships;

the short- and long-term benefits and losses that may result from the separation of your child from his or her community, local school, and family.

The first task in considering a special school or residential program is to determine what alternatives are available. Your child's placement team may have recommended a particular school or residential facility. However, you may want to investigate others as well.

Even if the placement team did not suggest a special school or residential program for your child, you may want to consider that alternative. Your school district should be able to provide you with listings. Also, many parent advocacy groups maintain lists of residential school programs.

The next task when considering a placement in a special school or residential facility is to learn all you can about the program offered prior to visiting the school or facility to observe the program in operation. You should find out all you can about:

the program's reputation for training children and young adults with handicaps similar to your child's;

the location of the facility, including the means of public transportation serving that location, the driving routes, and driving time;

the costs of the program, broken down by category (e.g., tuition, room, board, transportation, equipment, supplies);

the admission eligibility requirements and whether there is an admissions waiting list;

the accreditation of the school and whether it meets state certification standards.

Write or call those schools or facilities that you are considering and ask for a catalogue and other program description material. Talk with school personnel and other people you trust about the schools or facilities you are considering. If at all possible, talk to other families who have a child in the program. Ask these families:

how their child has benefitted from the program;

what they feel are the program's major strengths and weaknesses;

what factors they considered and deemed most important when making their decision to place their child in that program.

Talking with school personnel, friends, and other parents, and reading descriptive material may help you narrow the possible options down to one or two. You should visit these alternatives. During your visit you should talk with one or more of the school administrative staff to find out about the general program offered by the school or institution, and you should visit the class or classes in which your child may be placed.

In your discussions about the general school program you should learn as much as you can about:

the program philosophy and approach;

the staff training and experience, particularly with children with handicaps similar to your child's;

number and type of therapists and other specialists available, where they are located in the facility, how much time they spend with students with needs similar to your child's, and whether the contact is individual or group instruction;

the availability of in-service opportunities for staff; the incentives to participate; the number of staff involved, and the topics included;

the use of aides, paraprofessionals, volunteers, university trainees, including their roles and responsibilities and their methods of supervision;

the availability of recreational facilities and leisure time opportunities; such things as music, art, dramatics, athletics, dating opportunities, dances;

the opportunity for close companionship with individuals with similar capabilities;

medical programs available; nurses, physicians, and paramedics on duty and/or on call; drug-dispensing policies;

the standard student diagnostic testing and evaluation program, including the frequency of student diagnostic testing and other assessments used;

the nature and type of contact between students in special schools or residential programs and those in regular school programs;

the relationship of the special school or residential program to the community including the involvement of students in community youth programs, athletic teams, etc., and the use of community resources (library, bowling alley, skating rink, movie theaters);

the living arrangements including sleeping and dining arrangements (including quality of the food and assistance with eating);

the social policies, rules, and regulations such as "lights out" policies, freedom to move about and/or to leave the campus, family visiting periods, student housekeeping responsibilities, laundry, and personal hygiene;

the number and ratio of house parents, residence counselors, and attendants to students; their training and experience;

the program's involvement with innovation and program development activities; the names of the colleges, universities, and other organizations that collaborate or assist in these activities;

the nature and type of parent involvement (parent advisory groups, parent volunteers, openness of the school or facility to parent visitation, visiting hours).

Then visit the class or classes in which your child will receive instruction.

In considering whether a special school or residential placement is appropriate for your child you should consider realistically your child's needs. You should consider the capability of your family and your local school system to meet those needs and consider the resources and programs available from other agencies and organizations in your community to assist you. Contrast these capabilities and resources with the program available in the special school or residential facility.

After careful investigation and prayerful thought, many families decide that a residential or special day school is the only setting where their handicapped child can receive the specialized training, intensive care, and social companionship that he or she needs. Other families feel that their child will be able to progress satisfactorily and be happy while participating in the special program offered by the local school district.

Remember, as important and critical as this decision may be, it is not irreversible. You can request a change in placement if you feel that your child's present placement is no longer appropriate.

Who pays for a private school or residential placement?

If your local school system is unable to provide an appropriate educational program for your child, then the school system must pay for your child to attend an appropriate program in another school district, intermediate or regional center, private school, or state residential facility. This includes paying tuition, room and board, transportation, and any other nonmedical costs incurred as part of the instructional program. It does not include recreation expenses, laundry, and other personal expenses or medical costs.

If the school district offers an appropriate program (as determined by the placement team and supported in a due process hearing or court decision) but you elect to send your child to a private facility, then you must pay all costs, although the school district must pay for diagnostic evaluation and reevaluation (and your child remains eligible for all services offered students with similar educational needs).

Some school systems have instituted financial support policies for students placed in external programs at their parent's discretion. When you discuss the placement alternative for your child with school officials, you should find out what level and type of financial support might be available if you decide to place your child in an external (out of the local district) program even though the local district's program may be appropriate. You may be able, for example, to get the school system to agree to contribute an amount equal to the average (either regular or special education) cost per pupil to your child's tuition or fee.

The issue of exactly what constitutes part of the instructional program of a residential placement, and thus is cost borne by the school, and what constitutes medical, recreational, or personal expense is not clear-cut. Often, the answer to this question will be determined through a due process hearing or by the court. A common example of this issue is the psychological or psychiatric treatment needed by emotionally disturbed students. Before enrolling your child in a private facility, you should be very clear about what the school district is agreeing to pay and what expenses you must bear yourself.

What is mainstreaming and how does it relate to the least restrictive environment?

Mainstreaming is a popular, philosophical term that refers to the belief that handicapped individuals must be viewed as members of mainstream society with the same personal goals and the right to pursue them as nonhandicapped individuals; and that as members of mainstream society, handicapped individuals have the right to live, work, play, and study with their nonhandicapped peers. In education, mainstreaming is the belief that handicapped students are members of the school community and that, whenever appropriate, they should attend regular schools and classes and participate in normal school academic and social activities. Historically, mainstreaming as an educational philosophy developed out of a concern that special schools and classes resulted in the separation of handicapped students from nonhandicapped students.

Rhetoric surrounding early discussions of mainstreaming pictured special classes as dull, dead-end situations that should be abolished for all or almost all students in favor of regular classes which were thought to be more challenging, enriching, and vibrant. Handicapped students in special schools and classes were considered to be stigmatized academically and socially isolated in an artificial and protective environment, subjected to low teacher expectations and ignored potential, denied the more stimulating opportunities and experiences of a normal school program, and removed from their neighborhood schools and friends.

As an alternative to separate special schools and classes with their limitations, mainstreaming was proposed as a panacea. Mainstreaming was founded on the following basic assumptions:

Physical contact between handicapped and nonhandicapped will lead to more involvement and participation in worthwhile educational and leisure time activities at school, at home, and in the community.

Nonhandicapped students, with support and instruction from their teachers, will accept handicapped students into the school and class social structure.

Regular teachers, using supportive instructional materials, can individualize instruction enough to accommodate the diverse educational needs of both handicapped and nonhandicapped students.

Regular teachers, using carefully designed group projects and class discussion questions, can involve both handicapped and nonhandicapped students in the same instructional activities.

Nonhandicapped students will provide a more stimulating cognitive (intellectual) environment, and more appropriate behavior role models (examples) than will other handicapped students.

Handicapped students will develop more positive self-concepts when they are part of a regular class or school.

Special education resources (materials, equipment, personnel) are available to assist and support the regular class program.

Critics were quick to challenge some of these assumptions and point out that most special classes and special schools were not the dull, dead-end, depressing environments that early mainstreaming advocates had pictured them to be.

Although the basic belief in mainstreaming as a philosophy has not altered, the application of mainstreaming principles to education has become more practical and involves less rhetoric.

Educators now recognize the following:

Under certain circumstances, physical contact between handicapped and nonhandicapped students may not result in the assimilation of the handicapped student into the social structure of the class, but rather in his or her isolation and/or rejection from it.

Many regular classes are academically demanding and competitive and result, not in increased stimulation, but increased pressure and frustration for the handicapped student.

Many regular class teachers are not skilled in instructing handicapped students, nor are they all able to use individualized instructional practices effectively.

Not accustomed to having handicapped students in their classes, many regular class teachers feel anxious, resentful, and unprepared.

In many schools the patterns of social behavior exhibited by some nonhandicapped students (e.g., class absenteeism, alcoholism, drug abuse, vandalism) are not appropriate; thus, the use of nonhandicapped students as role models may not be appropriate.

The special education resources available to support the regular teacher and handicapped student in the regular class (e.g., special materials, equipment, aides, attendants, interpreters, resource or itinerant teachers, consultants) are not always adequate, sufficient, appropriate, or effective.

The coordination and communication between regular and special instructional personnel is imperfect. As a result, there may be gaps, overloads, inconsistencies, or disruptions in the handicapped student's instruction.

Some, if not all, of these limitations to mainstreaming can be expected to change as teachers become better prepared and more experienced in teaching handicapped students, as resources become available to support mainstreaming programs, as administrative mechanisms are developed to coordinate the regular and special education instructional programs, and as nonhandicapped students become accustomed to and tolerant of handicapped students in their classes.

In addition to pointing out some of the potential problems that might limit the successful integration of handicapped students into regular classes and schools, mainstreaming critics also presented a more positive picture of special education classes. Special classes offered the handicapped students:

smaller sized classes;

trained and experienced teachers;

individual or small group instruction;

special learning materials and equipment;

reduced academic pressure and competition;

training targeted toward social living and vocational skills;

a warm, tolerant, and accepting environment;

intensive instruction and therapy directed toward unique needs;

academic expectations based on realistic assessment of students' capability;

structured, controlled, tightly organized class activities.

Although educators have debated the methods by which mainstreaming principles can be applied to educational programs for handicapped students, the philosophy underlying mainstreaming has never been questioned. Handicapped students are part of the mainstream of the school community and are entitled to participate in all aspects of school life.

Educators are now in general agreement about the following mainstreaming principles:

All handicapped students should be integrated into regular schools and classes to the extent that they are able to benefit from such integration.

The degree and form of mainstreaming provided each student must be based on the principles of the least restrictive environment and must be determined individually, considering each student's needs.

Special classes and schools should be available for those handicapped students who require intensive individual instruction from highly trained professionals, free from the pressures and isolation of the regular class.

Even those students who need to be in special classes or schools because they require very specialized services and highly intensified instruction should have some opportunities to interact with nonhandicapped students and, whenever possible, participate in regular school activities.

Participation of handicapped students in regular classes and schools is to be facilitated and supported by sufficient architectural modification, special materials and equipment, aides, attendants, interpreters, consultants, and technical assistance to the regular teacher, and supplemental or remedial instruction from itinerant or resource teachers.

Mainstreaming benefits nonhandicapped students, offering them new insights into the nature of individual differences and human rights and the importance of tolerance, cooperation, and support. And the following are the important things for you to remember about mainstreaming for your child:

First, mainstreaming represents a conviction that handicapped individuals must be considered part of the mainstream of society and that handicapped students must be considered full members of the school community.

Second, the application of mainstreaming principles does not preclude the use of special classes or schools; these and other options must remain available for students who need them.

Third, the application of mainstreaming principles in the consideration of the placement for your child must be done on an individual basis with your involvement and consent.

Notes

1. Buss, W. G.; Kirp, D. L.; and Kuriloff, P. J. "Exploring Procedural Modes of Special Education." *Issues in the Classification of Children.* Edited by N. Hobbs. Washington, D.C.: Jossey-Bass, 1975.

2. A particularly comprehensive listing of alternatives has been developed by Gregory F. Aloia in "Assessment of the Complexity of the Least Restrictive Environment Doctrine Public Law 94–142," *Developing Criteria for the Evaluation of the Least Restrictive Environment Provision,* U.S.O.E. Bureau of Education for the Handicapped, State Program Studies Branch, 1978, pp. 79–150.

3. Yoshida, Roland K.; Schensul, Jean J.; Pelto, Pertti J.; and Fenton, Kathleen S. *Parent-School Relationships in Transition: Issues in Securing Informed Consent for Special Education Placement Decisions.* Technical Report, U.S.O.E. Bureau of Education for the Handicapped, 1978.

7

Instructional and Related Services

JUDITH ANDREWS AGARD

Your child has been evaluated and designated as eligible for special services, an IEP has been developed for your child, and he or she has been placed in an appropriate program where the needed services can be provided. You view your efforts on behalf of your child as having been successful, and you may feel ready to relax (and to stop reading this book). However, your work is not over; you have a major role to play in seeing that your child gets the needed instructional and related services and that the instructional program offered by the school is supported and reinforced at home. In this section, we answer some questions concerning the services available to your child and your role in assuring that your child receives and benefits from them.

What are the special services my child should receive?

Your child is entitled to those special education and related services which are provided in conformity with your child's IEP—the regular and special education–related aids and services that are designed to meet the needs of handicapped persons as adequately as the needs of nonhandicapped persons are met.

This somewhat technical definition can be interpreted to mean that all programs, services, instructional equipment, and materials indicated in your child's IEP must be provided and at no cost. Your child's IEP in turn must include all services your child needs to assure an appropriate educational program.

In the next few questions we detail some of the instructional and related services that might be appropriate for your child. If you think your child requires one or more of these services, be sure they are mentioned in your child's IEP. Remember, the best way to assure that your child obtains the services needed to receive an appropriate education is to have those services included in your child's IEP. Plan ahead, investigate the potential benefit of some of these services for your child, and be ready with your suggestions at your child's IEP conference.

First and foremost, there is *direct, intensive, academic instruction provided by special teachers* trained, certified, and experienced in teaching children with educational needs like those of your child. This means that your child will receive individually designed instruction directed toward achieving the goals and objectives listed in the IEP. Recent research on resource and special self–contained classes (Kaufman, Agard, and Semmel, in press) suggest that it also means the following:

small classes;

instruction of students individually or in small groups;

use of special curriculum materials and instructional aids;

attention paid to each child;

warm, supportive climate;

individually designed and structured instructional exercises and assignments;

active student participation in class activities;

teacher questions and assignments that are geared to the student's ability;

opportunity for directed, independent work;

disciplined, controlled group behavior;

special teaching and motivational techniques.

Second, there are *corrective and/or supportive personnel, equipment, and material resources* required to assist the handicapped student to benefit from special instruction. These include:

such personnel as aides, attendants, peer advocates or tutors (non-handicapped students who provide assistance), interpreters, and readers;

such equipment as adaptive equipment for the physically handi-capped, environmental control systems (e.g., voice activated ma-chines), special platforms, motorized vehicles, hearing aids, mobility aids for the blind, and reading devices (e.g., Opticon, Kurzweil machines);

such materials as brailled texts, taped material, recordings, instructional games, aids, special curriculum materials, skill practice materials (workbooks, programmed exercises), and prosthetic devices.

Third, there are *special diagnostic, therapeutic, and adaptive support services* provided by trained therapists and other specialists. These services include the following:

language and speech instruction;

speech pathology and audiological services;

aural rehabilitation;

mobility instruction;

special instruction for the visually handicapped;

physical therapy;

occupational therapy;

adaptive physical education;

special driver's education;

psychological counseling.

Fourth, there are also *regular education support services* offered by the school to nonhandicapped students which must be made accessible and available to handicapped students as well. These include:

physical education;

athletic programs;

career education;

vocational education;

college and job placement services;

counseling services;

psychological diagnostic services;

school aptitude, interest, vocational, and achievement testing programs;

school health services;

day care programs;

cultural and special interest programs (music, dance, dramatics, journalism);

employment opportunities (library aides, etc.).

A fifth consideration is the *social and recreational opportunities* that are offered as part of the general school program which must be made accessible to handicapped students so that they can participate along with their nonhandicapped peers. These include the following:

lunch, recess, free periods;

athletic teams;

music organizations (band, chorus, orchestra);

dramatic clubs, debate teams;

special interest groups and clubs (e.g., science club, chess club, language clubs);

school student government and service organizations;

school assemblies, pep rallies;

school journalism groups (newspaper, yearbook).

Sixth, there are *transportation services* required to assure that the handicapped student receives the educational program detailed in his or her IEP. This includes travel within the school building, travel between school and home, and travel between school and the community facilities where services are being provided. Furthermore, it includes the use of specialized equipment and attendants, if required.

Finally, there are *services to parents and families* such as:

school social services;

parent counseling;

parent education in child development;

assistance to parents in understanding the special needs of their child.

Will all the services my child needs be provided by the public school?

Many but not all services will be provided by the public school. Such agencies as mental health and mental retardation centers, city and county health departments, vocational rehabilitation agencies, crippled children's services, and university clinics may have services or programs that would benefit your child. These agencies offer such services as psychological therapy, therapeutic recreation, diagnostic and aptitude testing, and parent and family counseling.

The public school is responsible for coordinating the efforts of these agencies but often parents who have done careful sleuthing are more aware of the services provided by outside agencies than are the school staff. If you know where your child can get particular services, special equipment, or other support, be sure to share the information with the school. Make sure you inform school authorities about any services your child may be getting outside the public school and be sure to provide the names of those providing the service.

Will I have to pay for any of these services?

The law clearly states that a free, appropriate public education means special education and related services provided in conformity with an individualized educational plan. These services are to be provided at public expense, under public supervision, and without charge (P.L. 94–142 Regulations Section 121a.4). However, gray areas remain that will need to be clarified by school officials or, if you request one, through a due process hearing.

For example, medical costs, including psychiatric evaluations and examinations by other specialists, are paid for by the school if they are incurred for diagnostic purposes rather than for treatment.

Psychological counseling is considered an educational service but psychiatric counseling is not. If you do want psychological counseling or therapy for your child you must specify the psychological services desired (group therapy, guidance counseling, counseling with a chemical psychologist) and clearly state what the educational relevance of such services is.

Another example of a cost that might or might not be paid for by the school is room and board at a private facility. If your child needs 24–hour instruction in daily living skills, then room and board may be considered a part of the instructional program, and therefore paid for by the school.

If you have questions about these gray areas you should consult an experienced parent advocate, an attorney, or a law clinic.

A serious and as yet unresolved problem is that of who should provide and pay for the medical attendant services required by students who are incontinent or otherwise physically in need of periodic assistance but who are in all other respects capable of benefitting from a school–based (rather than home–bound) instruction, and in many cases from the regular class program. Some school districts are providing for attendant care as a related service; other districts are suggesting that the parents themselves provide this care if they wish the child to attend school.

You should try to negotiate with your school system to provide your child with all the special education and related services you believe your child needs to benefit from the educational program. If you believe your child requires services the school is unwilling to provide, you should consult an experienced parent advocate, an attorney, or a law clinic.

What is my responsibility as a parent in making sure that my child receives the services he or she requires?

You have several very important roles. First and most important, you should find out what instructional and other services are actually being provided to assist your child in meeting the educational goals and objectives specified in the IEP.

Second, you should share your insights on your child's problems and offer your suggestions on successful techniques you have used with your child with those individuals who are working with your child.

Third, you should facilitate the coordination of the services provided your child so that your child doesn't feel cast adrift into a sea of instructors, therapists, and specialists all popping in and out and up and down with no apparent pattern.

Fourth, you should learn what kinds of activities you can do with your child at home to support your child's instructional program.

How do I find out what services my child is actually receiving?

One answer to that question is that your child should receive those services that are indicated in his or her IEP. However, the answer is not that simple. The best way for you to find out exactly what services your child is receiving is to ask your child's teachers. And we suggest that you do that early and often. But discovering the appropriate person or persons to ask may not be straightforward. Often your child's IEP will indicate a teacher or other person such as a counselor who is responsible for implementing the IEP. You should arrange to talk with this person about your child's IEP and how it is being implemented.

If you are not clear about who coordinates your child's IEP, ask the school staff person who chaired the IEP conference whom you should talk with.

You will also probably want to talk with each of your child's teachers, therapists, counselors, and other specialists. Make a special point to talk with any regular educational program staff who instruct your child. These individuals may be less familiar with handicapped students and therefore your insights will be especially valuable.

When you talk with your child's teachers and other specialists, find out what these individuals are doing with your child on a day-to-day basis, what techniques they use, and what special materials and equipment. Ask questions about any aspect of your child's program you do not understand. Find out why your child's instructors use particular techniques or materials.

You might find it very helpful to observe your child in class and therapy to get a feeling for your child's program and to gain insight into the types of activities you can do with your child at home.

When you talk with your child's teachers, remember they have the principal responsibility for implementing your child's IEP and for assisting him or her in meeting the goals and objectives stated. They need your support and suggestions and they should answer your questions, listen to your suggestions, and provide you with information on your child's progress. Teachers represent a critical force in your child's educational program, and therefore you should cooperate with and support them all you can.

What type of assistance can I provide my child's teachers?

You have a wealth of information to share with your child's teachers. You are the person most familiar with your child and you have the following insights you should share with your child's teachers:

your child's skills, abilities, and interests;

how you go about teaching your child new skills;

what motivates your child to do difficult or unpleasant tasks;

the rewards your child likes to receive for doing good work;

how your child reacts when frustrated, bored, unhappy, or frightened;

your child's special personal needs (rest habits, toilet habits, special diet).

In addition to information about your child, you should also share any information you have about new and innovative materials, equipment, procedures, and teaching methods that you think might be useful with your child. If you have heard or read about a new procedure or adaptive device that you think might work with your child, discuss it with your child's teachers. They may be willing to try it; if they are not, they should have good reasons why it wouldn't be appropriate.

It is understandable that many school personnel are not familiar with all the disability definitions and may have only a limited and often incorrect understanding of what having a particular disability means. You may be able to provide your child's teacher with useful background information about your child's disability and the educational challenges it creates. You should answer any questions your child's teachers may have and alleviate any of their fears or anxieties so that they feel comfortable with your child.

The time you spend helping your child's teachers to understand and accept your child has a direct effect on the other students in your child's classes. Your child's classmates may be curious about your child's disability, or even worse, they may be afraid of or repulsed by it. Other students may need to be encouraged and instructed to be tolerant, accepting, and supportive of your child. You and your child can help in this process by being open and candid about the disability, what it means, how it happened, what can be done about it, and whether it will get worse. Explain what the disability means in terms of what your child can do alone and how and when he or she will need the help of classmates. Discuss any special equipment or prosthetic devices used by your child, what they do, how they work, and when they are to be used. Share with others what your child is and isn't able to do, both in terms of school, work, and play.

Try to anticipate and answer some hidden questions that children may have but are embarrassed to ask: Is the disability "catching"? Does it hurt? How do you feel about it? Does it make you angry? These questions may be difficult or painful for you or your child to answer. However, many social psychologists believe that a handicapped student will be liked and respected when his or her classmates have information about the disability and sense that the handicapped student is comfortable enough to talk openly with others. Furthermore, each time you and your child reach out to nonhandicapped students, you make it easier for the next handicapped individual.

What can I do to coordinate my child's educational program?

Technically, coordinating your child's program is not your responsibility, but there are certain circumstances in which you may find yourself assisting in that effort. In many instances, one or more of the teachers who will be responsible for implementing the IEP are not present when it is developed. Sometimes these teachers will receive a copy of the IEP, but more often they receive informal oral reports on the goals, objectives, placements, and instructional and related services to be provided.

These reports may be inconsistent, distorted, incomplete, or unclear. If you discover that one or more of your child's teachers does not know or understand what is in your child's IEP, you can share your copy with them and discuss your interpretations of the particular sections that are unclear. You might also want to refer them to the school staff person given overall responsibility for the implementation of your child's IEP.

Another situation which may arise (and which you may recognize before your child's teachers do) is a coordination breakdown. If responsibility for your child's educational program is divided among several teachers (one or more regular teachers, a special resource teacher, a speech therapist), you may find that no one person has a total view of your child's instruction. There may be gaps or overloads in your child's instruction. If you think this might be happening to your child, you should talk with your child's teachers to encourage them to coordinate their efforts.

Many times the programs of handicapped students in elementary school classes require that the students leave and return to their regular classes one or more times during the day. This can be bothersome to the teacher, confusing for your child, and disrupting to the class. You can help avoid some of these problems if you teach your child to enter and leave the class quietly, and to go directly and quickly to an assigned class. More mature children can even be taught to remember when their own special classes are and to keep track of the time. Talk to your child's teachers about your child's program problems and try to work out solutions. Attempt to set up times for your child to receive special instruction when it will not conflict with the regular class activities that your child really needs and enjoys.

What kinds of things can I do with my child at home to support the instructional and related services offered by the school?

The best people to answer this question are your child's teachers. First ask them to suggest books you might read on child development, psychology, and education; your child's handicap; special education; and the experiences of other parents of handicapped children.

Your child's teachers can also recommend toys, games, records, books, and other educational aids that might be useful and that would supplement the school program. There is an almost endless variety of commercial material being advertised as "educational," "cognitively enriching," "aiding in the development of psychomotor skills," etc. Your child's teachers can tell you which of this material might be useful and which might actually contradict the instructional approach being used with your child. It is particularly important to check before purchasing systems or programs for teaching your child reading or mathematics since they may be inconsistent with the approach used by your child's teachers, and may actually confuse more than help your child.

Check with your child's teachers about the homework your child should be doing and how you might help with it. Listening to spelling words, quizzing on arithmetic facts, practicing speech sounds, helping in physical therapy exercises, and reading aloud to your child are all possibilities. The most important way you can help your child with homework, however, is to clear time and a work space for homework to be done without disruption, to be sure that it gets finished, and to encourage your child.

Finally, there may be particular teaching activities or techniques you can do with your child. Ask your child's teachers for suggestions of activities that will relate to the school program. Be sure you understand and follow the procedure and approach the teacher recommends when you conduct these activities. Remember that you want your time with your child to be a positive, happy learning experience for both of you. If your child gets impatient, bored, frustrated, or angry, or you get impatient or feel pressured, then stop and ask the teacher for some assistance and/or something different to do. Whenever your child appears to have learned as much as possible from a particular activity and all its variations, ask for some other suggestions.

If my child attends a private school, will these special services still be provided?

The simple answer to this question is yes. P.L. 94–142 Regulations (Section 121a.400) state that a handicapped student who is placed in a private school by a public school must be provided with special education and related services in conformance with his or her IEP at no cost to the parents. The regulations (Sections 121a.403, 453, 454) further state that if a handicapped child has available a free, appropriate public education and the parents choose to place the child in a private school, the public school is not required to pay for the child's education, but must provide special education and related services. The type of special education and related services must be determined (after consultation with persons knowledgeable about the needs of handicapped students in private schools) on a basis comparable to that used in providing services to handicapped students in the public schools. The services provided do not have to be the same, but must be comparable in quality, scope, and opportunity for participation to those provided public school students with similar needs.

What can I reasonably expect the school system to provide in the way of transportation for my child?

The school system is required to provide transportation if it is necessary to ensure that your child receives an appropriate education. Usually this will mean bus service, but it could mean reimbursing you for driving your child or arranging with a community agency to drive handicapped students.

The transportation services required by your child should be described in your child's IEP, and depend upon your child's handicap and designated placement. You should find out (preferably before the IEP conference) the following:

transportation services to be provided;

who will be providing the transportation and whether that person is sensitive to the needs of handicapped students;

special equipment to be used;

whether an attendant will be provided;

travel time (in miles and hours).

Transportation considerations should not limit your child's placement alternatives, although they sometimes do. For example, a specially equipped van may only transport students to a special school. You may have to convince school officials to change the route so your child can attend a regular school.

The efficient routing of buses to transport handicapped students to their special programs often means that some children travel long distances or for long periods of time. At a minimum you should try to ensure that the time spent traveling is used productively (in singing, playing instructional games, learning social skills). If you live in a sparsely settled area, there is probably little you can do about the time your child must travel, but you can encourage the school to develop as efficient a routing system as possible.

If your child needs special transportation to attend a recommended program and transportation services are mentioned in your child's IEP, then there should be no transportation costs for you to pay even if special equipment or personnel are needed.

Will my handicapped child be able to participate in the school physical education and athletic programs?

The federal law is quite clear on the question of physical education (P.L. 94-142 Regulation 121a.307). Physical education, specially designed if necessary, must be made available to every handicapped student. Furthermore, each handicapped child must have an opportunity to participate in the regular education program available to nonhandicapped students unless the student is placed full-time in a separate special center or the student needs a specially designed program. This should be included in the IEP. Even if your child is in a special education center or other separate facility, appropriate physical education must be provided.

In providing both physical education and after-school athletic programs, schools may not discriminate on the basis of handicap; all qualified handicapped students must be provided an equal opportunity to participate in these programs [Section 504 Regulation 84.37(c)]. Furthermore, the Office of Civil Rights has recently ruled that students can participate in contact sports even if they have suffered a physical disability if they have parental consent and the approval of a physician who is familiar with the student.

If participation in the regular athletic program is not appropriate for your child, investigate the Special Olympics Program. Most public school systems have information about the program and support it. So tell your child to start warming up.

What kinds of services are available to help my child prepare for the world of work?

Every handicapped person has the right to participate in the world of work, to be a productive, contributing member of society. Even severely handicapped individuals should have an opportunity to participate in some form of worthwhile activity.

Your child has the right to receive appropriate training in those social and technical skills that are necessary to become employable and be productive in those vocational areas in which he or she has interest and capability.

Both P.L. 94-142 and Section 504 address the question of career and vocational education. P.L. 94-142 (Regulation 121a.305) states that the public school shall take steps to insure that handicapped students have available the variety of educational programs and services available to nonhandicapped students. Vocational education is defined [Section 121a.

14b(3)] as those organized programs which are directly related to the preparation of individuals for paid or unpaid employment or for additional preparation for a career. Moreover, vocational education programs must be specifically designed, if necessary, to enable a handicapped student to benefit fully from the training offered.

Section 504 makes the exclusion of handicapped students from vocational education programs a violation of their civil rights. It also states that schools that provide vocational counseling, guidance, or placement services must provide these services without discrimination on the basis of handicap. Furthermore, the law specifically warns that qualified handicapped students should not be counseled toward more restrictive career objectives than are nonhandicapped students with similar interests and abilities.

The federal government has backed up its concern for vocational education services for the handicapped with money. The Vocational Education Amendments of 1976 require that 10% of all vocational education funds allocated to each state be used for special education programs and services to help handicapped students achieve vocational education objectives that would be beyond their reach because of their disability. This means both special services and modifications of the regular program.

Included among the vocational services that can be supported with vocational education funds are vocational instruction, curriculum development and modification of equipment to assist handicapped students in the regular education program, and support services such as interpreters, readers, aides, vocational evaluation, job placement, and follow–up support.

Career and vocational education services should be a part of your child's program throughout the school years and should include more than training in a specific vocational skill. Instruction in the following work habits and job adjustment skills should be provided throughout your child's school program:

attendance, punctuality, and completion of work on time;

use of money (budgeting, checking and savings accounts, purchasing);

health and grooming habits;

social behavior (engaging in conversation, asking for help if needed);

ability to travel around the community independently;

use of the telephone to obtain information, make arrangements, request service.

An important part of the school program for developing appropriate work habits and skills is prevocational classes such as industrial arts and/or consumer education. In many school systems, these classes are required before a student can begin a more advanced vocational training program.

Part of your child's program should include those services needed to help your child explore various career and work opportunities. They include the following:

field trips to various places of employment where career opportunities can be discussed (factories, offices, shops, stores);

instruction in career opportunities, requirements, nature of work, salary;

opportunities to experiment with different work–related tasks;

conversation with other handicapped and nonhandicapped adults about their jobs;

participation in career fairs;

participation in career education classes.

Your child may need counseling services to help narrow down career options to a few that are interesting and appropriate. Vocational aptitude and interest diagnostic and evaluation tests might be useful for assisting your child in the selection of possible careers. You and the school should work together to help your child identify appropriate careers and/or jobs. This involves knowing about the nature of the work, the requirements, salaries, and opportunities available in one or more possible careers. It also involves taking a hard look at such things as labor union membership and licensure requirements. But don't let anything or anyone, including your child, limit career horizons on the basis of past discrimination, handicap stereotyping, or inflexible, pessimistic attitudes.

Once your child has identified a set of realistic career objectives, you, your child, and the school can determine the needed vocational skills and training. Your child should then be placed in programs, classes, or work situations where he or she will acquire the skills and training required.

If involved in a regular vocational education program, your child is still entitled to whatever services are needed to benefit from that class. This might include the following:

aides, attendants;

interpreters;

special materials (including easy-to-ready instruction manuals);

adaptive tools, work site modifications;

prosthetic devices;

alterations in the way tasks are performed;

extra supportive instruction.

In addition to specific vocational skill training, an important component of a vocational program is work experience in an actual work situation, simulated work environment (e.g., school auto body shop), or sheltered workshop. It is important for your child that the work experience be tied to a skill development program. Actual work experience will assist your child in developing good work habits, and provide an opportunity to practice the technical skills he or she has learned. Don't let your child get into a work situation that is not related to career objectives or does not provide opportunity for learning new skills.

Part of career or vocational education is learning how to get a job. You should be sure your child learns how to:

locate a job (through employment agencies, job placement services, newspaper ads);

inquire about the job (by phone or through a letter);

develop a resume or complete an application form;

request and prepare for an interview;

behave in an interview (by pointing out strengths, answering questions about his or her disability).

A key individual in vocational programs, particularly for programs that have handicapped students, is the job placement or career counselor or work-study or occupational specialist. These individuals act as an interface between the student and the job market. They study the job market and available jobs to discover employment trends and specific job requirements.

The job placement counselor should know the wage and salary scale of particular occupations, the long-range prospect for continued employment in these occupations, the educational requirements, and any labor union apprenticeship or professional licensure requirements. This person should also know about specific job placement situations, the willingness of particular employers to hire disabled students and, if necessary, to make alterations to facilitate the disabled worker's performance. Often the job placement counselor seeks out employment opportunities for students and makes necessary arrangements with the employer for the alterations required by the disabled student. The job placement counselor, if there is one in your school system, is an important resource for you and your child when your child needs a work/study placement.

Despite the persistent concern for handicapped students shown at the federal level, vocational education programs for handicapped students are not yet available in every high school or even in every school district. Often the programs that are available are conducted separately from the regular vocational education programs offered nonhandicapped students.

As a first step, you should investigate the career and vocational education opportunities available in your child's high school or school district. Investigate the programs available for both handicapped and nonhandicapped students. Find out what each program offers in terms of the following:

instruction in work habits and job adjustment skills;

prevocational classes (industrial arts or consumer education);

career exploration activities;

career counseling;

training in specific vocational skills;

special materials, equipment, and tools to facilitate acquisition of vocational skills;

opportunities for work experience;

training in job location, application, and interviewing skills;

job placement services.

You might find that your high school or school district offers just the right services for your handicapped child. If so, be sure that your child's IEP includes these services.

You might find that your high school has a good program for non-handicapped students that would be appropriate for your child if certain adaptations or special supportive equipment or materials were provided. Make sure your child's IEP places your child in this program and that the required adaptations, special equipment, or materials are indicated.

In addition to your public school, you should check with other agencies. Local branches of state vocational rehabilitation agencies may offer services, such as aptitude testing, counseling, training, special tools and equipment, prosthetic appliances, job placement, and follow-up. These services are available to persons who have mental and/or physical handicaps that interfere substantially with employment and who have a chance of becoming employable. Vocational rehabilitation agency services are available to eligible high school students. These services should be coordinated with the services offered by the school through your child's IEP.

Other agencies may have training programs or sheltered workshops—Easter Seal Centers, Goodwill Industries, local associations for retarded citizens, and mental health and mental retardation programs are all possibilities worth exploring.

My child makes great progress during the school year but slips back when not in a special summer program. Is there any way the school can be convinced to provide year-round instruction?

Actually, there are some court cases in process demanding year-round instruction, but there is not yet a definitive answer to this question. One court case, however, has already been decided in favor of the plaintiff (the children in a class action suit) and the court has ordered the school district not to limit the number of days of instruction whenever a child's IEP specifies that a longer period of instructional time is necessary to provide an appropriate educational program. This case is under appeal at present.

Prior to the development of your child's IEP, you should find out what summer programs your school offers. If there is an appropriate summer program (or even if there is not) request that year-round instruction be included in your child's IEP. If enough parents request it, the schools may be convinced to offer (or expand) a special summer program.

My child is in high school and really wants to join all sorts of school clubs—the jazz band, the Spanish club, the newspaper, and the pom-pom squad. Is this really possible?

Absolutely; schools must provide nonacademic and extracurricular services and activities in such a manner as is necessary to permit handicapped students to participate (Section 504 Regulation 84.37). This means that there can be no barriers restricting your child's access to these clubs on the basis of his or her handicap. Some of these organizations may have eligibility requirements that your child must meet (auditions for the jazz band, a minimum of two years of Spanish instruction, current enrollment in a journalism class, or an ability to master the pom-pom routine). But the school must provide interpreters, brailled music, physically accessible meeting rooms, or whatever is necessary to facilitate your child's participation in these activities.

8

Formal and Informal Review Processes

JUDITH ANDREWS AGARD

After your child has been placed in a special education program and has begun to receive special services, your role as an advocate becomes one of monitoring and reviewing your child's progress.

Children and adolescents never stay the same; they grow, mature, learn new skills, and acquire new interests. Teachers, too, learn new techniques and obtain new materials and equipment. New placement opportunities open up, vocational opportunities shift, and community activities change. Your child's progress must be reviewed formally and informally to determine whether his or her educational program is still appropriate. In this chapter, we answer questions regarding both the formal and informal review processes.

When should I review my child's program?

P.L. 94-142 requires the school to review your child's IEP once a year and to reevaluate your child once every three years. But you don't want to wait a year to learn how your child is doing. We believe you should check on your child's progress continuously. You should be aware of your child's school activity on a daily basis, be in contact informally with your child's teachers at least monthly, obtain formal updates (written and/or parent-teacher conferences) each school marking period (4-6 times a year), and formally review your child's IEP once a year.

These are not hard and fast rules. If your child is in a new program or has serious problems, or if you are providing a fair amount of instruction at home, you may wish to have more frequent informal contact. At any time you believe your child's IEP is no longer appropriate you may ask for an IEP review. If your school provides only semester or trimester reports, you may request some form of formal report more frequently. Remember, the IEP goals and objectives are just estimates, not guarantees. You need to monitor the progress your child is making toward achieving those goals and objectives.

In reviewing your child's program you should be concerned with changes in your child's behavior, attitudes, and skills that represent educational progress or problems. You should also be concerned with your child's program, be aware of any problems that may have occurred with its implementation (e.g., coordination of teacher activities) and any subtle changes in focus that may have taken place (e.g., gradual increases in the time spent in the resource class or on academic skills), and any designated services that may not have been provided.

How should I monitor my child's educational program?

There are several mechanisms available to help you monitor your child's educational program both formally and informally.

The most formal monitoring and review mechanism is to participate actively in your child's *annual IEP review*. A less formal, but also important, procedure is to study and, if necessary, question the *report cards or other periodic written progress reports* you receive on your child. If possible, you should supplement written reports with parent–teacher conferences.

In addition to using these formal methods you should locate one or more persons at the school to keep you posted on your child's progress. This *informal liaison person* may be a special education teacher, a regular teacher, or a counselor. It may be the person designated as responsible for the implementation of your child's IEP, or it could be your child's favorite teacher, a teacher who has taken a special interest in your child, the teacher with whom your child spends the most time, or to whom your child has the greatest difficulty relating. You might want to be in close contact with more than one teacher; for example, both a regular and a special teacher, or both an academic and a vocational teacher. Try to talk with these contact teachers often, at least by phone (take notes, of course), and ask them to keep you informed of any significant progress or important problems with regard to your child.

Ask your child's teachers to send home copies of your child's work (tests, class assignments, reports, exercise sheets) at least weekly. This *weekly folder of work* might be accompanied by brief notes indicating special accomplishments or problems surmounted. It could also contain ideas for new activities you can do with your child at home. If your child is having difficulty completing assignments on time, it might be helpful if you had a schedule of homework assignments so that you could help him or her keep track of assignments.

You may also want to *observe your child at school* to see how he or she behaves in class, responds to instruction, and gets along with classmates.

Finally, you should *talk with your child and observe home behavior.* Watch for evidence of:

skills learned;

attitude toward school and school work;

level of spirits;

type, content, and difficulty of school work.

These procedures, although differing in formality, are all important. Informal review allows you to monitor your child's progress more frequently so that you are not surprised when problems surface or when major program changes are recommended. Formal review provides you with important reports about your child's progress and permits you to take an active role in changing your child's program.

Whether your review information is derived from formal or informal means, you should do the following:

Keep examples of your child's work, and any teacher notes you receive with it.

Make notes of the things your child says about school work and things you observe about your child's behavior.

Keep a log of your conversations with your child's teachers.

Save your copies of report cards, progress reports, and any formal test results the school sends you.

Be sure to note the date when these conversations, observations, work samples, and notes were obtained. When recording notes on observations of your child's behavior, describe the specific event, when it happened, why it happened, the context in which it occurred, and what you did about it.

How do I arrange to have a conference with my child's teachers?

First, you need to decide which teachers you wish to confer with. If there has been one teacher designated as your informal liaison person or as the person responsible for implementing your child's IEP, then that person is a logical choice. However, it may be equally useful for you to confer with other teachers—regular teachers (if the liaison teacher is a special education teacher), your child's favorite teachers, teachers with whom your child doesn't get along, and teachers of important classes (reading, mathematics, vocational training, work/study coordination).

Second, arrange for the conference. You should check with the principal or school counselor about the policies in your school regarding communication between parents and teachers. In most schools you may call a teacher directly during school hours. Tell the teacher that you wish to meet to discuss your child and ask when and where that would be convenient. If there is a particular problem you wish to discuss, be sure to say what it is (e.g., to review a report card, to check up on your child's progress). If you want that teacher to gather information from other teachers, be sure to ask if he or she would mind doing that. Tell the teacher who will be coming to the conference. You may be able to schedule meetings with several teachers at the same time, although you should probably check with the principal before doing this.

Occasionally, when you call to set up a conference, a teacher will try to confer with you on the phone rather than agree to a personal visit. That's perfectly all right if you are prepared to do this. If you think you would prefer to wait for a personal visit, simply say so.

Most often, the teacher or school will contact you about a conference rather than you contacting them. You should find out the date, time, place, and purpose of the conference, who will be there, and whether your child should attend. If you are contacted by letter or school note, be sure to respond, confirming that you will be there or asking for a more convenient alternative date or time.

It is possible and in many cases helpful to invite your child's teacher to your home. Having a teacher visit your home permits the teacher to meet your family and to see how your child behaves at home. It also eliminates babysitting or transportation problems. However, a meeting at school may have fewer interruptions, and permit you to see what your child's classroom is like, to examine the equipment and curriculum materials, and to visit with other teachers or school staff. Certainly, at least once a year it's good to invite your child's teacher to a parent-teacher conference in your home.

Remember to prepare for the parent-teacher conference by observing and talking with your child, and reviewing your child's school work and other reports (report cards, IEP progress reports, test scores, and teacher's notes). Make a list of all the questions you wish to ask and all the information you wish to share with your child's teachers, and gather and organize the material that you need to take with you. And most important, review your child's IEP and take it with you.

What should I do at the parent–teacher meeting?

The principal purpose of a parent–teacher conference is to share information. The conference may result in minor modifications in how your child is instructed but probably no major changes in your child's IEP will occur.

Basically, the information you will share at this conference will be related to the two following questions:

How is my child doing in school?

What is the school doing for my child?

The conversation will naturally shift around but it might help you to organize your thoughts and prepare your questions and materials if you have an idea of what might be considered.

Your child's progress

The principal purpose of the conference is for you and your child's teacher to compare notes on your child's progress. You want to consider three questions:

What is your child learning?

How does he or she behave?

How does your child get along with classmates?

You and your child's teacher should examine and discuss the following:

examples of your child's school work—the best, worst, and most typical in several academic areas;

projects your child has completed in art, industrial arts, science, or social studies;

examples of work your child does at home—things your child has made, problems or exercises your child does for you;

new skills and improved behavior your child has shown at home;

reports of your child's progress, examples of work, and any comments on particular problems from other teachers or therapists;

your child's grades—those in the teacher's gradebook;

your child's status as compared with his or her potential, nonhandicapped students, and other students with similar handicaps—whether your child is learning up to potential; how your child's work compares with that of typical children that age (better, the same, one or more years behind); and how your child's work compares with that of students with similar handicaps;

your child's adjustment to the new placement—whether he or she feels rejected, confused, stigmatized, or frustrated;

your child's school behavior—class attendance, work habits, discipline problems, attention and participation in class, alcohol or drug abuse;

your child's friendship patterns at home and at school—number of friends, who they are, what they like to do together;

your child's accomplishments of the goals and objectives on his or her IEP.

You and your child's teacher should exchange insights and perceptions on the progress of your child, and how it relates to the goals and objectives of your child's IEP. In the areas in which your child has made progress, try to find out what techniques or approaches were used and which seemed to be effective. In the behavior problem areas, try to find out what might be causing the problems, what approaches to eliminating or reducing the problem have already been tried, and what new approaches might be tried. Ask the teacher to suggest approaches used successfully in the past with other students with similar problems and discuss how you handle problems like that when they occur at home.

Your child's program

A second purpose of the parent–teacher conference is to learn about your child's program. You and your child's teacher should discuss how the implementation of your child's IEP is going, including answering (or at least attempting to answer) the following questions:

Which goals and objectives have been completed, abandoned, or extended?

Have there been any minor changes in my child's placement (new teachers, new students in the class, more or less time spent there)?

Is my child receiving the designated services of therapists and other specialists?

Have my child's teachers received the special materials and equipment they need?

Are there any gaps or overloads in my child's program?

Who is presently coordinating my child's IEP?

Is coordination a problem? How often do my child's regular teachers communicate with the special education teachers?

Ask to see your child's daily and weekly schedule. Discuss the schedule with your child's teacher in terms of:

the services your child is receiving;

how confusing the schedule is to your child and how disruptive it is for teachers;

what instruction is missed when your child leaves the regular class, a resources class, or other special services.

Although your child's IEP specifies the general goals and objectives to be the focus of his or her program, you should view the parent–teacher conference as an opportunity to learn about the program in more detail. You should do the following:

Look around at the displays in the classroom to get a feel for the atmosphere of the class and the current topics being covered.

Examine the special equipment being used with your child; ask to see it operate.

Ask the teacher for an overview of the curriculum, the topics to be covered, concepts to be introduced, and skills to be mastered. Find out what has been done to date and what comes up next, as well as whether your child is expected to have difficulty in any of these areas.

Ask the teacher to show you the specific curriculum materials and textbooks being used and to indicate how far your child has progressed in these materials.

Find out what the class behavior expectations, rules, and regulations are, how much freedom is permitted, whether the students can move about the room, and whether they can talk with or help each other. Discuss whether your child is able to conform to these behavior expectations.

Find out how the teacher intends to grade your child's work (compared with some standard, compared with other students, or compared with his or her potential); find out what is required to obtain certain grades.

Learn as much as you can about the types of activities, assignments, projects, and discussion topics that the teacher uses. Find out which particular activities cause problems for your child.

Discuss with the teacher the program modifications that may be necessary for your child to succeed (e.g., more time to take examinations, oral rather than written reports).

From this conversation you should get a feeling for what instruction has already occurred and what instruction will occur next, and you and your child's teachers should be able to pinpoint potential problems and figure out ways to avoid or minimize them.

Remember, one of the most rewarding experiences a parent of a handicapped child can have is to engage in a fruitful discussion with a teacher who is genuinely concerned about the child. You want to do all you can to create a climate where that can happen.

Try to keep the tone of the conference informal and friendly. Let the teacher know you have respect for his or her knowledge and skill as a teacher and that you can sympathize with the problems in teaching your child, many of which (e.g., availability of special materials) may be beyond the teacher's control. Stress that you view the parent–teacher conference as an opportunity to share information and to develop cooperation. Your child's teachers must work intensely with your child and the satisfactions, while great, may be slow in coming. Take time to thank them for their work and praise their successful efforts.

How should the parent–teacher conference end?

The conference should end on a positive, constructive note. Review your list of questions (and your notes of the meeting) to be sure you've covered everything. Be sure your child's teacher has covered everything. A good final question is: "Is there anything I should have asked you but didn't?"

If you and your child's teacher discussed particular tasks or activities to be done either at school or at home, review these activities to be sure each of you remember what you agreed to do and when you would do it. If you have been working on specific tasks with your child at home, be sure to review your progress and get new ideas, new tasks, or a go-ahead to continue with what you have been doing.

Set up a tentative date when you will meet again, and make a general note about what you will discuss at that meeting.

If this parent–teacher conference is intended to be a formal report to parents (i.e., it replaces a report card), be sure to get a formal written report from the teacher about what was discussed. Your notes cannot substitute for a school-prepared written progress report.

If you went over your child's IEP at this meeting and completed any form of IEP update, get a copy. For example, in districts using a two–part IEP, you will have periodic parent–teacher meetings to update the more specific, short-term instructional plan. Be sure to get a copy of the new instructional plan and note on the previous instructional plan which objectives were met, and which were discontinued or extended. Indicate the reasons why certain objectives caused difficulty. Indicate, too, which services were and were not actually provided.

Finally, discuss the parent–teacher conference with your child. Relate all the nice things the teacher said about his or her work and behavior and discuss the problems that need to be worked on. Obtain your child's cooperation in whatever plans were made to work on those problem areas. Answer any questions your child may have about the meeting and convey all you found out about the curriculum, class rules, and grade requirements. Above all, explain to your child that, despite any earlier disagreements, you and the teachers are now in agreement on most things, that you are all trying to help, and that you expect with everyone working hard, he or she will continue to make progress in school.

What should I do to observe my child in school?

First, talk about your observation plans with your child. Many older students are embarrassed when their parents appear at school. However, if your child agrees to your idea, he or she can help orchestrate your visit.

Second, ask the teacher if it is all right for you to visit your child's classes and arrange a convenient day and time. If the teacher has asked you to observe, be sure you know what particular things to look for. Have your own list of things you want to observe ready.

When you arrive, try to remain unobtrusive until the teacher is free to greet you. Ask where you should sit and what you can do, (e.g., whether you can talk with the students near you, answer questions about their work, move about the room).

Be sure to observe the teacher and other students in the class as well as your own child. When you are ready to go, say good-bye to your child, thank the teacher, and leave quietly. Often the teacher will not have enough time to talk with you about your observations, unless it's at the end of the day or he or she has arranged to leave the class. But sooner or later you will want to share your perceptions with your child's teacher, so do try to get in touch at a parent–teacher conference or over the phone.

If your child is placed in a regular class with supportive services provided through a resource teacher or other specialist, try to observe your child in both settings so you get a feeling for how your child reacts in both types of situations.

What should I look for when I observe my child in class?

You should look at many of the same things you looked at when you were considering placement alternatives—the composition of the class, the emotional atmosphere, the nature and type of social activity, and the instructional techniques used.

It is important for you to observe your child's behavior in that setting:

Does your child behave well (i.e., pay attention, follow directions, work quietly and independently, contribute to group discussions, disrupt others at work)?

Does your child fit into the social pattern (i.e., have friends, seem to be accepted, cooperate with other students, share materials, books, cause trouble, appear to be alone or rejected)?

Does your child seem happy (i.e, have self–confidence, smile and laugh, seem eager to join in the activities, look frustrated or angry)?

Does your child participate in the class instructional program (i.e., volunteer to answer questions, complete the work assignments, use the class materials and books as directed, do the same work as the rest of the class)?

Observing your child in class will give you tremendous insight into your child's educational needs and the approaches that teachers are using to meet those needs. You will have some feeling for what the IEP really means from this experience.

When does my child's IEP get reviewed?

Your child's IEP must be reviewed at least once a year [P.L. 94–142 Regulations Section 121 (a) 343 (d)]. However, it may be reviewed and revised as often as necessary to assure that your child continues to receive an appropriate education.

You have a right to ask for a review of your child's IEP any time you have reasons to believe your child's needs have changed so that one or more of the original IEP elements is no longer appropriate and a new statement of goals and objectives, placements, and services is required to assure that your child continues to receive an appropriate program.

Remember, however, that adjustment and learning take time. Don't expect the special education program of your school to work miracles. Give your child a chance to adjust to the new program and give the school staff an opportunity to work with your child before you feel discouraged and ask for a review.

What will happen at the IEP review conference?

In many respects the annual review conference will be similar to the first IEP conference. You must be notified and invited to attend. The team may be similar but must include at least:

a representative of the school, other than the child's teacher, who is qualified to provide or supervise the provision of special education;

the child's teacher;

the child's parents.

You and the school may designate others to attend.

The procedure may be less formal since fewer people are involved and since often, but not always, no new evaluation information is being considered.

Since the purpose of the IEP review conference is to review and revise your child's IEP, that purpose should govern the agenda. We would expect the following events to occur, although not necessarily in this logical order:

review of your child's initial evaluation information, original IEP, and placement decision;

review of the progress your child has made toward meeting the goals and objectives specified in the IEP;

examination of report card grades, teacher reports to parents, work samples, standardized test scores;

consideration of teacher and parent observations of your child's behavior in class and at home;

presentation of new information from more recent evaluations or other sources;

discussion of the factors contributing to your child's progress;

discussion of the educational goals which are still appropriate and of high priority and those which need to be added or modified to reflect changes in your child's interests and skills;

reformulation of short–term objectives, leading to the development of new goals and a new schedule for attaining those objectives;

review of the instructional and related services your child has received and a discussion of the need to change, expand, or reduce those services;

introduction of new approaches, techniques, materials, equipment, and other resources that might be effective with your child;

discussion and selection of an appropriate placement for the following year (try to visit the placement before you give a final approval);

preparation of a revised IEP which includes a designation of goals and objectives, identification of services required, and selection of a placement.

What is my role at my child's IEP review conference?

You have a very important role to play in the review of your child's IEP just as you did in the development of the initial IEP.

You may be the person who requests the review. If you have new evaluation information to present, or if your child is unhappy or upset with the current program or placement, has made no progress, or has accomplished all of his or her objectives, you should request an IEP review. Other reasons for requesting a review may be if your home or family circumstances have changed or you have learned about new, promising placements, equipment, materials, or approaches you think would be appropriate for your child.

Regardless of who requested the review, you have critical functions to play at the review conference, just as you had at the initial IEP conference. Your role should be to:

provide information on your child's progress from your perspective;

introduce new ideas and make recommendations;

participate in the discussion regarding changes in goals and objectives, service, or placement;

give your consent to any proposed changes in placement.

You need to prepare for the IEP review by doing the same things you did to prepare for the initial IEP conference, especially the following:

Review all your own and the school's records on your child, particularly the evaluation reports and any new data that have been added since the previous IEP conference.

Study your child's existing IEP and consider which items should be revised, deleted, or added.

Gather together the material you wish to share, including:

samples of your child's work;

notes on your child's progress observed at home;

report cards;

records from parent teacher conferences.

Visit any new placements being suggested for your child.

Attend the conference; you will never be able to advocate for your child if you are not there.

In many cases, the annual IEP review will seem like a relatively routine procedure—everyone agreeing to continue with the same goals, objectives, placement, and services. But you should take the review as seriously as the initial IEP meeting.

Share your perceptions of your child's progress (or lack of it) based on your observations of your child at home and at school, the work samples you have collected, and the teacher conferences you have attended. Lay out your concerns squarely and ask questions about what was done that was effective and what new methods could be pursued.

Consider carefully the new goals and objectives proposed for your child—do they agree with your priorities? Consider the placement suggested for the following year. Find out what alternative placements are being considered. If any of the classes are different (and the regular classes are almost certain to be), visit them before you agree. Review carefully the proposed services and be sure any new materials, equipment, approach, or technique that you've heard about is considered.

As always, take notes, ask questions about terms or ideas you do not understand, and get a copy of the revised IEP. Be sure to identify who will be responsible for implementing the revised IEP and when the revisions will take effect.

Should my child attend the parent–teacher conference?

Whether or not your child should attend the parent–teacher conference depends on the school or teacher policy (or preference), the age and maturity of your child, and the purpose of the conference.

Young children are often confused, bored, and sometimes upset when present at meetings in which their behavior and school progress are being discussed. Older children, however, may appreciate being involved in the discussion of their progress, have useful insights into what teaching techniques they find helpful, and be more committed to doing school work assignments which they helped design.

An alternative to having your child present at the parent–teacher conference is to talk with your child before the conference to find out what questions he or she would like answered and then to share what you found out afterwards.

Are the standardized achievement tests that my school gives a good source of information about my child's academic progress?

Standardized achievement tests are designed to measure how well students have learned the skills and attained the knowledge considered appropriate for a child's age and grade level. Achievement tests do not cover all the skills and knowledge that might be taught but they do reflect the skills and knowledge that are common to the curriculum of most American schools.

Achievement tests are administered in a carefully standardized manner and there is a reference group of students selected to represent students in general or specific types of students with whom the scores can be compared. It is the standardized manner of administration and the standard comparison group that gives the achievement tests the name standardized. However, standardized does not mean that the tests represent a standard or model of what your child should achieve.

Achievement test scores may be reported as raw scores, percentile ranks, stanines, or grade equivalents. A raw score typically is the number of correct answers. A percentile rank represents the percentage of students in the norm or reference group who had a raw score lower than the score received by the individual under consideration. A stanine score represents one point on a nine-point scale formed by grouping the raw scores into equal intervals (except at the beginning and end). A grade equivalent score represents the grade level of the students in the norm group who obtained the same raw score.

For example, your child may have received a raw score of 40 correct out of 100, or 40 percent. The raw score could be translated to a percentile rank of 30 meaning he or she scored better than 30 percent of the students in the comparison group. The raw score might represent a score in the fourth stanine, meaning that your child scored in the fourth out of nine possible groups (in which nine is the highest). Or the raw score might correspond to a grade equivalent of 3.2, meaning a score that typical students in the second month of the third grade would obtain.

Many school districts give standardized achievement tests to all students as part of an evaluation of the school's program or as an initial screening to determine which students might need special help. Some schools exempt all handicapped students from these tests, some exempt some students but not others, and some provide alternative test forms or testing conditions.

You should find out what your school's policy is regarding the administration of standardized achievement tests to handicapped students. Find out what, if any, modifications are made in the test administration (e.g., braille or large print, extended time, reading of the questions, different levels).[1] If you have questions or reservations about your child's inclusion or exclusion from the testing program, be sure to share them with school staff. Most schools are flexible regarding the inclusion of handicapped students in the achievement testing program and will be responsive to your concerns.

We believe that when achievement tests are carefully selected and administered and the scores professionally interpreted, they may provide you with useful information regarding your child's relative performance in certain academic areas (e.g., reading compared with mathematics) performance in comparison with other students (e.g., a national norm group or one formed of other deaf or hard of hearing students), and the improvement of academic performance over time (e.g., your child may receive a percentile rank of 30 one year and a rank of 35 on an equivalent test the following year).

When you receive your child's achievement test results you should ask a school staff person to assist you in interpreting the scores. The meaning of your child's scores will vary depending on what level of test was administered, whether modifications were made in the test administration procedure, and what comparison groups were used to establish the percentile rank, stanine, or grade equivalent scores.

You will also want to find out how your child's achievement test scores are to be used. They are often used as criteria for placement into certain classes—advanced or gifted, vocational training, special art, music, or industrial arts. Don't let your child be eliminated from these programs on the basis of an achievement test score that was derived from an inappropriate test given under unfair conditions.

Are there any special things I should consider if the school recommends that my child no longer receive special services?

It is the dream of every parent of a handicapped child that the child will eventually be able to function successfully without a special education program. Some students make such progress that special services are no longer necessary in order for them to obtain an education equal to that of their peers.

However, more often the reason why many handicapped students are eliminated from special education programs or have their special services terminated is that there is no longer an appropriate program available. This may be particularly true when a student moves from elementary school to junior high or intermediate school, or from junior high or intermediate school to high school.

Before you agree that your child no longer needs special education or related services, take a long, hard look at his or her educational progress and the role that special education services played in assisting your child's achievements. Find out what your child thinks about the help provided by the resource teacher and other special teachers and therapists. Discover what programs and services exist and be sure your child would be eligible for them if needed. If you believe that the recommendation for termination of service is based on the lack of an appropriate program, then share your concern with the local director of special education.

What can I anticipate as being important issues in the review of my child's achievement before graduation?

Your school or state may have certain requirements that determine who may graduate and/or receive a regular diploma. Special requirements are particularly important for high school graduation, although some school systems are instituting elementary and junior high school promotion requirements as well.

Many states and some school districts have established minimum competency requirements that they expect students to meet before they may graduate from high school. Usually states or school districts with these requirements have developed standard competency tests which students must pass before graduation. Students who do not pass these tests either do not graduate or they graduate but are awarded a different, more limited diploma.

There has been no clearly defined policy about applying the competency requirements to handicapped students. At least four approaches are available.

One approach might be to require all handicapped students to demonstrate competency prior to graduation by passing the standard competency test administered to all students. Those students who either did not take the test or did not pass would either receive no diploma or would receive a special diploma that is distinguishable from the regular diploma in some recognized way.

A second policy might be to require all handicapped students to demonstrate competency prior to graduation by passing an appropriately modified version of the standard competency test. Modifications might include braille or large print test booklets, provision for oral responses, or extension of the time limits. Students who did not take or pass the modified version would be awarded either no diploma or a special diploma.

A third possible approach might be to require all handicapped students to demonstrate competency through some alternative to the standard competency test. For example, one might argue that competency means the ability to perform adequately in real life situations (e.g., handling money, locating a job, making consumer decisions), and therefore a better measure of the competency of a handicapped student is behavior on a direct performance or situation test. Students who did not take or pass the standard competency test, but who did pass the alternative direct performance or situational test, would be awarded a regular diploma; other students would receive no diploma or a special diploma.

A fourth approach is to define different (and presumably less stringent) competency standards for handicapped students to meet. These standards could, but need not, be individually determined, and could also be part of a student's IEP. Thus, competency for a handicapped student could be defined as the attainment of those individually specified skills that are incorporated into the student's IEP. Those handicapped students who achieved the goals specified in their IEP could be awarded either a regular or specially designated diploma.

If your child is approaching graduation, you should try to determine what options are available for your child.

Based on this information, you may decide on one of the following options with regard to testing the competency of your child:

You can request that your child be included in the competency testing program with no alterations made for his or her handicap.

You can request that your child receive a modified or alternative version of the standard competency test.

You can request that different, individually determined competency standards be established for your child.

Regardless of which option you select, be sure you understand its implications for a diploma.

If your child has worked hard and achieved the IEP objectives, he or she should be entitled to participate in graduation and receive a diploma. You may, however, have to negotiate on the type of diploma your child can receive. If you believe your child has acquired the general competencies specified for all students, but think the competency testing procedures discriminate against your child, suggest that appropriate modifications or alternative testing procedures be used.

Notes

1. Some school districts use out-of-level testing with handicapped students; that is, they select a test level based on the student's performance level rather than grade placement. Thus, your third grade child might be administered the second grade level test if his or her teacher thought that level would provide a more reliable indicator of achievement. This affects the interpretation of the score.

9

Dispute Settlement

JUDITH ANDREWS AGARD

In previous chapters we described your role as an advocate for your child within a parent–school partnership. In any partnership there may be disagreements, and in the process of developing and implementing an appropriate educational program for your child, you and the school may have different opinions. There are several procedures available for settling these differences. In this section we answer questions you might have about these dispute settlement procedures.

What is the philosophy underlying dispute settlement procedures?

The dispute settlement procedures are derived from due process theory which, briefly stated, acknowledges that identifying and evaluating students, placing them in special classes, and assigning them a categorical label may cause social stigmatization and unnecessary segregation, thus depriving them of their civil rights. To protect the civil rights of students, schools are required to provide certain due process safeguards: prior notification, parental consent, and impartial dispute settlement procedures. These safeguards are intended to insure that the concerns of the parents, child, and school are considered before a placement or program decision is made.

What are some dispute settlement procedures?

There are several different procedures you might use when you are not in agreement with the decisions the school has recommended with regard to your child's identification, evaluation, placement, or program. You may use one or more of these procedures; some may be more appropriate than others at different times and for different problems.

One dispute settlement procedure involves a *discussion or conference with school staff*—teachers, counselors, the school psychologist, principal, director of special education, and superintendent. One or more of these individuals should know your concerns and your proposed alternative to the decisions suggested or already made. Often, persistent requests presented in a cooperative but concerned manner will convince school personnel of the reasonableness of your position faster than a more formal process. Whenever you believe that the procedures used by the school have been unfair, you should discuss your concerns with school staff; often, this will be enough to get the procedure changed.

A second procedure is *negotiation or mediation*. Mediation is a dispute settlement process in which a third person tries to negotiate a solution or compromise to the dispute. The mediator listens to the argument presented by both sides and tries to convince one or both sides to make a concession or compromise. The mediator may be a school staff person (an ombudsman or other person with negotiation skills) or an independent third party. The federal law does not require mediation as a dispute settlement process although it recognizes that it may serve a useful function. Many states, however, require mediation. Mediation is only effective if there is a spirit of compromise on the part of the parents and the school; without some flexibility and openness to change, mediation will not resolve a dispute. The nature of the compromise might be on the basis of time—to try something on a temporary basis or to wait for a period (e.g., until the new school year) before making a change; on the basis of intensity—to adjust the number of hours with a resource teacher or other specialist or the size of the group in which the instruction or therapy is provided; or on the basis of location—to provide similar services but in a different setting (e.g., intensive play therapy as part of a public school resource class rather than in a private facility).

A third dispute settlement procedure is an *independent evaluation*. (See Chapter 5.) If you disagree with the decision regarding the eligibility of your child for special education or the categorical classification of your child, then you should request an independent evaluation. An independent evaluation is also appropriate if you believe that certain learning or behavior problems were not diagnosed correctly or the implications of the diagnosis for determining the educational needs of your child were not fully explored. Sometimes it may appear to parents as if the school evaluation results are being dictated by program availability. (For example, when the speech therapist has openings, more students are designated as speech impaired.) If you suspect this process might be occurring, ask for a second independent evaluation. When you get the results of the evaluation, share them with the school and ask for changes in your child's eligibility or classification status. If the evaluation results suggest a modification in your child's placement or program, ask for a new placement team meeting or IEP review conference.

A fourth procedure is an *IEP review*. (See Chapter 8.) If your child is already receiving special services and/or is placed in a special education program but is not making adequate progress or is not receiving all the services indicated on the IEP, you may request a review. At the review you can present your reasons for wishing changes made and get the school to agree to the modifications you request in the IEP. If your child already had an IEP before you obtained an independent evaluation, then an IEP review conference would be an appropriate mechanism for considering the results of that evaluation.

A fifth procedure is a *formal complaint to the state and federal government*. Under P.L. 94–142 (Regulation 121.602) every state education agency is required to investigate complaints submitted to it regarding noncompliance with the procedures being used to implement the law. Thus, complaint procedure is being used with increasing frequency, particularly when the problem is related to school district special education policies or procedures (rather than a judgment regarding an individual child).

If you believe that your problem is general and occurring throughout the system (e.g., parents are being asked to consent to placement on the basis of an incomplete IEP) you should file a 602 complaint with the appropriate person in your state education agency. You should also send a copy of your complaint to the Office of Civil Rights (if it concerns a violation of Section 504) and to the Bureau of Education for the Handicapped.

A sixth, and the most formal, mechanism is a *due process hearing*. A due process hearing involves an impartial third party who serves as an arbitrator and resolves disagreements between the parents and school. A due process hearing is a quasi–legal procedure in which the parents and school present evidence and logical argument to support what each believes is an appropriate classification, placement, and program for a particular child.

The due process hearing is adversarial, that is, it forces the school and parents to confront each other in an argumentative situation. It should, therefore, be used only when other methods to resolve the dispute have been unsuccessful. Furthermore, a due process hearing is appropriate for resolving disputes about educational programming decisions but not for situations in which procedural rights have been violated. For example, if you were not notified of the IEP conference in time to make arrangements to attend, and you don't agree with some of its provisions, you should request a new IEP conference, not a due process hearing. If your request is denied, contact your state director of special education. If you still disagree with the content of the IEP that was developed when you were present, then you can request a due process hearing.

If I have a disagreement with the school, what should I do first?

As a general rule, you should use every available channel of communication to settle disagreements with the school informally through understanding, compromise, constructive criticism, and persuasion.

Discuss your disagreement informally with other parents who have experienced a disagreement similar to yours. Your local parent advocacy group may be able to suggest such a parent or other knowledgeable person. That person can discuss your options with you, as well as give you an idea of what results you might get with each option and the important factors which must be considered when deciding what action to take.

A parent who has had experience communicating with the school can help you to organize your thoughts, arrange for a parent–school conference, and develop your presentation. And an experienced parent or parent advocate may even go with you to important parent–school conferences to help you present your case, take notes, and make suggestions about questions to ask. It is helpful to have a second person's view of the discussion that took place and any agreements that were made.

You should also *discuss your problem with professionals who know your child.* Find out if they agree with your view and think your concern is reasonable. If they do agree, they may be willing to support you by sending the school a letter or personal statement.

After you have discussed your disagreement with others and have gained a better perspective of what your various options are, you should then *talk your problem over with those directly involved—your child's teachers.* Explain the problem to them, offer possible solutions, and listen to the suggestions they may offer. You should be prepared and organized for such a meeting and ready to discuss the problem openly, sincerely, and cooperatively without anger or frustration. Your child's teachers may be able to make the changes you request or offer reasonable alternatives.

Sometimes, however, teachers will be sympathetic but unable to make the requested changes. Be sure that you inform them of any further action you take and enlist their support. You may also discuss your problem with other school staff who are familiar with your child (school nurse, social worker, counselor) to obtain their understanding and support as well.

If your meetings with teachers have not resulted in a resolution of the problem, you should *arrange to meet with the principal* since he or she is responsible for the instructional programs and activities within the school building. You should prepare for this meeting by outlining the problem, being ready to present whatever evidence you have in your records that is related to the problem, and offering your suggestions for the program and services changes which you think are necessary.

If any of your child's teachers are sympathetic, ask them to be present and to support you. If the problem is with one of your child's teachers, you may want to present your own position first without the teacher present and then meet with both the principal and the teacher at a later date.

When meeting with the principal it might be helpful to have a knowledgeable friend or parent advocate with you. Take notes of your meeting and summarize (and write down) any decisions and agreements reached. If you are not satisfied with the outcome of the meeting, tell the pricipal that you are going to discuss the problem with the director of special education and/or the superintendent of schools.

Explain your problem to your district director of special education and ask for an investigation. You may be able to do this over the phone or you may prefer to make an appointment for a personal conference. In either case, you should follow up your request with a written letter—and don't forget to keep a copy for yourself. In this letter you should describe your problem (including as much background information as possible), the action you have taken to date, and the action you wish the school to take. Often your phone call and letter will be enough to prompt an investigation by the special education director or his or her staff. You should be informed of the results of that investigation within a week or two.

Discussing the problem with the school district superintendent may be productive since, occasionally, your disagreement may stem from the application of a district-wide policy established by the superintendent. (For example, no more students who might be placed in a learning disabilities resource class are to be referred for an evaluation until a new resource teacher is hired.)

If you wish to understand, influence, or change administrative regulations or procedures, you will need to confer with the superintendent of schools or other top level administrators. In discussions with these people it will be important to know the state and federal laws related to special education and the administrative organization and policies of your school district. An experienced parent advocate also can be of real value at this point. Your presentation to the superintendent should indicate the particular school policies or practices that are posing barriers to your child's obtainment of the free, appropriate public education to which he or she has the right.

You may also find it helpful to *talk to members of your school board*. Try to locate a school board member who is sympathetic toward special education and explain your disagreement with the school, indicating those general school policy or administrative regulations that are causing problems. The board member may be able to take specific action on your behalf; if not, he or she may be influential in obtaining support for changes in the special education programs offered by your school.

This may seem like a long chain of meetings, letters, and conferences. You don't have to go through each step for every problem or disagreement. If your problem is specifically related to your child's evaluation, placement, or IEP, you may decide after several conferences with teachers and the principal that you have no other recourse but a due process hearing. If your problem is related to a school district policy, you may not find it useful to confer with teachers or the principal about a policy they cannot change, although you want to keep school staff informed and to elicit their support.

What do I do if the school district refuses to change its policies or practices?

Once you have discussed your problem with the superintendent and school board members, your next recourse is to contact the state department of education. If your problem is related to general practices or procedures that you believe are not in compliance with P.L. 94–142 or Section 504, you should contact your state director of special education and request an investigation. Be as specific as possible in your request about the practice in question and what actions you have taken. You can also request a due process hearing. This section of the P.L. 94–142 Regulations states that each state education agency must develop procedures for reviewing, investigating, and acting on any complaints made by private individuals or public or private organizations about the actions of any public agency that are contrary to the provisions of P.L. 94–142. The state education agency must provide for negotiations, technical assistance, and remedial action, including sanctions to achieve compliance.

If you believe your school district's policies or practices are not in compliance with P.L. 94–142 you can request an review.

First, contact your state director of special education to find out the name of the person to whom you should address your complaint, and specific procedures you should follow.

Second, develop your complaint as completely and specifically as possible. Describe your attempts to persuade your local district to change its policies or practices, and the results of your efforts. Provide the names of the persons you have contacted and dates of your contacts. Local consumer and parent advocacy groups can be very helpful at this point. Many other parents may have experienced the same problem you have and can add additional details and examples to support your complaint. Advocacy groups, particularly those with legal representatives, can help you frame your complaint so that it is clear, accurate, and commands attention.

Send a copy of your complaint to the designated person in your state education agency and, as a courtesy, to your local director of special education. Also, send a copy of your complaint to the U.S. Office of Education, Bureau of Education for the Handicapped.

What should I do to develop a persuasive case for my position?

Regardless of what dispute settlement process is used, you want to present a persuasive argument in favor of your position. This means you should be able to present evidence that your child requires the particular placement, program, or service you recommend in order to assure that he or she receives an appropriate education. This evidence will come from several sources:

records of your child's progress or lack of it, including tests given by the school, your own written observation of your child's behavior, or samples of his or her work;

information from diagnostic evaluations, the evaluation conducted by the school, and an independent assessment that supports your position;

testimony from special education professionals who are familiar with the needs of children like yours who will lend credibility to your position;

written observations that contrast the alternative placements or programs for your child along with any statistical information to back up the success of the program or placement you think is appropriate.

Your goal is to develop a reasonable, logical set of arguments in support of your position in the dispute.

One method for building a systematic case might be the following:

Discuss your child's educational needs in terms of the evaluation findings and other records.

Present what you believe are reasonable educational goals for your child, based upon diagnosed strengths and weaknesses.

Outline the progress your child has shown to date as determined by report card grades, class test scores, achievement tests, teacher behavior reports, your own written observations of behavior, and work samples.

Describe the instructional and related services you believe are necessary for your child to make satisfactory progress toward meeting the educational goals. Explain what you think are the barriers to your child receiving those services and offer evidence on the potential value of those services. Research articles and testimony from special education professionals can substantiate your opinion.

Describe the services the school provides or has recommended for your child and discuss the discrepancy between what is provided and what is required.

Discuss the placement alternatives where the services required may be provided. Present information from your own structured observation of the placement alternatives on the appropriateness and restrictiveness of each placement; expert testimony and evaluation reports can be used to support your observations. Contrastive, quantifiable descriptions (e.g., number of trained staff) should also be used.

Discuss how your alternative in the dispute fits into a long–range educational plan that will prepare your child to live as productive a life as possible.

When you present your case at a due process hearing, you and your attorney or counsel will help you prepare a presentation along this or similar lines. However, even in informal dispute settlement situations like a parent–school conference or IEP annual review, you should go through a similar process of preparing your position, considering the points you wish to make and the evidence available to document those points.

You will be more persuasive if you have extensive records and other written documents on your child to support your points and research or evaluation reports on alternative placements and services to support your personal observations. Your arguments should be logical and rational and not based on anger or emotions, and your position must be derived from a realistic concern and understanding of your child's needs.

Under what circumstances can I request a due process hearing? ⌐

The federal law is fairly specific about this (P.L. 94–142 Regulations Section 121a.506). You can request a due process hearing regarding the identification, evaluation, and placement of your child, as well as the type of free, appropriate public education given him or her (as defined by your child's IEP). Some common disputes you might request to be resolved through a due process hearing are the following:

You believe your child's evaluation was inadequate or unfair and your request for a second evaluation at no cost is denied.

You disagree with your child's categorical classification.

You believe your child is eligible for special education and the school does not.

You believe your child's placement is not appropriate for his or her needs.

You don't believe the goals, objectives, and/or services indicated on the IEP are appropriate.

You don't think your child is receiving the services indicated on the IEP.

You believe the delay in placing your child in a particular program and/or delivering the specified services is unreasonable.

You believe your child is being excluded from certain educational opportunities or services available to nonhandicapped students because of physical or programmatic accessibility barriers.

Your request to have your child readmitted after a suspension or expulsion is denied.

Your request to amend or delete information from your child's records is denied.

The school may also request a due process hearing, particularly for the following reasons:

You refuse special education services and keep your child out of school.

You fail to respond or refuse to consent to a placement the school recommends as necessary.

You fail to respond or refuse to consent to requests to conduct an evaluation.

You request a second evaluation and the school believes its evaluation is adequate.

Although there are differences among the specific disputes that may lead to a due process hearing, there is a common thread that runs through most parent–school disputes: you, the parent, want those services and placements that you believe your child needs to make satisfactory progress and the school, on the other hand, has to balance your request for services for your child against the needs of and services required by other students. What you view as appropriate is what you feel your child needs; what the school views as appropriate is what the school feels it can provide within the limitations of its financial resources.

What difficulties are associated with a due process hearing?

A due process hearing creates an adversarial relationship; that is, it forces the parents and the school to oppose each other in a conflict situation. In most due process hearings the adversaries are the parents who represent a particular child and who want the placement and services they think are appropriate for their child; the school represents all other handicapped and nonhandicapped students and wants all students to have an appropriate education.

An adversarial relationship has the advantage of permitting full and complete evidence to be offered in support of both positions and requiring an impartial third party to make a fair and unbiased decision. However, an adversarial relationship also has the potential disadvantage of arousing anxiety, defensiveness, and hostility on the part of both parents and the school.

Some of the resentment and distress can be eliminated if parents and school staff act reasonably by recognizing that, although a dispute exists, both you and the school staff remain committed to your child's educational welfare. You should also remember that after the hearing is completed and a decision rendered, you and the school must resume your cooperative relationship. Don't jeopardize your relationship with your child's teachers, principal, and other school staff by being critical, getting angry, or making personal attacks.

The emotional tone of the due process hearing should be rational and constructive, not personal. Simply because there is an honest difference of opinion does not mean there has to be hostility or anger. Try to share with school personnel your understanding that you know they are doing all they can under the circumstances but that you believe your child needs something different, something more intensive, and that you must do everything you can to see that your child gets what you believe is needed.

What should I do to request a due process hearing?

First, you should be aware that once you request a due process hearing you may not have much time to prepare for it, so you should prepare your case before you make your formal request. Begin your preparations for it just as you did for the evaluation and the IEP process by gathering as much solid information to present as possible.

After gathering this information and talking to those who have had experience with these hearings in your school district (e.g., parents, advocates) you should decide whether your position is correct and whether you have enough evidence to support it.

If you still believe that a due process hearing is your only recourse, submit a request. Your written request should be addressed to the person designated as responsible for administering the due process hearings in your school district—the superintendent of schools, the director of special education, or a designated staff person. You should send this letter by registered mail (because the date the letter is received is important), and you should send copies to other concerned school staff (e.g., principal, IEP conference chairperson). You should state your child's name, address, telephone number, birth date, and present school placement. State your reasons for wanting a hearing, as well as the individuals involved in the disagreement and the modifications you are seeking. See Figure 9.1 for an example of such a letter.

The impartial hearing officer is responsible for making arrangements for the hearing—the date, time, and place. But you or your representative should provide the officer with a list of the witnesses (names, addresses, and telephone numbers) whom you will request to attend the hearing, including any school staff, and you should indicate the information you will present as evidence. Inform the hearing officer whether your child will be present and whether you want the hearing open or closed to the public. Even if the hearing is closed, you may still have present any individuals you specifically invite. It is also important to tell the hearing officer any needs you may have for an interpreter.

Figure 9-1
Sample Letter—Due Process Hearing Request

2542 Winding Road
Austria, Virginia 23270

March 15, 1979

Dr. Elizabeth Filbert
Director of Special Education
Austria Public Schools
7920 Municipal Road
Austria, Virginia 23270

Identification

Re: David Ajar, Age 9, Born August 10, 1969
Mr. José Garcia's Special Education Class
James Monroe Elementary School

Dear Mr. Filbert:

Purpose
of Letter

We, the parents of David Ajar, wish to request a due process hearing to review the appropriateness of his special education placement.

On February 19, 1979, we met with Dr. Dunn, Dr. Lorton, and Mr. Garcia to review David's educational progress in Mr. Garcia's class. At the meeting we reviewed the reasons why we believe that class was inappropriate for David and asked that David be readmitted to Ms. Murphy's regular classroom with some supportive instruction from Mr. Martin, the learning disabilities resource teacher. However, the school members of the IEP team did not agree. Since the IEP meeting we have met with both Dr. Dunn and Dr. Lorton (the school psychologist) but we have not been able to resolve our disagreement.

Summary of
Disagreement

As you may recall, we signed the written consent to David's placement on November 25, 1978. This placement was to be for a two-month trial period. At that time we were concerned that placement in Mr. Garcia's class would separate David from his friends in Ms. Murphy's class and not provide the intensive reading instruction David needs. Although Mr. Garcia has tried to work with David, the disruptive behavior of the other students has required that Mr. Garcia spend most of the class time disciplining other students.

History
(Parents'
Prior
Action)

Personnel
Involved

We have arranged with Ms. Maryann Hobb, a parent advocate from the Association for Children with Learning Disabilities, to be our counsel at the due process hearing.

Logistics

We wish the hearing to be closed to the public; however, our son David will attend. We will be contacting the hearing officer regarding the list of witnesses and evidence to be submitted. We would appreciate it if the hearing could be held early in the morning or late in the afternoon to facilitate our work schedules.

Figure 9-1
continued

Request to   As part of our preparation for the hearing, we would like to
Review   review and obtain copies of David's school records. Could you
Records   arrange for an appointment for this?
Thank you for your efforts on our behalf.

Sincerely yours,

Judith Swerdna

Robert Ajar

What should I do to prepare for the due process hearing?

You must prepare carefully and thoroughly to assemble the evidence needed to present a persuasive case. You will need evidence to support your arguments and you should begin assembling that evidence even before you request a hearing.

First, gather written materials. Obtain copies of the school's written records pertaining to your child, including those kept by teachers or specialists. Ask for minutes or summaries that the school maintains on IEP and other parent–school conferences. Obtain copies of the evaluation reports and other records from private professionals who have examined your child. Add to these records from your own file on your child, your observations of behavior, work samples, your own notes from parent–school conferences, and copies of letters you have written and received about your child.

Review all of this material to determine what items will be useful in building a case. Check to be sure that the evidence is appropriate—that it is related directly to your child and your child's program. Share the information you intend to present with the school at least five days before the hearing.

Second, contact witnesses. You should talk with those individuals who have evaluated and taught your child and who are supportive of your position. Your physician, the psychologist who conducted your child's independent evaluation, your child's teachers (if supportive), and other supportive persons who have worked with your child should be asked to testify or prepare a written statement of support. You may also wish to have the testimony of other expert witnesses (recognized special educators, social workers, psychologists, and medical and mental health personnel) to help support your position. For example, a representative from the nonpublic school program you are recommending as a placement should be present to discuss that program and indicate how it would meet your child's needs.

When you arrange for witnesses, you should indicate to them the kinds of questions you will ask them and get some indication of how they will respond. You will want to have questions you intend to ask witnesses carefully prepared before the hearing, including follow-up questions and probes. You must inform the hearing officer and the school district of the names of those witnesses who intend to testify. You can call school system employees as witnesses if you want.

What do I need to do to assemble evidence?

First and foremost, gather together your own records on your child and obtain copies of all school records. You should also obtain the following:

research articles or other professional descriptions relating to any equipment, materials, instructional approaches, or therapeutic services you are recommending for your child;

notes and copies of published articles by specialists recommending the particular placement or program you believe is appropriate;

copies of state and local policies and regulations related to the education of the handicapped, procedural safeguards and due process hearings, including the material used to train impartial hearing officers;

written descriptions of the programs and services available in your school district or community;

descriptions of the alternative program you believe is appropriate and statistical or other data to support your belief.

You should have as much of this material as possible assembled before you visit with your attorney or parent advocate representative.

Do I need to have someone represent me at the due process hearing?

Yes. No matter how cool, rational, and persuasive you think you are, you will still need a person whom you can trust to assist you in making your presentation.

There are several factors to consider when selecting a person to represent you. The person should be knowledgeable regarding the federal and state laws and regulations pertaining to the education of handicapped students and be familiar with standard educational practices and approaches used in special education. He or she should be sensitive to and supportive of the needs of handicapped children and yet recognize your need not to alienate or antagonize the school staff with whom you must continue to work.

Certain skills are needed to prepare a well-documented case, present evidence, examine and cross-examine witnesses, and present your argument in a persuasive manner. The person you choose should possess such skills. The person should be committed to assisting you in the entire dispute settlement process including careful preparation of your case, attendance at the hearing, and follow-through to assure the decision is implemented. Finally, be very sure that the cost of this person's services is within your financial means.

Because the due process hearing is a quasi-judicial process, an attorney is a reasonable person to select as a representative. But you should select an attorney with successful experience in educational dispute settlement cases. Your school district should be able to recommend legal aid clinics, university law school clinics, and developmental disability law clinics that may provide legal services you can afford. Often parent advocate groups, community agencies, or local colleges and universities have trained persons who can act as parent advocates in a due process hearing or can recommend an attorney. If you can afford it (and especially if the dispute has sizable financial implications), you should try to locate a skilled attorney.

When you contact prospective attorneys, ask them about their experience in special education due process hearings, the legal approach they use, and their success rate. Try to get a feeling for their sensitivity and level of commitment—will they antagonize school personnel by the manner in which they present your case; will they stick with you after the hearing to be sure the decision is implemented?

What are my rights at the due process hearing?

You and the school both have the following rights:

to have access to and copies of your child's school records;

to be accompanied by and advised by counsel;

to be accompanied by and advised by individuals with special knowledge or training with respect to handicapped children;

to compel the attendance of witnesses, including school employees,[1] and to examine and cross-examine them;

to present evidence;

to prohibit the introduction of evidence that has not been disclosed at least five days prior to the hearing;

to obtain a written or electronic verbatim record of the hearing;

to obtain a written finding of fact and decisions.

The due process hearing must be conducted within a reasonable amount of time. The law requires that a decision be reached within forty-five days after receipt of a request for a hearing (P.L. 94–142 Regulations 121a.512).

Remember, a school may request a due process hearing on certain dispute issues. If the school requests the hearing you must be given adequate notice to prepare your case.

Who will be present at the due process hearing?

At the hearing will be:

due process hearing officer(s);

the parents and their representative (an attorney or advocate);

a designated school spokesperson (usually the director of special education), and often the school attorney;

witnesses for both the school and parents;

any friends or advisors the parents wish to invite.

If you request the hearing to be open, the press may be present, and if you request it, your child may be present. Occasionally, attorneys are present to advise witnesses (e.g., a teacher may wish to have an attorney present to advise on testimony). Recent opinions from the Office of Civil Rights, however, suggest that it is a violation of your rights to privacy to have these individuals present, so you may ask that they not attend.

What is the role of the hearing officer?

The hearing officer is an impartial arbitrator responsible for listening to the evidence and testimony at the hearings and making a reasonable decision based on that evidence and testimony. The hearing officer is also an administrator responsible for arranging for the hearing and notifying both the parents and school personnel involved.

The hearing officer must be independent, cannot be employed by the school district or have any vested interest in the outcome of the dispute, and must have an understanding of the relevant issues.

Most important, the hearing officer must be impartial. Individuals with definite biases (e.g., in favor of intensive instruction in more restrictive environments) should not be hearing officers. Hearing officers may be attorneys, university faculty members, psychologists, educators, or community leaders. In some states a hearing panel rather than an individual is required.

You should find out who the hearing officer(s) for your dispute will be. Check their qualifications and possible conflicts of interest or strong philosophical biases. You may ask to have a hearing officer replaced who you believe will not be sufficiently knowledgeable, impartial, or independent.

What will happen at the due process hearing?

The due process hearing is relatively formal and the agenda is usually structured. The best source of information on the agenda that will be followed in your state is the guidebook or training material prepared for hearing officers. Usually the agenda proceeds as indicated in Table 9.1.

The opening remarks by the hearing officer establish the formal purpose of the hearing, introduce the participants in the hearing, and establish the agenda and procedures to be followed. The opening arguments by parents and school or their representatives should provide an outline of the issues, a summary of evidence, and the rationale for the recommended courses suggested by both parties. The opening remarks cannot be included as evidence although they will provide a frame of reference for organizing the evidence when it is presented.

The order in which the evidence is presented may vary. Some hearing officers will have all written evidence introduced first, followed by examination of expert witnesses while others will allow each party to introduce the written evidence and expert witnesses in support of his or her position followed by evidence and witnesses in support of the alternative position.

The presentation of evidence is the heart of the hearing. In the presentation of documentary evidence, it is helpful if each document is identified and its contents briefly described and highlighted. It is not permissible for either party to introduce new evidence at a due process hearing, although

Table 9.1 Illustrative Agenda for a Due Process Hearing

I. Opening Remarks by Hearing Officer

Statement of the purpose of the hearing

Introduction of the parties involved (child, parents, and school), their names, and positions

Description of the due process hearing procedure

Description of the role of the hearing officer

Review of the procedures to be followed

Announcement of the order to be followed

Determination of whether parents were informed of procedural rights

Identification and seating of witnesses

II. Opening Arguments by or on Behalf of the Parents and of the School

III. Presentation of Evidence

Presentation and identification of documentary evidence

Brief description of documentary evidence provided

Presentation of witness

The following should occur with each witness:

name, address, and position stated;

relationship to child;

reason for appearing;

responses to questions from party requesting the witness' testimony;

responses to questions (cross-examination) from other party;

responses to questions posed by the hearing officer.

IV. Concluding Remarks by or on Behalf of the Parents and of the School

V. Concluding Remarks by Hearing Officer

Announcement of when decision may be expected

Overview of rights to appeal

Statement of right to receive a verbatim record

---

the hearing officer can request additional documents and even another independent evaluation. After the evidence is presented, each party may present a summary of the argument in his or her case and the evidence offered in support of those arguments. The hearing officer will then make some concluding remarks and the hearing will be adjourned.

If the hearing officer has requested additional documentary evidence, or an independent evaluation, he or she may reconvene the hearing. The decision of the hearing officer is final and it must be implemented.

What happens to my child during the due process hearing?

Your child will remain in the present placement unless the parents and school agree to another placement. If out of school before the special education process begins, the child should be placed temporarily in a public school program that the parents agree to until the hearing is completed. If the child is currently in a nonpublic school at parental expense, the parent will continue to bear that expense.

What are some of the possible outcomes of the due process hearing?

On the basis of the evidence presented at the hearing, the hearing officer or panel will decide the dispute and will order the school to provide whatever placement, program, or services are appropriate. The hearing officer is not limited to accepting the parents' or the school's position; he or she can recommend a third alternative if that seems appropriate. The hearing officer can require the district to start a new program or provide a new service, or he or she can require the district to pay for the child to attend a private school.

The hearing officer's decision should also state why specific alternatives were rejected or accepted, as well as the specific evidence that was considered in developing the conclusions. The opinion should be directed toward the issues of the case and should be specific and practical. The opinion may be on a trial basis, or delayed placement may be ordered. The decision cannot specify a particular teacher or school but it can be a recommendation for a particular type of program or placement including a suggestion of where this program is available.

The hearing officer's decision is final (unless a party appeals) and it must be implemented. The school must change its practices to conform to the hearing officer's findings. A new IEP must be written for your child which incorporates the hearing officer's decision. You should be invited to and attend the IEP conference when the IEP is developed.

You will also want to institute some review procedures to be sure your child is receiving the services and placement the hearing officer concluded were appropriate.

Can I appeal the decision if I don't agree with it?

You have the right to an administrative appeal to the state department of education. The state department officer will review the due process hearing to be sure that your legal rights were protected and all appropriate information was considered. This hearing appeals officer then makes an independent decision in accordance with the evidence presented. The hearing appeals officer may (but does not have to) request additional written information and/or oral testimony, and has thirty days to review your case and issue a new opinion.

Is the decision of the hearing officer always followed?

We are becoming aware of instances where school districts have not implemented the decisions of the hearing officer. There does not at present seem to be a recourse for the problem. You could contact the hearing officer and request his assistance in obtaining school district compliance; you could bring continued pressure on the school district; or you could go to court to ask for a court order forcing compliance with the hearing officer's decision. Keep in touch with your attorney or parent advocate group until you are sure that the decision of the hearing officer has been implemented. These people may be able to help you apply pressure to the school system.

Is it possible for me to take my dispute to court?

You might consider going to court under several circumstances: you were unsuccessful in both the hearing and the appeal processes, but you still believe your child is not receiving an appropriate education; you may have been successful in the hearing process but the school has not implemented the hearing officer's decision; you believe some aspect of the evaluation, placement, and/or hearing process was unlawful. (In the latter case the court may issue a direct order to the school to provide you with the services to which your child is entitled.)

Before going to court, you must consult an attorney. Often the threat of going to court and getting on the docket is enough to force school district reconsideration and agreement.

Notes

1. In some cases, the school may request that written testimony be taken if the appearance of the witness would interfere with school operations.

10

Techniques for Changing the System

MARY S. AKERLEY

After having carefully read the first nine chapters, you should now be better able to deal with the system. You should feel much more comfortable about requesting a conference with your child's school principal, counselor, or teacher, or even writing or calling the local or state special education program director.

However, even if you *are* able to deal effectively within the system, you are likely to find that it does not always respond rapidly enough to meet your child's special education needs. The question, then, is how you, as an individual, can change the system. This chapter should help you answer that question.

Suppose that I've followed all the advice you've given me up to now but I'm still not satisfied with the services my child is getting. What more can I do?

Then it's time to turn your attention to the system itself. Up to now, we've been talking about *individual* advocacy—making sure an eligible person (your child) gets all that he or she is entitled to under present laws and regulations. But sometimes the laws and regulations just aren't adequate. Then you have to work to change them, and that's called "systems advocacy."

If you've just been through some of the procedures we've been talking about, you've been dealing with public officials and you've gotten some valuable experience. You're more ready than you realize to take on bigger things; you're ready to lobby.

The word lobby may sound frightening to many of you, but it shouldn't. You don't have to buy favors or threaten your representatives. Any citizen has the right to present views to public officials. In fact, that's an important part of the governmental process, and that's all lobbying is.

People in government are essentially process people; they know the mechanics of passing laws and writing and implementing regulations. Lobbyists are content people; they supply the subject matter. And remember that you can deliver at least one vote: your own. And your influence, as well as your friends', and family's, is also important. In other words, if your lobbying is successful, the lawmaker who helped you feels confident that you will support and spread the word about him or her.

I thought lobbying just referred to getting laws passed or changed, but you said something about regulations. Can you lobby agencies, too?

Yes, indeed. In fact, sometimes that's the best place to start because it's easier to get a regulation changed than to amend a law or pass a new one. So we really are talking about two types of lobbying—legislative and administrative. Maybe it would help to go through the process from start to finish and find out which steps of that process you can affect, because there are certain steps you cannot change.

Many citizen lobbyists get frustrated because they haven't learned some important wheres, whens, and whos. Let's start with three ground rules:

1. *You can effectively lobby only someone over whom you have some control.* In other words, if you live in Ohio, you can't make a senator from Mississippi vote your way. You have to know who *your* representatives are, and use them.

2. *You must exert citizen pressure at the right level.* If your local school system isn't doing right by your child, writing your congressional representative won't do much good since he or she is concerned with national issues. You need to contact your city council members or county commissioners because they're the ones with *local* control.

3. *You must speak up at the right time.* When a bill is in committee, when regulations are being drafted, when public hearings are held—these are the times to make your views known. After the fact is too late.

Where do I start?

Let's take basic governmental structure for starters because it's pretty much the same at the local, state, or federal level. There is a legislative, or lawmaking, branch and an executive, or implementing, one. The executive branch is usually much larger than the legislative one, whose size is limited by law and whose members are all elected. For example, Congress is the legislative branch of the federal government; the President, the Cabinet, and its departments and agencies make up the executive branch. In other words, congressmen represent specific citizens while the executive branch serves everyone. Every state has two senators. However, the number of representatives in a state depends on its population. For purposes of electing representatives, each state is divided into congressional districts, with a member of the House of Representatives from each. Hence, everyone has two senators but only one representative, the one elected from the district in which he or she lives.

There is the same kind of system at lower levels. States are divided into legislative districts from which state senators and delegates or assemblymen are elected. You can find out what legislative district you are in and who your state senators and delegates are by contacting the local central committee of either political party, the board of elections, or the League of Women Voters. This information is also available at public libraries and any librarian can help you look it up.

While some people may say they will "feel dumb" asking questions about things they should already know, they should realize that most people don't know much about their government, and never even bother to find out. So you needn't feel embarrassed about asking. When you make inquiries by phone, all you need to give is your address. If you still want a "cover," just say you are new to the area.

By the way, if you are not a registered voter, become one before you read another word. Call your board of elections (look under the county government listing in your phone book) and find out the registration procedures in your area. In many states you can now register by mail. If you can't vote, you can't lobby.

I'm feeling overwhelmed by all this information; can you make it any simpler?

Let's try some charts. First, we'll break down the executive and legislative branches. (See Table 10.1.)

Here is an illustration which will clarify what has been stated about election districts. The square represents a state and an election district for the United States Senate.

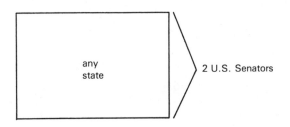

Table 10.1 The Executive and Legislative Branches of Government

	FEDERAL	STATE	LOCAL (County or City)
EXECUTIVE	President and Cabinet* Departments: (Labor; Agriculture; Interior; Health & Welfare; Education; Housing and Urban Development; Transportation; Commerce; etc.)	Governor and "Cabinet"* Agencies (Health, Education, Social Services, etc.)	County Executive, Board of County Commissioners or Mayor Agencies* (most are local branches of state agencies)
LEGISLATIVE	Congress Senate and House of Representatives	Legislature Senate and Lower House (except Nebraska, which has only a Senate)	Council - County or City

* = Appointed officials (all others are elected)

ELECTION CYCLES:

President—every 4 years
U.S. Senate—6 year, staggered terms (both senators would never be up for election at the same time)
House of Representatives—every 2 years
State and Local—varies from state to state

Now we'll divide the state into congressional districts, each of which elects *one* member of the House of Representatives.

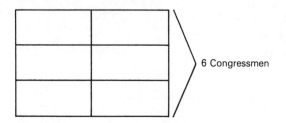

Remember, in reality the lines will not be straight, nor will they necessarily conform to jurisdictional boundaries. Districts will not all be the same size but they will all contain roughly the same number of people—about 450,000.

Next, we'll add state legislative districts. Again, the lines will not necessarily conform to city, county, or congressional district lines, but they will define areas that are equal in population.

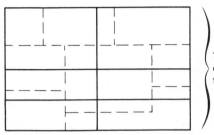

The number of state senators and delegates from each district varies from state to state.

Councilmanic districts are a little easier to explain. They do conform to existing city or county boundaries; they are simply political entities which have been divided into smaller areas (again, based on population) for the purpose of elective representation.

Okay, now how do I use all of this information to get something done?

You need to learn the process that is involved in making a citizen's idea become a law or regulation. Let's take a specific idea and observe the process.

Suppose you want your state to provide all medical services listed in a handicapped child's IEP free of charge. You have already found out that the state education agency is not required to provide medical services, so you need to focus attention on the state and local health departments. You would begin by making an appointment with the state director of Crippled Children's Services by calling your state or local health department. However, a more productive initial approach might involve discussing the matter first with your state or local director of special education. You may win yourself a valuable ally who can help you get an appointment, and who may even go with you to explain the situation and lend support to your idea.

Suppose I can't get an appointment?

Call or write your state delegate, explain the situation, and ask for help in getting the appointment. Be sure to write a note of thanks for the help, even if the person is not successful. This is a good way for you to get to know each other, as well as a way of documenting the history of the problem if your administrative lobbying is not successful. And remember, keep copies of everything you write or receive, and start a file. You may need that copy of a letter you filed two years later. You should also keep a telephone log, and follow up important calls with a letter confirming the contents of your conversation. (See Figure 10.1.)

Since we've already digressed, this is a good time to point out something on technique. Even though you may be ready to murder the person to whom you're writing (in this case an unresponsive bureaucrat), be nice—or at least civil. Remember, nasty letters can be used against you. They can be used as proof that you're just another "hysterical parent." Moreover, today's adversary may become tomorrow's ally if you play your cards right.

Let's assume that, one way or another, you've gotten your appointment. Before you go, you must do your homework. Besides knowing the restrictions in the federal laws and regulations, you should know as much as possible about your state Crippled Children's Plan. (Crippled Children's Services is a federal program; however, states are given considerable latitude in implementing it.) You may have to explain the federal special education law to a health department official, since it may be possible that he or

Figure 10–1
Sample Telephone Log

> Your address
> City, State, Zip
> Date

Dr. Titus Tourniquet, Director
Crippled Children's Services
State Department of Health
100 Main Street
Capital City, State 00000

Dear Dr. Tourniquet:

I appreciate your returning my call yesterday and your very clear explanation of the regulations governing school-based services to handicapped children. I also appreciate your candor in telling me that you saw little possibility of changing the regulation to allow coverage of services listed in a child's individual education plan at no cost to the family.

I will take your advice and seek other avenues of service and will, of course, keep you advised of any progress I make. Thank you for your time and interest.

> Sincerely,
>
> Signature
> (Type Full Name)

she is not familiar with it. The chances are not very good that you will get what you want on the first try; what you will most likely be given is a reason why whatever you want can't be done.

The most frequently given reason is a financial one. If you are told that the health department doesn't have the money for all the services that would be required, ask if there are "discretionary" funds which could be used to start at least a pilot or demonstration project in one local school system. Your cohort from the department of education could be extremely helpful here. If this person has gone along with you to the health department and doesn't have wit enough to speak up at this point, do it yourself: "Dr. Bookworm can help with this, can't you, Dr. Bookworm?"

Whatever the result, you should also be asking questions about next year's budget: Can provisions be made for funding IEP medical services? Will the health department request those funds? Where can pressure be exerted to help get results—the governor's office, the legislature, or both?

Clearly, you will need to educate yourself about your state's budget process; however, you are not expected to become a fiscal expert. In most states the legislature controls the purse strings, but some states do have an executive budget which gives the governor the ultimate say in how much is spent and where.

If you get even a moderately positive response, you must follow through. Establish yourself as a reliable person of serious intent; be sure the director of your state's Crippled Children's Services is kept aware of your activities. If you are successful in obtaining additional funding, he or she will be in your debt. You may need to use that advantage for further negotiations or simply to insure that the "new" money is spent as intended.

What if the bureaucrat says the problem is the regulations or the state plan you mentioned earlier?

Discuss changing the regulations. If you meet with resistance, you will have to take your case to a higher level. But be sure to let this person know you intend to do so. Remember, never go over anyone's head without giving fair warning! While you are still in the office you can say something like: "Dr. Tourniquet, I can see you are as frustrated as I am over this impasse. Perhaps we should see Commissioner (or Secretary) Scalpel about it." By using this technique, you are including Dr. Tourniquet in the solution, not identifying him as part of the problem.

However, in spite of your efforts, Dr. Tourniquet may insist on being the problem. If so, don't lose your cool. Make an appointment with Secretary Scalpel and let Dr. Tourniquet know you've done so.

Perhaps Secretary Scalpel will listen. Oddly enough, the higher one goes, the more responsive the officials seem to be. However, remember that you cannot start at the top; you must begin at the level where the problem exists.

Even if you fail to get the funding increased or the regulations changed, the state plan is fair game and it's open season once a year. Every federal program which requires a state plan (e.g., Developmental Disabilities, Vocational Rehabilitation, Special Education, Crippled Children's Services) also requires that the plan be updated annually. This is usually done in the last quarter of the fiscal year, and there must be a period (usually 30 days) for public comment before the revised plan is approved and adopted.

Take advantage of this period. Prepare a written statement and submit it. If there are public hearings, request to be put on the list of witnesses. If the schedule is already full, go to the hearing anyway. It's helpful to know what other people are saying, and it's a marvelous opportunity to find like-minded souls who might join in your efforts. You can find out when and where the hearings are being held by calling the particular department you are concerned with. When you do, also ask when the draft of the plan will be available. You may not be able to get a copy for yourself. (They are generally lengthy and therefore expensive to reproduce.) However, the plan must be available for public perusal. This means you may have to spend a day or more at the health department just reading it and taking notes so that you can make comments on it.

You should be aware that the availability of the plan and the provisions for public comment must be publicized. Don't expect prime time TV coverage; instead watch the "Public Notices" sections of the local newspapers.

What happens if a state doesn't do all that is specified in the state plan?

If you have good reason to believe your state has not complied with any of these requirements or with its own approved plan, you can and should file a complaint with the federal agency that administers the program. Prior to making contact with the agency responsible for administration of the plan, you should let the state agency know what you're doing. For our example, that would be the Division of Maternal and Child Health of the Public Health Service. If your complaint is found to be valid, the state will be given an opportunity to mend its ways. Should it fail to do so, it is subject to penalties—usually the loss of all or part of the federal money due it for that particular program.

But wouldn't the loss of federal funds result in even less service?

Yes, if it actually happens. However, usually a warning from the federal government is enough to turn things around or at least make them better. But the complaint process is a very slow one, and one you can't be sure will go your way. So instead of filing a complaint, write to your state legislators. Advise them of the situation (especially the potential loss of federal monies) and ask them to intervene. Send carbon or photocopies to your governor and to all the agency people you have been dealing with. Be sure to indicate on the original letters, by name, those persons you are sending copies to. That in itself has been known to change official minds.

You should also be aware of the fact that federal officials may support the state. Then you will have exhausted all administrative remedies. But because you have been documenting your efforts, you are in an excellent position to attempt to get a law passed in your state to provide the needed medical services.

Do I have to write the law myself if I want it considered?

You can if wish (and if you have a working knowledge of legal language), but you don't have to. The first step is to get an appointment with your state delegate or senator so you can describe the problem and explain your solution. Your appointment request letter should state briefly why you want to see your senator, delegate, or assemblyman. That way he can "bone up" on the subject.

Does it matter whether I start with the upper or lower house when lobbying?

It could. Generally it's easier to begin with the Senate; it is smaller, so your lobbying job should be easier. It is also often the more liberal body. For these two reasons it is easier to get a bill through. Of course, it must pass *both* houses *in the same form* in order to become a law; nevertheless, it makes sense to give your bill momentum by doing the easier half first.

Of course, that generalization may not apply to your state so you must have some sense of the local political climate in order to lobby successfully. And certainly, if you have already worked with, or even just met, your delegate, he or she is the logical person to start with. What's more, you run the risk of offending your legislator if you do not seek help from him or her first.

If you think it sounds as though legislators have rather fragile egos, you're right, and the smart lobbyist takes great care not to inflict any bruises. For example, when it becomes obvious that you know more about a subject than your senator does, choose your words with care. You can indicate that the situation you're trying to rectify is not well known or understood by anyone, or that it has developed very recently.

What should I hope to accomplish from an appointment with my legislator?

After you have given the background and discussed the situation, ask the legislator to introduce a bill. It is a good strategy to have the points you want covered by the bill written down. It can be in very simple language; the legislator's staff will put it all into legal form.

What if my bill request is refused?

That's not very likely. But if the legislator feels that, for political reasons, he or she cannot support your bill, you can do one of two things: find someone else in the legislature sympathetic to your cause and ask this person to do it. (Remember to tell *your* senator that that's what you're going to do.) Or ask your legislator to introduce it "by request." That simply means that the legislator is introducing it as a courtesy to a constituent (or sometimes to the governor). You should be aware, however, that this is not a good way to proceed. The words "by request" after a legislator's name on the bill act as a flag, signaling to everyone else in the legislature that your bill is not one he or she cares about or will push.

Could both a senator and a delegate introduce the bill? Wouldn't that speed things up?

The answer to the first part is "yes." And when that happens, you have two separate bills, each with its own number. They are called companion bills. Because one of them must pass *both* chambers in order to become law, joint introduction doesn't necessarily speed up the process.

The senate bill must first pass the Senate then the House or vice versa. The only time it may be useful to have companion bills is when you really aren't sure which chamber is going to be more responsive, so you have your bill introduced on both sides to test the waters, then push the one that seems to have the best chance of moving.

After my bill gets introduced, do they debate it and vote on it?

Not right away. Figure 10.2 should help you understand what will happen to your bill.

The arrows show how a bill moves through a legislative body. Notice that some of the arrows are broken. They indicate a step that may, but does

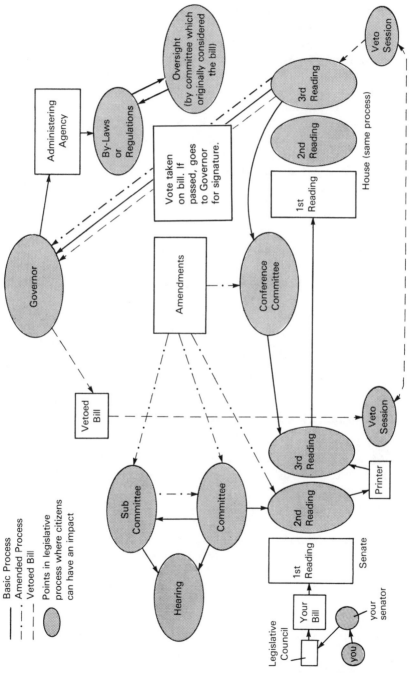

Figure 10-2
How a Bill Becomes a Law
(A Sample Process)

not have to, take place. The areas that are shaded show where the public can influence the legislative process.

Let's start at the beginning, down in the lower left hand corner. You present your idea to your senator; he or she refers it to staff (legislative counsel) who draft the bill; then your senator introduces it. That introduction is called the bill's first reading. It is really just a formality; the entire bill isn't even read. The sponsor presents it and the president of the Senate (or Speaker of the House) gives it a number and assigns it to a committee.

If your state also has subcommittees, assignments to them will be made by committee chairpersons. These committees and subcommittees are where most of the real work gets done. Through them legislators are able to keep themselves well informed on a variety of subjects. The committees, at least in theory, are made up of people with expertise or an interest in a particular area. They handle legislation related to that area and then recommend action to the entire chamber. Your greatest opportunity to affect legislation is while it is in committee or subcommittee.

Most of the time, assignment to a particular committee is fairly cut-and-dry. However, there may be times when there is more than one committee which could have jurisdiction over a bill. For example, if your legislature has both a health and an education committee, your bill could be assigned to either one. If you believe one would handle your bill more favorably than the other, you could—and should—lobby for it to be assigned to that committee.

How would I lobby for my bill to be assigned to a particular committee? How would I know which committee to ask for?

If your senator is on one of the two committees, that's the one to ask for. As the bill's sponsor, your senator would be in an ideal position to move it along. Actually, any connections you have (another senator, if you have more than one; a friend or relative's senator; a social acquaintance; someone you've worked with before) may be able to help you make a correct committee choice. Another factor to consider are the reputations of the committees. Some committees are known as "graveyards" because so few bills ever come out of them. Since it is the president of the Senate who will make the assignment, you must communicate your committee preference to him or her. This is best done via someone (constituent, a senator to whom he or she is indebted) who has some influence.

You may also have to deal with dual jurisdiction, that is, your bill may be assigned to two committees. They may work on it jointly or sequentially.

Some legislatures assign all bills which call for spending new money to the Ways and Means or Finance Committees, but only after they have been considered and received a favorable report from whatever committee reviews them for program content.

Basically, the committee must study the bill, amend it, if necessary, and recommend action. The committee must also respond to public input, and will usually hold a hearing at which witnesses present formal testimony.

Can anyone testify for my bill at the committee hearing?

Theoretically, yes. Often, however, there is not enough time to allow everyone with an interest in a particular bill to speak. Witnesses are scheduled on a first come, first heard basis. Those who don't get on the schedule may submit written statements. Or, if witnesses are not prescheduled, the chairperson may ask that those present condense their statements and discuss only those points not covered by a previous speaker. Certain witnesses are given preference: the sponsor of the bill, who is always the first witness; the head of the agency which will be administering the new law if the bill passes; witnesses representing organizations with a special interest in the bill (lobbyists); and, where applicable, private citizens like yourself.

How do I get on the witness list to present my testimony to the committee?

If you are the one who started the ball rolling, you will probably be invited to testify, either by your senator or by the committee chairperson. If that doesn't happen, you will have to follow the usual procedure of calling or writing the committee and formally requesting the opportunity. If witnesses are not scheduled in advance, you will simply be told of the time and place of the hearing. When you arrive for the hearing, you may be asked to sign a witness list; if so, you will be called in the order of signing. Generally, all witnesses supporting the bill are heard first.

When you inquire about testifying, you may be told that no hearing has been scheduled yet. You should then ask to be notified as soon as the hearing date is set. Hearings for bills are often listed in local newspapers. You can frequently keep track of committee hearings by reviewing daily the committee hearing schedule.

If a week goes by and you have heard nothing, call again. You may have to do this several times. If still nothing happens and there are fewer than four weeks left before adjournment, you may have to lobby for a hearing. More bills die in committee than get voted down on the floor, so you may need to work at getting the committee to act, and the best way to do that is to keep contacting the chairperson. If you are not his or her constituent, find someone who is and ask for help. Or, if your senator is on the committee, ask him or her to push for hearings.

Is there any special format for testimony?

Yes, but it's fairly loose. You should begin by introducing yourself to the committee: "Mr. (or Madam) Chairperson, and members of the committee, I am (your name), a (your occupation), and the parent of a child with (disability)." Mention any other things about yourself and your background that give you credibility relative to the bill, then conclude your opening paragraph by saying you appreciate this opportunity to testify on Senate Bill number _____.

Briefly describe the present situation of handicapped children—that they are entitled by federal law, and state law in most cases, to a free, appropriate public education. (Know your state code.) For many disabled children, "appropriate" includes specialized medical services (physical therapy, for example). However, the state education agency is not required to provide them.

Then explain how the bill being considered would solve the problem. You can describe your administrative lobbying efforts here as a way of demonstrating the need for legislative remedy.

If you anticipate objections (possibly from Dr. Tourniquet or Secretary Scalpel, who may not want to do any more work) try to answer them during your testimony. This weakens the opponents' arguments and enhances your credibility. One point the administering agency is almost sure to raise is the lack of money to implement the new program. You should acknowledge that need in your statement. Don't minimize it; instead you can stress how expenditures now could result in long-term savings of public dollars. For example, you could make the point that for the already mandated education dollars to have the maximum effect, some support services are going to be needed. Conclude by thanking the committee and offering to answer any questions.

Should I write my testimony out word-for-word or just talk from notes?

Both. Your formal testimony should be typed, double-spaced. If possible, you should have copies for each member of the committee. Some legislatures require you to submit your testimony in advance. In most cases, though, you can just bring it with you. Give the copies to the staff person in charge of the committee before you speak. If you can't find the right person, or if you arrive after the hearing has started, you can pass them out yourself when your turn to speak comes. If you introduce yourself while you're doing it, you will not be taking up too much time and you will be deviating from the usual routine in a way that's acceptable—a very good way to draw attention to your testimony and give it a better chance of being remembered.

When you actually give the testimony, don't read it! The committee members all have copies and are, presumably, all literate. Highlight it in your own less formal words. You may find it helpful to make yourself a "working copy" of your formal statement; you can underline major points and take notes on it, which you can use in making your oral presentation.

Don't be afraid to use humor or pathos; just don't make emotion the basis of your statement.

The amount of time you will have to testify depends on how many other people want to speak and how many other bills are being heard. Usually a committee hearing lasts about two hours and covers several bills, or groups of bills, all pertaining to the same general area. You may leave when you've finished speaking, but you really shouldn't. Listen to what the other witnesses have to say, particularly those opposing the bill. Take notes on the issues they raise so you can refute them or show why your arguments outweigh theirs. In some states, the "pros" may speak again after the "cons." In any event, you will have plenty of opportunity for rebuttal via letters, calls, and personal visits while your bill is in committee.

What if I don't know the answer to a question that is asked about my testimony?

Say so, but then offer to get the information and submit it as soon as possible. Never lie or fake an answer—those are the kinds of mistakes that can come back to haunt you, and hurt your cause. You need never feel embarrassed about not knowing something; after all, the person who asked didn't know the answer either.

Can I attend the committee sessions?

The rules on that vary from state to state. If your state has open sessions (sunshine laws), by all means attend. Although you may not speak, often just your presence can make a difference, and you may even be asked some questions. Legislators have actually changed their votes because of who was in the audience. Even if the "mark-up" sessions are closed, committee votes are recorded in most states, so be sure to check the voting record on your bill and let the right people know you've done so. If you find that someone did not vote as you expected, ask why. Don't be nasty; assume there was a good reason and remind the person nicely that you have a right to know what that reason was.

What if the committee amends the bill in a way I don't like?

If the amendments have been introduced but not voted on, lobby the committee members in the ways just mentioned. Each amendment must be voted on separately, so you can be very specific about what you want. This whole process will be repeated when the bill has its second reading on the floor, so if you fail to get the amendment killed in committee, you will get a second chance.

This might be a good place to talk about the necessity for compromise, which is an important part of the political process. Even if you don't like the amendment, you may have to live with it in order to get your bill passed. Of course, if the amendment absolutely "guts" the bill, you may wish to stick to your guns, knowing full well you may wind up with nothing. Bad legislation is usually worse than none.

Another alternative is to go along with the amended bill with the intention of making some changes in a year or so, after the new program has been in operation. Any problems, especially if they have resulted from the amendment you opposed, can be used as proof that further amendments are needed. Existing laws get amended every legislative session. In fact, that's technically what most bills are all about. And it is usually easier to amend an existing law than to start from scratch. Most legislative change is incremental, that is, it happens a little at a time. It can (and often does) take a legislative body several years to pass an entirely new program. The first two or three times such legislation is introduced, it is frequently allowed to die in committee because the matter "needs further study." However, once the program is enacted and becomes law, modifying it via legislation is relatively easy.

How do I get a law amended?

You have a bill introduced which amends a specific section of your state code—the collection of state laws. In fact, before you begin lobbying, you should visit your state capitol to get familiar with the various buildings, offices, and legislative chambers, and learn where the "bill room" is. Get copies of a few of the bills currently under consideration so you can familiarize yourself with the format. You will see that most of them amend existing law, either by removing things, adding things, or both. Anything added is printed in italics, capitalized, or underlined. Material to be deleted is put in brackets or parentheses.

You should go to the information desk in your state capitol and ask for a synopsis of bills. You will find them listed by number, which indicates the order in which they were introduced. The House and Senate will have separate synopses. Read through the list and pick a few which are of interest to you; then order them by number from the bill room.

How does the bill get out of committee?

The committee must take a formal vote on the bill itself, after voting on any amendments. Then it is "reported out," that is, the committee chairman notifies the president of the Senate (or the Speaker of the House) that the bill is to be put on the Senate (or House) schedule for a second reading. This is not the same as the first reading; it's much more important. The committee chairperson presents the bill, with the committee's recommendations, to the entire Senate (or House). There may be considerable discussion or actual debate. This is the *only* time a bill can be amended on the floor, that is, when it is before the entire chamber. If floor amendments are offered, they are debated and voted on individually, then a straw vote is taken with whatever amendments have survived. If the vote (which is not binding) is favorable, the bill is sent to the printer for a final printing with any changes which have been made. This straw vote is taken because printing is both expensive and time consuming; if this vote is negative, there is no need to reprint the bill.

Is a bill likely to be amended during the second reading?

Not as a general rule. Usually the entire body goes along with the committee's recommendation whether it is favorable or unfavorable. That is another illustration of the need to rely on the committee's expertise because the individual legislators cannot study each and every issue in depth. Exceptions occur when a bill is very controversial or when some parliamentary maneuvering is going on.

Often a floor amendment is enough to kill a bill because it raises doubts in the minds of those who were not on the committee, and since they don't have the time to research the points on their own, they take the "safe" way out and vote the bill down. For that reason, you should try to avoid floor amendments—either deletions or additions.

Is it a good idea to use the second reading to rectify any committee actions I didn't like?

You should be aware of the pitfalls in that particular technique. If you are really unhappy about the way your bill came out of committee, you should approach a legislator *who is not a committee member* in much the same way you initially sought out a sponsor for the bill. Explain the situation and ask this legislator to offer an amendment on the floor. Here again you need to do some research. Obviously, you are not going to get help from someone who usually works closely with the committee chairperson or who, for political reasons, cannot risk a confrontation. It will be much harder to find a sponsor for a floor amendment than it was for the bill itself.

The second reading box is shaded. Are calls and letters important here too?

They are *very* important if your bill is not a shoo-in. Since citizens cannot testify at this point, calls and letters are their only way of letting their senators and delegates, especially those who were not on the committee, know how they want them to vote. Even if your bill's chances look very good, it doesn't hurt to communicate your wishes. Get as many people as you can to call or write; ideally, every member should be contacted. Sometimes just one call or letter can make a real difference. Here again, it's crucial that they be contacted by their own constituents. It certainly can't hurt to do this for the third reading as well, especially for those who didn't vote your way on the second reading. However, the third reading is more a formality, the final technical approval of the reprinted bill. Bills that pass the second reading are, almost without exception, home free.

Then do I have to go through the whole complicated process all over again with the other half of the Legislature?

Yes, you do (unless you live in Nebraska where there is a one-house legislature), but it should be a little easier. For one thing, you don't have to find a sponsor; as soon as a bill passes one chamber, it is automatically referred to the other for consideration. You don't have to write testimony because you can use the same statement you wrote for the first hearing, although you may want to make some minor revisions. (You should retype at least the cover sheet and perhaps the first page because you'll want to change the name of the committee, e.g., from "Senate-Finance" to "House Ways and Means," and the date.) And finally, your bill has now gained some momentum.

What is the conference committee?

That is a special committee put together solely for the purpose of resolving any differences between the House and Senate versions of a bill. It is made up of some members from each of the two committees who had responsibility for the bill in the first place. Notice that the arrows to the conference committee are broken, which means that referral there does not always happen. For example, if the House passes a Senate bill in exactly the same form, there is no conference; the bill goes directly to the governor for signature.

However, if the House amends the bill in any way it must be referred to conference committee. The final version of the bill will usually be some sort of compromise between the two versions, unless the Senate accepts the House amendments.

Once the conference committee agrees on all points, the bill is reprinted and sent back to each chamber for final approval. Only one vote on the so-called clean bill is required. If both chambers pass the bill, it is sent to the governor.

If the Senate amended my bill in a way I didn't like, could I get the original language restored by the House?

You could certainly try, but remember that there will be senators on the conference committee. Also, keep your eye on the clock. If you are nearing the end of the session, House amendments may cause time to defeat your bill. In fact, amending a bill near the end of a session may be politically more acceptable than opposing it, and it may have the same result: the bill dies because there isn't time for the conference.

In any event, you will have to lobby the conferees just as you did the members of the original committees.

The governor's box is shaded, too. How do I lobby the governor?

The same way you've lobbied in the Legislature. After your bill has passed both chambers, write to the governor urging him or her to sign it. This is good practice any time, but it is vital if there's any chance of a veto. As before, get as many people as you can to write. Also, even if the governor does veto the bill, the legislature may override the veto.

Can the state legislature override the governor's veto right away?

Not as a rule. Some legislatures have special veto sessions; they reconvene just long enough to consider all vetoed bills from the regular session just concluded. Others make vetoed bills the first order of business in the new session. Veto sessions will vary based upon the length of time a state legislature meets. All-year-round legislatures (California and New York, among others) may have more frequent veto sessions than do those legislatures which meet for one 60-or 90-day session per year.

Does the vote to override have to be unanimous?

No, but it does take more than the simple majority it took to pass the bill. Here again, states vary in their requirements, but two-thirds or three-fourths of the legislature is commonly needed to override a veto. The process is similar to that used for voting on amended bills. Vetoed bills are considered first by the chamber in which the bill originated. A single vote of the entire body is taken. If there are enough votes to override, the bill is sent to the other chamber for its vote; if the veto is sustained, the bill is not sent on. This override period is a time when you need to lobby even more than before because you need more votes. Since time is short, you might want to send telegrams. There is a special low rate lobbyist's special called a "Public Opinion Message." It is limited to ten words plus your name and address; however it costs only $1.25 from anywhere in your state to your capital ($1.50 from anywhere in the country to Capitol Hill). If both chambers vote to override the veto, it does not go back to the governor, but automatically becomes law. As soon as that happens, it is referred to the implementing agency, which prepares regulations or a bylaw. These regulations and by-laws are written because it is usually not wise to make legislation deal with the nitty-gritty. A good law sets forth policy; how that policy will be implemented is detailed in bylaws, rules, or regulations. And while these do have the force of law, they are much easier to change, because the agency which wrote them can revise them without going back through the legislative process.

That part of the chart is shaded—what can I do about the bylaw?

The process is virtually identical to the one described for commenting on a state plan. The thing to watch out for is a bylaw, rule, or regulation which is more restrictive than the law itself. For example, if your enacted bill mandates medical services for all children as prescribed in the IEP, the bylaw cannot arbitrarily exclude psychiatric services simply because they are very expensive. Yet this kind of limit is not uncommon in regulations.

So I'm back to administrative lobbying. It looks as though we've come full circle.

Not quite. If the final regulations are unsatisfactory, or if the law and regulations are not being fairly and properly implemented, you can invoke "legislative oversight." To set the oversight process in motion, you might go back to the bill's sponsor, who will take the problem to the committee which originally considered the bill. They will conduct oversight hearings, which are similar to the original hearings, and determine what corrective measures are needed. Usually they tighten up the legislation itself by amending it.

You must realize that getting your bill passed is only half the battle. The other half is getting it implemented. Besides regulations, there is the ever-present funding problem. The best program in the world is useless unless there are resources available to implement it. So you are going to have to learn how the budget process works in your state, and lobby there for appropriations.

Does this mean that even if the bill passes, the program might not be funded?

Exactly, or it may be only partially funded. Even if the bill calls for specific sums of money (authorization levels), the actual sums allocated (appropriation levels) may be considerably less.

Are there other things I should know about?

It is important to know how to adequately thank the people who help you in your efforts. Earlier it was suggested that thank you letters be sent to administrators as a way of documenting their behavior and as an actual expression of gratitude. You should also send a thank you letter everytime a legislator votes your way, introduces an amendment, or contacts a colleague on your behalf. And remember, you are dealing with public people, so your thanks should be expressed as publicly as possible. In addition to your personal letter to the senator or delegate, you could, for example, write a letter to the editor of the local paper, praising the responsive legislator(s). Be sure to send copies to the legislators in question; if the paper doesn't print your letter, the lawmakers will know that at least you tried.

You should also help in reelection campaigns in whatever way you can; a contribution is the minimum you can offer. There are many other campaign jobs for nonprofessionals, such as telephoning, distributing literature, covering polling places. You may discover that most of these jobs are actually fun. They are also an excellent way of strengthening your position as a lobbyist.

All of this may seem like more than one person could ever do, and it probably is. One person, especially a volunteer who has other responsibilities such as a home, family, and job, usually doesn't have the time, or the energy, to take on another full-time commitment. Most of the active and successful volunteers work with other like-minded souls, usually through an organization.

These organizations are not lobbying groups, but volunteer organizations for the handicapped, founded by parents of handicapped children or by handicapped adults. While they do lobby, that is not their main function. For that very reason, they are extremely effective; they are perceived as "pure" compared to, say, the oil lobby, yet they are very powerful because they represent the collective voice of hundreds, sometimes thousands, of voters. Most are organized in tiers which correspond with governmental levels (local, state, federal) so their lobbying efforts are very precisely directed.

The older, established organizations (and some of the newer ones) represent a kind of collective wisdom. They are a splendid source of support and information. The "old timers" help younger parents learn more about their child's disability, locate services, and, in general, make the system work better. It is through organization activity that most parent lobbyists get their training. Public officials, too, have come to depend on this collective wisdom and use it as *the* source of the latest information on a particular disability.

Finally, working within the organization structure gives you personpower: more people to write letters, to make phone calls, to draft and present testimony. Therefore, there will be more legislators with whom you can have direct, personal contact since every member of the organization is someone's constituent. Even if none of the members live in a particular legislator's district, you still have some clout because no delegate or senator can afford to ignore a lobbyist who represents all the blind or deaf or retarded persons and their families and friends in the state. And communications on an organization's letterhead automatically get more attention than private letters for just that reason.

When you work through an organization, you also have at your disposal the potential for public influence and recognition. This works for administrators as well as legislators. If Mary Lou Underserved complains to the press that Dr. Tourniquet isn't doing his job, she will probably be ignored. If the United Cerebral Palsy Association of Obstacle County complains, it will in all likelihood be attended to.

The organizational thank you is also useful. Because it is public it makes it very difficult for an official to change his policy or go back on his word. In fact, it can sometimes be used to maneuver a reluctant or undecided policymaker into the position you want. Of course, this kind of thing must be done with discretion. Virtually every disability has a consumer group working on its behalf. Join the one which most closely meets the needs of your child and volunteer to serve on its legislative or public action committee. And, if organizations are good, coalitions are better. If your county or city doesn't have a coalition of handicapped groups, make starting one a project for the legislative committee. Once it's going well, turn your attention to a similar effort at the state level. There will be problems because the member organizations won't always be able to agree on a position or course of action, but even just being cognizant of one another's needs and points of view is very helpful. A bill that has the support of every state organization for the handicapped is virtually assured of passage.

Of course, not every bill or administrative problem will be of interest to every organization. However, coalition activity means that "I'll help your bill now, because I know you'll help mine later."

Coalitions also help to do away with the kind of parochial thinking that hurts the cause and, in the long run, can mean less service. For example, a federal law that benefitted just one disability expired in the late 1960s and the chances for renewal were not good. (Many laws mandating specific services are time limited, so you may have to be aware of renewal cycles and be prepared to lobby for the same benefits periodically.) The national organization representing this disability was acknowledged to be one of the most effective in influencing public policy. It also had the reputation of suffering from tunnel vision. Its leaders realized that, powerful as they were, they couldn't save their program alone, so they went to two other national groups, much less powerful but equally worthy. The "big guys" offered to rewrite the legislation to include the "little guys" if the latter would help lobby to get the act renewed. It worked and everyone benefitted. In fact, this premier cooperative effort has had far-reaching effects. It led to the formation of a very powerful national coalition of organizations, recognized and respected on Capitol Hill and in the federal agencies dealing with the handicapped.

11

Summary

STANLEY I. MOPSIK

Those of you who have read this book from cover to cover have been given a great deal of information, and some advice. Others may have used this book as a reference guide, dealing only with specific issues of importance to them. You represent a variety of backgrounds. Some of you have worked actively to provide programs and services for the child with special needs; others of you, although less experienced, are fervent in your desire to attain whatever information and skills are necessary to improve the quality of opportunity for your child.

There are a multitude of options that you may be considering as you consider your future role. You can:

sit back and hope that federal, state, and local education and related agencies meet their mandated responsibilities to improve services for the exceptional child;

join with the responsible implementation agencies in working for increased budgets to insure increased programs and services;

become a gadfly of the bureaucracy and challenge all that is tried, if it does not fit in with your own goals and objectives;

gain clout through numbers and become active in organizations and coalitions that foster the interests of children with special needs;

totally remove yourself from the growing numbers of committed parents by telling yourself that you don't have the verbal, writing, or interpersonal skills to effectively function as an advocate for your child.

Which role or roles you wish to assume is up to you. However, you have come this far. By reading this and other books, and by interacting with the myriad of people and organizations who have acquired a high level of awareness you can go even further. Action is much more difficult even though the satisfaction from achieving progress is great.

Perhaps you're personally drained from all those years of single-handedly working to improve the system on behalf of your child. You now believe that since all this wonderful new legislation is in place and awareness is high, you can now take a rest. Indeed, it is our contention that we are now in an entirely new ballgame and the odds are moving in our favor. In reflecting upon our past and the potentially bright horizon ahead, a statement made by Andrew Carnegie seems appropriate. An employee reported that, "All records were broken yesterday." Carnegie quickly asked, "But what have you done today?" Your role as a parent and an advocate has not ended and will not end. It is a continuous process that requires doing as much today as you did yesterday.

We hope that this book has provided you with information that can be utilized today and tomorrow and tomorrow and tomorrow. . . .

Index